T0261137

Learning Microsoft Power Automate

Improving Productivity for Business Processes and Workflows

Paul Papanek Stork

Beijing · Boston · Farnham · Sebastopol · Tokyo

Praise for *Learning Microsoft Power Automate*

Paul leads readers on a methodical and insightful journey into constructing automated business processes with Power Automate. This comprehensive book covers everything required to kickstart your journey and empowers you to create a wide range of solutions. By the end, you'll have the skills to build, troubleshoot, and seamlessly integrate with other Power Platform tools.

—*Jason Rivera, Author and Microsoft 365 Collaboration Architect*

Power Automate has a low barrier to entry in the Power Platform and Microsoft 365 set of tools. Users with little to no experience can create their first approval with a few clicks in SharePoint and start adding value to their work.

Power Automate also has a depth of functionality that can be daunting for new users having to implement business logic into their flows using actions, expressions and integrations into other apps and services that can seem like more of a traditional IT skill set than that of a maker or citizen developer.

Paul's book *Learning Microsoft Power Automate* does an incredible job at bringing users along on a Power Automate journey: from new maker to seasoned Power Automate developer. This book should be a key resource for anyone wanting to learn and implement Power Automate into their working lives.

—*Norm Young, Microsoft MVP and Senior Strategic Consultant at AvePoint*

Learning Microsoft Power Automate

by Paul Papanek Stork

Copyright © 2024 Paul Papanek Stork. All rights reserved.

Published by O'Reilly Media, Inc., 1005 Gravenstein Highway North, Sebastopol, CA 95472.

O'Reilly books may be purchased for educational, business, or sales promotional use. Online editions are also available for most titles (*https://oreilly.com*). For more information, contact our corporate/institutional sales department: 800-998-9938 or *corporate@oreilly.com*.

Acquisitions Editor: Andy Kwan	**Indexer:** Judith McConville
Development Editor: Jill Leonard	**Interior Designer:** David Futato
Production Editor: Jonathon Owen	**Cover Designer:** Karen Montgomery
Copyeditor: Nicole Taché	**Illustrator:** Kate Dullea
Proofreader: Piper Editorial Consulting, LLC	

October 2023:   First Edition

Revision History for the First Edition

2023-09-26:   First Release

See *https://oreilly.com/catalog/errata.csp?isbn=9781098136369* for release details.

The O'Reilly logo is a registered trademark of O'Reilly Media, Inc. *Learning Microsoft Power Automate*, the cover image, and related trade dress are trademarks of O'Reilly Media, Inc.

The views expressed in this work are those of the author and do not represent the publisher's views. While the publisher and the author have used good faith efforts to ensure that the information and instructions contained in this work are accurate, the publisher and the author disclaim all responsibility for errors or omissions, including without limitation responsibility for damages resulting from the use of or reliance on this work. Use of the information and instructions contained in this work is at your own risk. If any code samples or other technology this work contains or describes is subject to open source licenses or the intellectual property rights of others, it is your responsibility to ensure that your use thereof complies with such licenses and/or rights.

978-1-098-13636-9

[LSI]

Table of Contents

Preface

This book will show you how to use Microsoft Power Automate to automate repetitive, manual, and time-consuming tasks. You're about to take your first steps on a journey that will change the way you handle information every day. But, like all journeys, we need to start at the beginning. That means we need to understand what Power Automate is and how it fits into the broader Microsoft ecosystem. If you already know the basics, please feel free to skip ahead to the next section.

Power Automate, which was originally called Flow, is a cloud-based application that can be used to create workflows. These cloud-based workflows (flows) can use connectors to access information stored in a variety of systems. If a connector does not exist but an API does, then you can create your own custom connector. If an API doesn't exist, then you can use a desktop flow to interact with the data. The result is a workflow engine that works with almost any information source, whether that system is designed by Microsoft or a third party.

Here are just a few examples of the kinds of everyday tasks that Power Automate can transform:

- Automating the collection and processing of information
- Managing the approval of documents and data
- Sending automatic reminders for past-due tasks
- Archiving emails and attachments in an indexable system
- Automating interactive computer tasks that are normally done manually
- Visualizing a staged process consisting of multiple steps

Power Automate is one of five applications included in the Microsoft Power Platform. The other four applications are:

Power Apps

Quickly build custom applications that are accessible on personal computers, tablets, or mobile phones.

Power BI

Create reports and graphs that supply data-driven insights for making informed business decisions.

Power Virtual Agents

Easily build chatbots to engage your customers and employees, using a conversational pattern.

Power Pages

Easily build a website to showcase your business data to internal or external users.

These applications are integrated, and, working together, they can do more than any one application alone.

Who Should Read This Book

There are two primary audiences who will find this book useful. The first is a group Microsoft calls "citizen developers." Citizen developers are defined by the following characteristics:

- They work in a position that is not part of the Information Technology (IT) organization in their company.

- They are not trained as professional developers.

- They use information in their daily work.

- They create software tools, for consumption by themselves or others, to make their work easier.

Citizen developers were clearly the audience that Microsoft focused on when designing and building Power Automate. But they aren't the only ones who can benefit from using it. Professional developers and other technical users like IT administrators will also benefit from Power Automate. By using it, they can quickly develop prototypes or personal productivity aids that will free up additional time to concentrate on their main duties.

In essence, Power Automate puts automation tools in the hands of every employee. It can transform the way your company deals with information and makes it possible for people to create their own problem solutions within an easy-to-use, low-code/no-code platform. Reading this book will help you learn how you can use Power Automate flows to automate the use of information in your own workload.

Why I Wrote This Book

Power Automate is a constantly changing product. At least every six months, Microsoft releases a new set of features and enhancements. It's impossible for any book to keep up with that level of constant change. As a result, this book will concentrate on teaching you how Power Automate works and what role its various components play. I'll also include lots of references to additional documentation and online resources that you can use in the future to enhance your knowledge. Once you've learned how Power Automate works, you'll be better prepared to take any new connector, action, trigger, or feature and use it to enhance your flows.

Reading a technical guide is often like reading a cookbook. It's filled with good recipes to help you handle specific scenarios. By following the recipe, you can produce an outstanding meal, or in this case automate a specific manual task. But what if your scenario doesn't match the recipe exactly? In that case, you need to have learned "cooking" skills that you can use to adapt the recipe or to create your own recipe.

In this book, I will focus on teaching you how to "cook" with Power Automate. I'll focus more on the basic ingredients in a flow and how they interact with each other. I'll explain connectors and the triggers and actions they contain. You'll learn how to understand what fields need to be filled in for each action and how to determine what kind of data is needed. Yes, there will be examples and demos. But the point of those examples will be to demonstrate the skills you need to work with Power Automate in general, and not to just to follow a step-by-step recipe. I'll also discuss where to go to get documentation on the various ingredients that go into a flow. Along the way you'll learn more than just a couple of specific recipes. You'll begin to learn the skills you need to use Power Automate for yourself to create some amazing workflows.

Navigating This Book

Now that you understand the approach of this book, let's look at a summary of what is in each of the chapters. Knowing what is coming will help you build your knowledge and skills using Power Automate as we go through each chapter.

Chapter 1: What Is Microsoft Power Automate?

In the first chapter, I'll introduce the Power Automate application. We'll look at what it is, who should use it, and what they will use it for. I'll describe some typical business scenarios where we can use Power Automate to replace inefficient manual processes—improving both the quality and quantity of information available to an organization. By the end of the chapter, you will be ready to learn how to employ Power Automate to streamline manual processes in your own environment.

Chapter 2: Getting Started: What You Need to Know

In this chapter, we'll focus on the background information you'll need to know before you create your first flow. We'll start by reviewing the licensing required for building different kinds of flows. I'll demonstrate how to sign up and access the Power Automate website the first time and some special programs that will let you learn Power Automate without having to buy a license. I'll help you understand the basic building blocks that make up a flow and the different types of flows that are available. By the end of the chapter, you'll have everything you need to get started developing your first flows.

Chapter 3: Building Your First Flow

Now that you have access to a learning environment, we'll look at how to build your first Power Automate cloud flows. We'll examine how to create a flow using one of the many prebuilt templates. I'll also discuss the potential issues of using templated flows in a production environment. I'll then walk through how to build your first simple flow without using a prebuilt template. This will be the way you will create most of your flows going forward. Finally, I'll demonstrate how to use Microsoft Visio as a planning tool to map out a flow before building it. Once the high-level Visio template is designed, I'll show you how to export it from Visio and import it into Power Automate to create a flow.

Chapter 4: Working with Triggers and Actions

Once you have learned how to plan and create a basic flow, we'll move on to discuss the basic building blocks of flows in more detail. There are more than 600 different connectors available in Power Automate, and each connector supports multiple triggers and/or actions. Because there are so many connectors, it's impossible to cover all the potential combinations and settings available. Instead, we will focus on understanding how triggers and actions work. We'll look at how to use the Dynamic content dialog to select values from previous actions in a flow. I'll also show you how to modify those values using a variety of functions. Since these values are recorded in JavaScript Object Notation (JSON), I'll demonstrate how to manually enter values into the functions if the Dynamic content dialog doesn't show the value you need. Finally, we'll look at how to configure action and trigger settings. We'll also examine other options available on the context menu.

Chapter 5: Implementing Logic

Simple flows often start at point A and flow to an end at point B, following a straight line. But what if your flow needs to do something different depending on a value that changes while the flow is running? For that, we need the ability to branch or loop, based on those values. In this chapter, I'll cover the different ways to implement logical processing in a flow using conditional actions, loops, and parallel branches.

Chapter 6: Integrating with Other Power Platform Applications

Power Automate is one of four applications in the Power Platform. The level of integration between the different applications in the Power Platform can make Power Automate an even stronger application. In this chapter, we'll review how to do the following:

- Trigger a flow from a Power App and return a value or array to the application
- Invoke a flow from a Power Virtual Agent bot and retrieve information for display
- Use Power Automate to process data used in a Power BI report or dashboard
- Start a flow from a Power Page using a button to retrieve information using Power Automate

Chapter 7: Troubleshooting Tips

It would be nice if every flow worked perfectly the first time, every time. But, of course, that's not what happens in real life. In this chapter, I'll present some tips to help you figure out what is going wrong with a flow so you can get it running. I'll also discuss how to design and structure a flow to automatically recover from errors without user intervention.

Chapter 8: Desktop Flows

Power Automate has more than 600 existing connectors. But what do you do if a connector doesn't exist for a legacy desktop application or web page? Power Automate Desktop is a robotic process automation (RPA) application that can be used to overcome this limitation. Using Power Automate Desktop, we'll review how to record or build a desktop flow that can interact with a user interface (UI) on a computer to simulate actions normally done by a person. These desktop flows can then be scheduled using a cloud flow and even run unattended, meaning without human intervention, to accomplish a task.

Chapter 9: Business Process Flows

Automating a business process is often bigger than just one flow. Frequently, it involves multiple people doing a variety of tasks. Sometimes there are even manual steps involved that can't be easily automated with Power Automate flows. That's where a business process flow can help. These flows define a set of steps for people to follow to achieve a specific outcome. Many of the steps will involve regular cloud flows, but some can also be manual tasks that are not otherwise automated. In this chapter, I'll examine how business process flows can be created to pull together a disparate group of cloud flows, desktop flows, and other tasks to achieve an overall goal.

Conventions Used in This Book

The following typographical conventions are used in this book:

Italic

> Indicates new terms, URLs, email addresses, filenames, and file extensions.

`Constant width`

> Used for program listings, as well as within paragraphs to refer to program elements such as variable or function names, databases, data types, environment variables, statements, and keywords.

`Constant width bold`

> Shows commands or other text that should be typed literally by the user.

`Constant width italic`

> Shows text that should be replaced with user-supplied values or by values determined by context.

This element signifies a tip or suggestion.

This element signifies a general note.

This element indicates a warning or caution.

O'Reilly Online Learning

 For more than 40 years, *O'Reilly Media* has provided technology and business training, knowledge, and insight to help companies succeed.

Our unique network of experts and innovators share their knowledge and expertise through books, articles, and our online learning platform. O'Reilly's online learning platform gives you on-demand access to live training courses, in-depth learning paths, interactive coding environments, and a vast collection of text and video from O'Reilly and 200+ other publishers. For more information, visit *https://oreilly.com*.

How to Contact Us

Please address comments and questions concerning this book to the publisher:

O'Reilly Media, Inc.
1005 Gravenstein Highway North
Sebastopol, CA 95472
800-889-8969 (in the United States or Canada)
707-829-7019 (international or local)
707-829-0104 (fax)
support@oreilly.com
https://www.oreilly.com/about/contact.html

We have a web page for this book, where we list errata, examples, and any additional information. You can access this page at *https://oreil.ly/learning-mspa*.

For news and information about our books and courses, visit *https://oreilly.com*.

Find us on LinkedIn: *https://linkedin.com/company/oreilly-media*

Follow us on Twitter: *https://twitter.com/oreillymedia*

Watch us on YouTube: *https://youtube.com/oreillymedia*

Acknowledgments

I would like to start out by thanking my wife, Sharon Papanek Stork, for letting me have the time to write this book. She has supported me throughout this journey, taking care of our grandchildren and giving me time to work on this book. She is the love of my life, and I look forward to spending more time with her now that the book is complete.

I would also like to thank all the people who ask questions about Power Automate on the Microsoft Power Platform forum. Your questions have driven me to look deeper into and learn more about Power Automate than I ever would have on my own. I hope this book will add to your knowledge and help you follow in the learning path I've been on.

Finally, I would like to thank all the fantastic crew members from O'Reilly for their support and trust. Jill Leonard, you have been a joy to work with as an editor. Your comments were always an improvement to the book and I'm proud of what we produced together.

I also want to thank the technical reviewers who checked my work for accuracy: Benedikt Bergmann, Damien Bird, Nicholas Bratttoli, Sheryl Netley, Jason Rivera, Scott Shearer, and Norm Young. As a developer, I learned a long time ago that having a separate set of eyes review my work is crucial to "getting it right." Your cross-checking has helped make this a much better book.

CHAPTER 1

What Is Microsoft Power Automate?

Working for an organization is…well, it's work. Even if you have a job doing what you love, there are still a lot of repetitive, manual, and time-consuming tasks. You may have to process reports or invoices that are sent to you by email and enter them into an accounting system. Or you may have to fill out travel expense reports and send them to someone for approval. Or you may have to take old files and information and move them to archive locations to make room for more up-to-date information. Every job includes processing information and distributing it to the right people and places. Frequently, these mundane tasks can keep you from doing the parts of your job that you love or growing your abilities by learning new things.

Welcome to this introduction on how to use Microsoft Power Automate to automate tasks in your daily work life. You're about to take your first steps on a journey that will change the way you handle information every day. But, like all journeys, we need to start at the beginning. That means we need to understand what Power Automate is and how it fits into the broader Microsoft ecosystem.

Power Automate is a cloud-based application that can be used to create workflows. These cloud-based workflows (flows) use connectors to access information stored in a variety of systems. Using these connectors, you can take manual tasks and convert them to automated workflows. Here are just a few examples of the ways in which Power Automate can transform everyday tasks:

- Automate the collection and processing of information
- Manage the approval process for documents/information
- Send automatic reminders for past-due tasks
- Archive emails and attachments in an indexable system

- Automate interactive computer tasks that are normally done manually
- Visualize a staged process consisting of multiple steps

These are just a few of the many varied tasks that you can transform using Power Automate. The only real limit is your creativity and whether a connector is available for the data you are working with.

 When Power Automate was originally released in October 2016, it was called Microsoft Flow. It was renamed Power Automate in November 2019 to better align with the other Microsoft Power Platform products. But the workflows created by Power Automate are still called "flows."

Power Automate is a powerful application, but it can do even more when used with other Power Platform applications. It is one of five applications included in the Power Platform. The other four applications are as follows:

Power Apps
Enables the user to quickly build custom applications that are accessible on personal computers, tablets, or mobile phones.

Power BI
Allows the user to create reports and graphs that supply data-driven insights for making informed business decisions.

Power Virtual Agents
Helps users to easily build chatbots to engage customers and employees using a conversational pattern.

Power Pages
Provides users with guidance on how to easily build a website to showcase business data to internal or external users.

These applications are all integrated. For example, you can use Power Automate to periodically send reports generated by Power BI. Or you can use Power Apps to create a mobile-ready application to collect information that is then processed and stored using a flow. We'll look at these possible integrations in more detail in Chapter 6. You can read more about the rest of the applications in the Power Platform on Microsoft's website (*https://oreil.ly/sKXXr*).

Power Automate is an advanced integration tool that can connect to a growing list of more than 600 out-of-the-box data sources, such as Google Sheets, Dynamics 365, SharePoint, Salesforce, and OneDrive. More data sources are being added every quarter. When this book was written, there were 645 connectors available in Power

Automate from Microsoft and third-party vendors. If a connector doesn't exist, but there is an API for a system, then developers can create their own custom connector.

 Custom connectors are an advanced topic and won't be covered in this introduction to Power Automate. You can read more about custom connectors in Microsoft's documentation (*https://oreil.ly/ VENCj*).

There is even a way to access information stored in legacy systems for which there is no connector or API available. Power Automate desktop flows can be used to interact with this legacy information using a regular computer user interface. We'll cover Power Automate desktop flows in Chapter 8. All these options provide you with a workflow engine that works with almost any information stored in a computer system, whether that system is designed by Microsoft or a third party.

Now that we've conducted a high-level overview of what Power Automate is, let's move on to the question of why you should use Power Automate to automate your manual processes. You probably have some sense of its capabilities and how it can improve workflows and make task management easier, or else you wouldn't be reading this book. However, it's important to be sure you are using it because it will solve your problems and not just because it's an industry buzzword.

Why Use Power Automate?

It's no secret that before the nternet, business profits were determined by commodities sold. This profitability has now shifted and is driven largely by digital assets and information profiles, leaving organizations dependent on the efficient processing of information. This is true for service organizations, like financial advisors, that focus on the production of information. But it's also true for traditional manufacturing companies that depend on computer systems to efficiently manage the procurement of raw materials, oversee the manufacturing process, and direct the delivery of finished goods. In today's world, every organization, regardless of its business model, depends on being able to process information quickly and accurately. But that very dependence leads to challenges.

Creating computer programs to efficiently process information has traditionally required professional developers. But there are never enough professional developers to do all the work that needs to be done. The good news is that, with the introduction of low-code/no-code development environments like Power Automate, much of that work can now be done by "citizen developers."

What is low-code/no-code? Well, it's essentially exactly what it sounds like. *Low-code/ no-code* are terms used to describe the development of software applications, generally for business solutions, without the need for a traditional programming background or knowledge of a programming language. For example, when building a flow in Power Automate, the "maker" creates the flow by choosing triggers and actions from a list. Then, they fill in blanks in the trigger or action to configure what it does. When these actions are executed in order, a process can be completed by the flow.

Conversely, traditional coding is an approach to software development where a professional programmer or a team of programmers who are trained to use a programming language like JavaScript or C# are employed to build software and applications. The ability for non-developers to use low-code/no-code tools frees up professional developers to focus on applications that require the use of more complex coding environments, like C# or JavaScript.

Who Are Citizen Developers?

Who are citizen developers? According to Gartner's Information Technology glossary (*https://oreil.ly/ePBf4*), a citizen developer is:

> an employee who creates application capabilities for consumption by themselves or others, using tools that are not actively forbidden by IT or business units. A citizen developer is a persona, not a title or targeted role. They report to a business unit or function other than IT.

That means a citizen developer is someone who has business knowledge that a professional developer in the IT department doesn't have. Although they aren't trained to do the same kind of development as a professional, citizen developers can accomplish a lot with a simpler low-code/no-code environment like Power Automate. For example, a sales representative might use Power Automate to consolidate monthly sales reports (received as Excel attachments to an email) into a more comprehensive report to be emailed to senior management. The sales representative understands the sales reports, since they work with them often. A developer would need an explanation of what the figures mean to be able to summarize them for a report.

The cost benefits of using citizen developers are substantial. Chiefly, businesses won't need to hire quite so many professional developers who have the expertise in building extensive enterprise applications. Professional developers with that level of experience are a limited, expensive resource. Using citizen developers for personal productivity or departmental applications can stretch the use of the limited number of professional developers to cover the essential enterprise development efforts that require that level of expertise.

But there are also significant benefits for the citizen developer, too. Using a tool like Power Automate, citizen developers can automate repetitive tasks that used to take them hours of manual effort. Automating these repetitious tasks improves reliability and lets the citizen developer concentrate their time on more interesting, productive endeavors. By doing these tasks themselves, instead of waiting for a professional developer, they also improve the turnaround on delivery of the application. Their involvement also guarantees that the design of the workflow is exactly what the citizen developer wanted.

The use of low-code/no-code development can also improve collaboration between internal departments by removing the professional developers as intermediaries. Citizen developers who speak the same business language can work together to implement new solutions to shared business problems. The result is an organization that runs more efficiently and can access necessary information more quickly. In almost every case, leveraging citizen developers is a net positive for both the organization and the citizen developer.

Migrating from SharePoint Designer to Power Automate

Power Automate is not Microsoft's first low-code/no-code workflow engine. SharePoint Designer (SPD) is a discontinued web design application that was used to build and customize SharePoint sites. One of the additional capabilities added into SPD was a low-code/no-code workflow designer that could automate the processing of information in SharePoint sites, lists, and libraries. Power Automate is the official replacement for SPD workflows, but it isn't a perfect match. In some ways, Power Automate is more powerful since it is not limited to processing SharePoint data alone. But SPD's tight integration with SharePoint made it easy to use. SPD could also do some things that Power Automate can't. So, why should citizen developers use Power Automate flows with SharePoint instead of the more established SPD workflows?

Why Not Use SPD Workflows?

Since its introduction, there have been two different versions of the SPD low-code/no-code workflow engines. The original version is now called SPD 2010 and ran within the software context of SharePoint. This made it susceptible to slowdowns if your SharePoint site experienced load-related issues. The newer version, called SPD 2013, ran as a separate, parallel process. It didn't have the performance issues inherent in SPD 2010 workflows. Since SPD 2013 workflows didn't contain all the actions available in SPD 2010 workflows, the ability to invoke a 2010 workflow from a 2013 workflow was added. SPD has been the established workflow engine for SharePoint for years. But on August 1, 2020, Microsoft announced that all SPD workflows were being deprecated. This deprecation called into question the viability of SPD workflows as a workflow solution. You can read about the deprecation schedule in Microsoft's documentation (*https://oreil.ly/gFi21*).

There are currently no utilities that can migrate existing SPD workflows to Power Automate. So, migration of workflows is a manual process. This makes it imperative that organizations make the switch to Power Automate as soon as possible, instead of waiting and creating additional SPD workflows that will need to be rewritten in 2026 when SPD support ends.

Power Automate Limitations and Workarounds

There are some things that SPD workflows can do that Power Automate can't, and the reverse is also true. Power Automate is a broader product that can access more than just SharePoint as a data source. It can also do more things with the data it accesses. Overall, Power Automate is an improvement on SPD workflows. But there are some limitations that you need to be aware of and some workarounds that may help if you are converting from SPD workflows to Power Automate. Table 1-1 summarizes the limitations and provides some potential workarounds.

Table 1-1. Power Automate limitations and workarounds

Power Automate Limitation	Explanation	Workaround
30-day timeout	Flow instances will tim eout and stop after 30 days. SPD workflows can run indefinitely.	Build flows with recurrence triggers that store their current state In a data source and wake up periodically to do processing.
HTTP connector	Calls to web services, like REST, require a premium license if they aren't to SharePoint. SPD workflows can make HTTP calls without additional licensing.	This licensing change reflects the broader scope of Power Automate. One way to minimize the cost is to use a Service Account with a premium license for flows that need to make general HTTP calls.
Reusable flows	With SPD you can create flows that can later be added to a variety of SharePoint lists. But Power Automate connections are bound to a specific data source when they are created. So, you can't have a single flow that works with multiple dynamic connections.	There is no easy way to duplicate reusable flows. But Power Automate does have a Save As function, which can be used to save a template that can be duplicated in other lists and modified.
Workflow history	SPD stores the workflow history for 60 days in a hidden list in the SharePoint site where the workflow runs. Power Automate stores workflow history for 28 days in a Dataverse table.	You can create a flow that periodically transfers workflow history from Dataverse to a storage location of your choice.
Impersonation (security)	SPD 2010 workflows include an impersonation step that lets you run a series of actions with elevated permissions. Power Automate doesn't support impersonation in cloud flows.	Flows can be created using a Service Account that has the permissions necessary to run the actions needing elevated permissions.

How This Book Will Teach Power Automate

Now that you've been introduced to what Power Automate is and who should learn how to use it, let's turn our attention to what you will learn from this book. Power Automate is a constantly changing product because Microsoft frequently, at least every six months, releases a new set of features and enhancements. It's impossible for any book to keep up with that level of constant change. So, this book will concentrate on teaching you how Power Automate works and what part its various components play. Once you've learned that, you'll be better prepared to take any new connector, action, trigger, or feature and use it to enhance your flows.

Learning to work with Power Automate is a lot like learning to cook. When I'm not sitting in front of my computer, I love to cook. Like most cooking hobbyists, I have acquired a lot of cookbooks over the years. The problem with learning to cook using cookbooks is that they focus primarily on recipes rather than cooking techniques. They may demonstrate the skills required for a specific recipe, but they don't show you how to cook in general. So, you learn how to make a few specific dishes, but it can be difficult to adapt what you learn to make other things.

Many technical guides and videos on Power Automate are designed to function like cookbooks. They walk you through examples of flows that solve a specific scenario, like creating an approval request when a new file is uploaded to SharePoint or sending a monthly report by email to a select group of managers. They are usually quick and make you feel like you've accomplished something when you follow along and produce the same results that they do. But what if you really need to do something that isn't quite the same scenario? Maybe you need to send an approval when a new contact is added to Dataverse. Or maybe you need to send a different report to each manager in the group. Now you're back to scouring the internet for a post or video that shows you how to do that specific scenario. If you can't find exactly what you need, then you have a problem—because you learned how to follow a recipe, not how to cook.

In this book, we will focus on learning how to "cook" with Power Automate. We'll focus more on the basic ingredients in a flow and how they interact with each other. I'll explain connectors and the triggers and actions they contain. You'll learn how to understand which fields need to be filled in for each action and how to determine what kind of data is needed. Yes, there will be samples and demos. But the point of those samples will be to demonstrate the skills you need to work with Power Automate in general, and not to just follow a step-by-step recipe. We'll also discuss where to access documentation on the various ingredients that go into a flow. You can find almost anything you need within Microsoft's Power Automate documentation (*https://oreil.ly/iSUCi*). As we go through the book, I'll explain how to sift through the wealth of available information to find what you need. Along the way, you'll not only learn how to complete a couple specific recipes, but you'll also begin to learn how to use Power Automate for yourself to create some amazing workflows.

Summary

In this chapter, I've talked about why Power Automate can change the way you process information every day. I've enumerated the different groups of people who will find it useful and discussed why it's a necessary replacement for existing SPD workflows. I've also promised that this book will do more than teach you a few simple recipes for doing common tasks. My goal with this book is to give you the tools and skills you need to grow your knowledge of Power Automate so you can use it to truly transform your daily workload.

CHAPTER 2

Getting Started: What You Need to Know

Now that we've explored what Power Automate is and why you might want to use it, you are ready to start working with Power Automate. But before you create your first flow, there are some other things you should know.

In the last chapter, I mentioned that there were more than 600 different connectors available in Power Automate to connect to various data sources. Because each of these connectors has different requirements, there are different levels of licensing available in Power Automate. The first thing you will need to figure out is which level of licensing is right for the scenarios that you will be automating.

You'll also need to gain access to the Power Automate website (*https://make.powerau tomate.com*) to build your first flow. Several different types of accounts can be used to log in to Power Automate. Some account types include what is called a "seeded license," which means they include some level of access to Power Automate for free. There are also free accounts that can be used while learning Power Automate. Each account type has different advantages, disadvantages, and limitations. I'll help you figure out which account is right for your situation.

The last thing you'll need to understand before you start building your first flow is what kinds of components make up a flow and what types of flows you can create. Flows are constructed using triggers and actions. I'll explain where to access them and what they do later in the chapter. I'll also cover the various types of flows available. Cloud flows can be instant, automated, or recurrent depending on how they are triggered. There are also desktop and business process flows that are completely different from regular cloud flows. The type of flow you create can affect the security context of the connections it uses. That security context can also affect whether users of the flow need to be licensed or just the original developer (maker) of the flow.

After completing this chapter, you'll have all the background information you need to get started and create your first flow. I'll show you how to do that in the next chapter, but first let's cover the foundational topics that you need to understand.

Key Licensing Terms

Before I begin discussing the licensing requirements for using Power Automate, I want to provide you with a list of the related key terms so that you understand what is covered by the different license types (see Table 2-1). I'll provide more detail on licensing later in this chapter, and in other chapters throughout the book.

Table 2-1. Key terms related to Power Automate licensing

Licensing term	Description
Microsoft 365	Previously called Office 365, this is a cloud-based subscription service that extends the Microsoft Office product line. It includes services like SharePoint, OneDrive, and Microsoft Teams.
Dynamics 365	A cloud-based product line of enterprise resource planning (ERP) and customer relationship management (CRM) business applications.
Power Apps	A graphical application for writing low-code/no-code custom business applications.
Power Virtual Agents	A low-code/no-code application for creating AI-powered chatbots that can be embedded in web sites or Microsoft Teams.
Flow types	Power Automate can support a number of different flow types. Each type will be explained more fully later in this chapter.
Desktop flows	Also known as Robotic Process Automation (RPA), these flows allow users to interact with Windows or web application user interfaces (UIs) on their desktop.
Business process flows	These flows provide a set of steps for people to follow to complete a complex business process, like onboarding an employee.
Standard and premium connectors	Connectors, which are used to connect to and process content stored in data sources, are categorized to require one of two licensing levels: standard or premium.
On-premises data gateway	A software service running on a local computer that provides cloud flows with access to data stored in on-premises computers.
Dataverse database	Microsoft Dataverse, originally named the Common Data Service (CDS), is a cloud-based data store originally designed for Microsoft Dynamics business applications, like CRM.
Power Platform environment	Power applications, Power Automate flows, and Dataverse tables are stored in dedicated areas called environments.
Storage capacity	Each Microsoft 365 or Dynamics 365 tenant includes a default environment. Additional environments can be created based on available storage capacity. Additional storage capacity is provided for each license purchased.

Licensing Options

Preparing to begin using Power Automate is fairly intuitive, but the many potential licenses available can be intimidating. Common questions include the following:

- Which license do I need to cover what I want to do?
- Can I start off with the least costly license until I learn how to use the product?
- Should I buy the most expensive license to make sure I have access to all the features?
- Is there a way to get started learning Power Automate for free?
- Is the Power Automate license included in Microsoft 365 licensing?

In this section, I'll review the different options for licensing Power Automate. There is quite a variety—from a free license to those included with other licenses like Power Apps or Microsoft 365, all the way to standalone Power Automate licenses. I'll explain what each type of license covers and what it doesn't. We'll examine different usage scenarios and which license is needed for each scenario. By the time we are done, you will have a good understanding of exactly what you need to get started, when you might need to upgrade, and generally what it will cost to use Power Automate.

Power Automate Free

Anyone can sign up and use Power Automate without buying a license. This is known as the Power Automate free license. All you need is an email address that can be used to create a Microsoft account. The problem with relying on this free license is that it severely limits what connections you can use in your flows. The free license does give you access to any standard connector, but most of the data sources you could connect to require their own licensing. The data source licenses are not covered by the free Power Automate license. For example, there are connectors that let you access Share-Point lists and libraries, but you'll need a Microsoft 365 license for the site, list, or library to access SharePoint. So, although the Power Automate free license is tempting, its practical uses are very limited. You'll likely find, however, that many of the data sources you wish to use, like SharePoint, include some Power Automate licensing in their licenses.

Microsoft 365 Licensing

One of the most common licenses used when working with Power Automate is the seeded license included with Microsoft 365 (previously called Office 365 and commonly abbreviated to M365) licenses. There are millions of Microsoft 365 users, and all of them have access to both Power Apps and Power Automate.

These seeded licenses are included so that Microsoft 365 users can easily create workflows and customize Office 365 applications. They cover the use of any standard connectors in Power Apps and Power Automate, with connections to things like SharePoint, OneDrive, Excel Online, and Microsoft Planner. These capabilities are summarized in Table 2-2 and will be covered in more detail later in this chapter.

Table 2-2. Microsoft 365 (seeded) licensing

Feature	Covered
Create and run cloud flows	Yes
Create and execute business process flows	No
Create and run desktop flows	No
Use standard connections	Yes
Use premium and custom connections	No
Access on-premises data using a gateway	No

However, there are limitations on these seeded licenses. For example, these licenses do not cover the use of on-premises gateways. So, if you or your organization uses non-cloud resources like SharePoint servers or network file servers, this may not be the best license for your needs. You also can't create your own custom connectors based on API calls or access data sources that require premium connectors like SQL databases or Dataverse. For those, you'll need a different license. There are a number of potential licenses that can cover these scenarios.

Dynamics 365 Licensing

Like Microsoft 365, some Dynamics 365 licenses include a seeded license for Power Apps and Power Automate. The following include a seeded license:

- Dynamics 365 Enterprise
- Dynamics 365 Professional
- Dynamics 365 Team Member

These licenses are intended to be used to customize and extend Dynamics 365 applications like Customer Relationship Management (CRM). The difference is that since Dynamics apps use Dataverse as a database, these seeded licenses include access to the premium Dataverse connector. The capabilities included in the Dynamics seeded license are summarized in Table 2-3.

Table 2-3. Dynamics 365 (seeded) licensing

Feature	Covered
Create and run cloud flows	Yes
Create and execute business process flows	Yes
Create and run desktop flows	No
Use standard connections	Yes
Use premium and custom connections	No
Use Dataverse database	Yes
Access on-premises data using a gateway	No

There are limitations on your use of the Dataverse connector, though. It must be used to customize or extend your Dynamics 365 application, but it cannot be used to avoid licensing costs by replacing existing Dynamics functionality. For example, you can't use the Dataverse connector to build your own CRM system based on a less expensive Dynamics license like a Team Member license.

The Dynamics seeded license also includes the ability to create business process flows in addition to cloud flows. Business process flows are normally a Premium feature. I'll take a deeper look at business process flows in Chapter 9. Like the Microsoft 365 seeded license, the Dynamics seeded license does not cover desktop flows or the use of on-premises gateways.

Power Apps Licensing

One of the most common ways to use premium connectors with Power Automate is to purchase a Power Apps license. Both the Power Apps per-user and per-app licenses include Power Automate use rights. This covers Power Automate when it is used in connection within the context of a related Power App. You can find more detail about the Power Automate use rights included with Power Apps licensing by downloading the Microsoft Power Apps and Power Automate Licensing Guide (*https://oreil.ly/5tIuj*). Unless you are building a solution that only uses Power Automate, this will probably be the only licensing you need.

What Is a Related Power App?

There is no firm definition of what a "related Power App" is when dealing with Power Automate. The idea is that you can use Power Automate to support and enhance what a specific Power App is designed to do. The clearest example of this is when an application manually triggers a cloud flow to process some data and return a result. But a flow can be in the context of a related Power App without actually being triggered by the application. Flows that are triggered using an automated trigger or a recurrence trigger are also covered if they use the same data source as the related Power App.

For example, if you had an application that let employees upload an annual self-review, you might have a related flow that triggers when a new file is created or modified, to submit it to the user's manager for approval. The flow isn't manually triggered by the application, but it is clearly used to enhance the business process that the application is automating. So, it would be considered a related Power App. But if I created a flow to take information submitted using a Microsoft form and save it to an SQL database, this would be considered a standalone flow because there is no Power App involved in any part of the process.

Power Apps per-user versus per-app licensing

Power Apps provides two licenses, both of which include the same use rights for Power Automate. A per-user Power Apps license covers an unlimited number of applications for a single user. A per-app Power Apps license lets a user run a single application that has been shared with them. Per-user licenses are assigned directly to the user, while per-app licenses are allocated to a pool of licenses in a given environment. Users will automatically get a license from the pool when they run an application for which they don't have adequate licensing.

There are three specific points that should be noted when dealing with Power Automate licensing based on Power Apps use rights:

- Since per-app licensing is tied to a specific application, it will normally only cover flows that are triggered directly by the application.
- Premium licensing isn't required to create an application, only to run it. But users will often be prompted to start a trial license when making an application or a flow if they don't have a Power Apps per-user license. Microsoft is working to correct this anomaly.
- Many users who have a Power Apps license find purchase of an additional Power Automate license to be unnecessary.

Power Automate Standalone Plans

For many Power Automate users, Microsoft 365, Dynamics 365, or Power Apps licensing will be enough to meet all their needs. But if the scenarios I've already covered don't apply to you, then you can also purchase Power Automate standalone licensing. There are three different Power Automate standalone plans: per-user without RPA, per-user with RPA, and per-flow. RPA stands for robotic process automation, for which Power Automate uses desktop flows. What each license covers is summarized in Table 2-4.

Table 2-4. Power Automate standalone licenses

	Per-user without RPA	Per-user with RPA	Per-flow
Premium connectors	✓	✓	✓
Cloud flows	✓	✓	✓
Business process flows	✓	✓	✓
Run desktop flows (Attended)	—	✓	—
Run desktop flows (Unattended)	—	Add-on (*https://oreil.ly/YkSOG*)	Add-on (*https://oreil.ly/YkSOG*)

The per-user license without RPA gives you the ability to create as many cloud and business process flows as you like, using either standard or premium connectors. This is similar to the Power Apps per-user license except there is no requirement for a related Power App context. The one limitation for this license is that you can't trigger desktop flows from a cloud flow.

The per-user license with RPA has all the capabilities of the regular per-user license but adds the ability to trigger desktop flows from a cloud flow. The desktop flows can be either attended flows (run on the user's computer) or unattended flows (run on a remote computer or virtual machine). Unattended flows require an additional add-on license for each computer (known as a bot) where you run them. I'll provide more detail about desktop flows in Chapter 8.

The last standalone Power Automate license is a per-flow license. Whereas the per-user licenses let a single user run multiple flows, the per-flow license covers many different users running one flow. The base license covers up to five flows. Additional licenses can be added on for each additional flow over five.

Pay-as-You-Go Licensing

All the paid licensing I've discussed so far requires an annual commitment, at minimum. Users are charged either a monthly rate for 12 months or a discounted yearly rate paid in advance. But in 2022, Microsoft released a new pay-as-you-go license plan for both Power Apps and Power Automate. With pay-as-you-go licensing, users are charged a slightly higher licensing fee, but only for the months when they actually use an application or a flow that requires a premium license.

Pay-as-you-go is configured at the environment level in the Power Platform. To enable pay-as-you-go, you link a Power Platform environment to an Azure subscription using a billing policy. The billing policy creates a meter to track the usage of applications and flows in the environment. It also provides 1GB of Dataverse storage.

Pay-as-you-go storage allocations are separate and do not count against existing Power Platform storage capacity.

If a user uses an application or a flow that requires a premium license in a particular month, then a charge is added to their Azure subscription. Charges are not added if the user has a license that would cover the usage. An explanation of the various charges recorded by the meter is presented in Table 2-5. Please refer to the pay-as-you-go documentation (*https://oreil.ly/hwYYV*) for the most up-to-date pricing.

Table 2-5. Pay-as-you-go charges

Meter type	What is counted?	Retail cost
Power Apps	Active users for each Power App who open an application at least once in that month. Users with existing Power Apps premium licenses are not counted.	$10 per active user/app/month
Power Automate	Cloud and desktop flow runs using premium connectors. Flow runs covered by existing licenses are not counted.	$0.60 per cloud flow run $0.60 per desktop flow run (attended mode) $3.00 per desktop flow run (unattended mode)
Dataverse storage	Usage of Dataverse database, file, or log storage above 1GB.	$48 per GB/month for database storage $2.40 per GB/month for file storage $12 per GB/month for log storage

Common use cases for the pay-as-you-go licensing plan include the following:

- Applications or flows that are used only occasionally but by a large number of users
- The need to evaluate costs when just starting to use the Power Platform without incurring an annual commitment
- The need to allocate costs across business units within an organization using an existing Azure subscription

Special Case Licenses

I've now covered all the licenses that you might normally use to add a Power Automate flow into a production environment. There are, however, a few special situations that we should discuss. These special case licenses are as follows:

- Power Virtual Agents license
- Power Automate trial license
- Power Apps Developer Plan
- Windows licensing

Power Virtual Agents License

A Power Virtual Agents (PVA) license grants limited-use rights to Power Automate, similar to the use rights included in the Power Apps per-user license. It lets you create flows that are triggered by actions in a PVA bot. But the use rights are more limited in PVA than they are in Power Apps. For example, PVA doesn't include the concept of a related Power App. To be covered by the PVA license, the flow must be triggered from an action in the bot. Power Automate can only be used to extend the functionality of the PVA bot itself to retrieve or process information. The PVA license does not cover any other types of flows.

Power Automate Trial License

Trial licenses are available for both the per-user without RPA and per-user with RPA Power Automate licenses. There are no trials available for the per-flow license. Trial licenses are also available for the Power Apps per-user license. They provide all the same functionality as the paid licenses, with one exception. The one thing you can't do with the trial licenses is create additional environments. But any of these trial licenses will give you access to premium connectors.

There are two ways users can obtain a trial of Power Automate. Microsoft 365 global admins can request a trial license using Purchase Services on the Billing page of the Microsoft 365 admin center (see Figure 2-1). After requesting a trial license, the admin can assign it to a specific user.

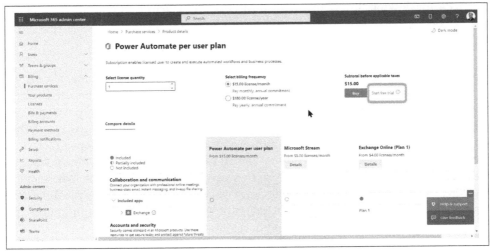

Figure 2-1. Requesting a Power Automate trial as an admin

Users can also sign up for a trial directly through the Power Automate website (*https://oreil.ly/1PWfj*) using the "Start free" button. But to get a full Power Automate trial, you must have a work or school account. If you sign up with a generic email or a Microsoft account, you will get access to the Power Automate free license discussed earlier, not a Power Automate per-user trial license.

These per-user trial licenses expire after 30 days, but you can extend the trial twice, so the upper limit is 90 days. Once your trial expires, you are given the option to purchase a plan. If you're already using one of the other licenses that don't include premium connectors, this is a good way to test the premium functionalities of Power Automate.

But 90 days may be too short a time frame if you are trying to learn Power Automate from scratch. Microsoft also offers a license for development called the Power Apps Developer Plan. This development-only plan may be a better alternative when learning Power Automate.

Power Apps Developer Plan

The Power Apps Developer Plan provides access to all the premium features in both Power Apps and Power Automate. Like a Power Automate trial, it is free, but it never expires. It does have the following limitations (but these won't interfere with using it to learn Power Automate):

- Currently limited to a single developer environment
- Dataverse database capacity limited to 2GB
- A limit of 750 flow runs per month
- RPA for desktop flows not included (needed to trigger desktop flows from cloud flows)
- Does not provide any AI Builder credits (advanced add-on feature)

The Power Apps Developer Plan provides the user with a single developer environment. The most important limitation is that this environment can't be used to run production applications or flows; it can only be used for learning and development. Any applications or flows that are developed here will need to be moved to another environment if you want to run them in production. Since the Developer Plan only covers one developer environment, that means any flows that use premium features will require an additional license before they can be run in production. Microsoft is working to change the limit on a single developer environment to allow the full use of Application Lifecycle Management (ALM). But that won't alter the requirement that the plan's use be limited to learning and development only.

Signing up for a Power Apps Developer Plan (*https://oreil.ly/zzClR*) requires a work or school email address. A work or school account is created by an organization that has an Azure Active Directory for authentication and authorization. The most common scenarios for this are organizations using Microsoft 365 or Dynamics. You can also sign up for a Developer Plan using the "Try free" link on the website, which we'll cover later in the chapter.

If you are using this book to learn Power Automate and already have a Microsoft 365 or Dynamics license, this is the best way to get a license that gives you access to almost all the premium features in Power Automate without an additional charge.

Windows Licensing

The licenses for Windows 10/11 operating systems include a license for Power Automate Desktop (PAD). PAD is related to Power Automate, but it is not the same thing. PAD is the RPA feature that is included with some of the Power Automate standalone licenses. RPA flows are known as desktop flows in Power Automate. Windows 10/11 includes a license for manually running attended desktop flows. The inclusion of desktop flow licensing in Windows 10/11 is designed to allow users to automate repetitious tasks on their own desktop. Unattended desktop flows or desktop flows triggered from a cloud flow are not included in this licensing. I'll provide more details on Power Automate desktop flows in Chapter 8.

Anatomy of a Flow

Now that you understand a bit about the licensing you will need to make use of Power Automate, there are a few other pieces of background information that you will need to understand before creating your first flow. Power Automate cloud flows are assembled out of relatively simple building blocks called triggers and actions. These triggers and actions are encapsulations of the APIs available for a particular data source. They all follow the same basic pattern. Both triggers and actions contain required and optional fields that are used for configuration. Figure 2-2 shows the configuration fields for a Dataverse trigger and a SharePoint action.

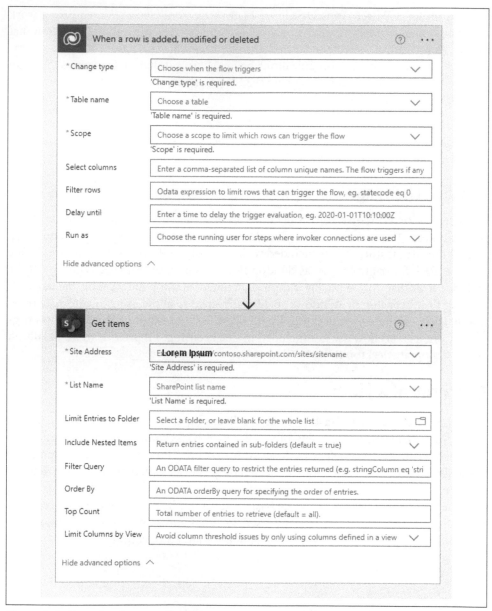

Figure 2-2. Sample trigger and action

Once you understand the pattern of configuration fields, you'll be able to use any trigger or action necessary to complete the logic of your flow. You'll learn more about how to use triggers and actions in Chapter 3. For now, you should concentrate on understanding what they are, where they come from, and how they fit together to create a flow. Desktop flows and business process flows are made up of different components. I'll discuss what desktop flows look like in Chapter 8 and business process flows in Chapter 9. For now, I'll focus on triggers and actions as they relate to cloud flows.

Triggers

A *trigger* is an event that initiates a cloud flow run. For example, you might want to start an approval process whenever a new file is added to a SharePoint document library. Or you might want to process an invoice that is received as an attachment when a new email arrives. Triggers aren't always automated events. A trigger event can also be a manual event, like a user pressing a button in a Power App, or a recurring event that happens at a specific date and time. The events that can be used as triggers are varied, but a specific trigger is always the first step in a cloud flow.

Triggers can either be webhook triggers or polling triggers. Webhooks will fire as soon as the event takes place, but polling triggers may take a few minutes before the change is detected and the trigger is fired. Unless it's a very special circumstance, a flow can only have one trigger.

 When testing a flow, it's usually a good idea to wait at least 5–10 minutes for a trigger to fire before assuming there is a problem. You may be working with a polling trigger that fires on a schedule.

Actions

Since there is only one trigger in a flow, most of what makes up a flow are actions. *Actions* are the steps that perform the work of the flow. Each action receives input from the action before it, does its processing, and outputs information to the actions that follow it. Some actions create, update, retrieve, or delete information in a data source. There are also actions that control the logical path the flow takes. For example, a conditional action may compare a value to a constant and decide which of two branches to follow. Other actions can be used to process multiple items in a loop or establish variables to hold temporary values. I'll provide some specific examples of simple flows later in this chapter. For now, I'll stick to a more abstract discussion of how triggers and actions fit together to build a cloud flow.

 One of the most common problems faced by flow developers is not having a clear idea of how to translate the logic of a business process into a series of flow actions.

Figure 2-3 shows how a flow might start with a trigger, perform an action, evaluate the result of that action in a condition, and then perform different actions based on the output of the condition. Other than the trigger, everything in the diagram is an action.

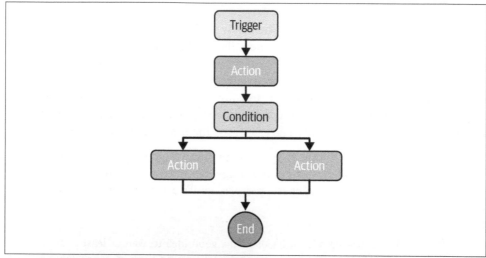

Figure 2-3. Generic flow

Connectors

We've already talked about the fact that there are more than 600 connectors that provide access to different data sources. Each connector provides access to triggers and actions that are specific to the data source that it connects to. For example, the Office 365 Outlook connector has a trigger for "When a new email arrives," and the One-Drive for Business connector has an action for "Delete file." Triggers and actions are classified as either standard or premium based on their connector. To use premium connectors, you will need a license that includes premium connectors. For some connectors, you may also need an account with the company that makes the connector. These accounts may be either paid or free.

To find a specific trigger or action, you must first know which connector it might be in. Standard connectors are available to all users, but premium connectors are only available to users with a premium license like a Power Apps or Power Automate per-user license.

Types of Flows

There are a variety of different types of flows. When you create a flow, the first thing you are asked is what type of flow you want to create. You'll need to understand the differences between the various types of flows to be able to pick the right one. The primary focus of this book is cloud flows, which are the most common. There are three types of cloud flows based on the type of trigger is used to trigger them:

- Automated cloud flows
- Instant cloud flows
- Scheduled cloud flows

There are two additional, special flow types that will be covered later in the book:

- Desktop flows
- Business process flows

Any of the five types of flows can be created in the Power Automate design studio (*https://oreil.ly/0gMOl*). Let's look at explanations and examples of each.

Automated Cloud Flows

Automated cloud flows are triggered by an event in a data source, such as the arrival of an email or modification of a record in a Dataverse table. The advantage of an automated flow is that it happens without human intervention (see Figure 2-4). Automated flows are probably the most common form of flow.

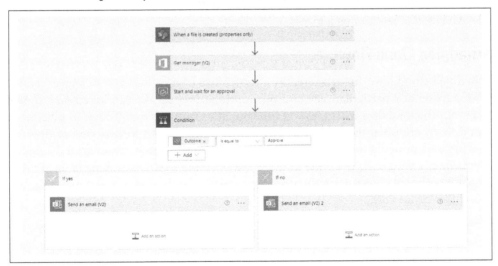

Figure 2-4. Sample automated flow

The steps in the flow shown in Figure 2-4 are as follows:

1. The flow is triggered when a file is uploaded to SharePoint.
2. The manager of the person who uploaded the file is notified.

3. An approval is sent to the manager.

4. Whether the file is approved or rejected, an email is sent to the original requestor.

Instant Cloud Flows

Instant cloud flows are triggered by a user action, such as a user clicking a button in a Power App or a button in the mobile flow application to run a cloud flow. Figure 2-5 shows a simple instant cloud flow.

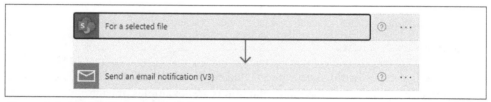

Figure 2-5. Sample instant cloud flow

The steps in the flow shown in Figure 2-5 are as follows:

1. The flow is triggered manually after the user selects a file in a SharePoint document library.

2. The user enters an email address in the side panel in the library.

3. An email is sent to that address.

Scheduled Cloud Flows

Scheduled cloud flows are triggered by a recurrence trigger. Recurrence triggers run a flow starting at a particular date and time and then repeat the run based on a timed interval. All cloud flow instances will time out after running for 30 days, so scheduled cloud flows are often used as a way of running a flow over a long period of time by starting and stopping it on a schedule. For example, a flow that retrieves all the documents that haven't been modified in the last six months and moves them to an archive might be scheduled to run on the first day of each month. Figure 2-6 shows a simple scheduled cloud flow.

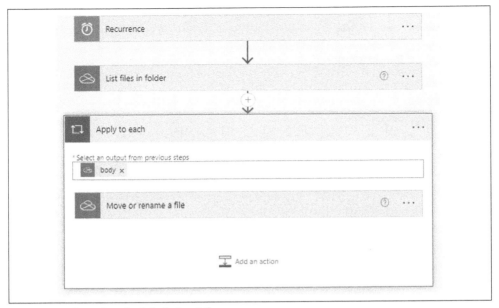

Figure 2-6. Sample scheduled cloud flow

The steps in the flow shown in Figure 2-6 are as follows:

1. The flow is triggered on the first day of each month at 5:00 a.m.
2. The flow retrieves a list of files that have modification dates of more than 30 days ago.
3. Each file in the list is moved to an archive location.

Desktop Flows

Desktop flows are Power Automate's entry into the world of robotic process automation (RPA). They can be used to automate all repetitive desktop tasks. They are best used in situations where a connector with appropriate triggers and actions does not exist, such as cases where you need to enter data into a website or a legacy desktop application that has no defined API. Figure 2-7 shows an example of a desktop flow.

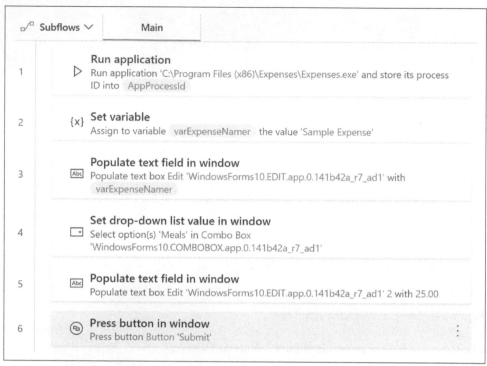

Figure 2-7. Sample desktop flow

The steps in the desktop flow shown in Figure 2-7 are as follows:

1. Run a legacy application called *Expenses.exe*.
2. Set a variable with the name of the expense (this could pull from another source like Excel).
3. Enter the expense name in the appropriate text box.
4. Select the expense type from a drop-down menu.
5. Enter the amount of the expense in the appropriate text box.
6. Submit the expense.

Business Process Flows

Business process flows provide an overview of a set of tasks, organized into stages, that need to be completed by one or more people. Some of the tasks may be manual, while others may include running cloud or desktop flows. The goal is to outline a repeatable set of tasks that can be followed to guarantee a high-quality result each time. Business process flows are created in Power Automate, but they are hosted in a Power Apps Model Driven application or Dynamics 365, which provides the user interface. Each stage is a checklist of tasks to be completed before moving to the next stage. When all stages have been completed, the process is complete. An example of a business process that could be automated this way is an employee onboarding procedure that combines tasks completed by a manager, the information technology team, and human resources. Figure 2-8 shows a sample business process flow.

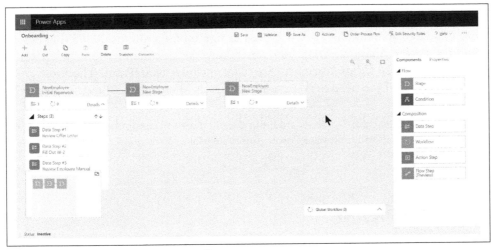

Figure 2-8. Sample business process flow

What follows is a brief description of the overall stages and tasks in the business process flow shown in Figure 2-8. This is a simplified example, but it does demonstrate how different people and groups cooperate to complete an overall process by doing their individual tasks in order:

- A manager reviews and signs required paperwork with the new employee, including the following:
  — An offer letter
  — Tax withholding paperwork
  — Company policies and procedures manual
- The IT team readies the resources that the new employee will need, including the following:
  — A user account
  — A configured laptop
- An HR representative reviews and signs additional paperwork, including the following:
  — Health insurance withholding
  — Company parking procedures

Accessing Power Automate

Now that you've learned about the licensing options and flow types, it's time to look at how to log in to Power Automate. If you already have one of the licenses discussed in the previous section, you can skip this section and go right to Exercise 2-3. If you don't have a license that has access to premium features but do have access to Microsoft 365 or Dynamics 365, then follow the steps in Example 2-2. If you don't have a work or school account, then you will need to sign up for a Microsoft 365 trial before getting a Power Automate trial. You can follow the instructions to sign up for a Microsoft 365 trial (*https://oreil.ly/cFFc6*) that includes SharePoint. The most cost-effective license, if you need to go beyond 30 days, is Microsoft 365 Business Basic.

 Microsoft 365 trials are limited to 30 days and cannot be renewed. This will limit your Power Automate trial to 30 days also.

Power Automate Trial

There are several ways that you can obtain a Power Automate trial license. Using the "Try free" link on the Power Automate website, you can sign up for a Power Automate free license (described earlier in "Licensing Options" on page 10). If you then create a flow that uses a premium connector and share it with another user, you will be prompted to start a 90-day trial. To start a trial, which includes premium connectors, you must be using a work or school account. Microsoft accounts and other email-based free licenses can't access premium features. Another way to start a trial is to use Power Automate Desktop (PAD), with a work or school account. Clicking on the "Go Premium" link inside the Desktop client will start a trial that includes attended RPA. Finally, you can ask your Microsoft 365 global administrators to sign up for a Power Automate trial through the admin center.

Exercise 2-1. Signing up for a Power Automate trial

To sign up for a Power Automate trial with a work or school account, do the following:

1. Open a web browser and navigate to the Power Automate website (*https://oreil.ly/TIUDJ*). Select "Try free" in the upper-right corner of the screen (see Figure 2-9). This will take you to a page where you can sign up for Power Automate.

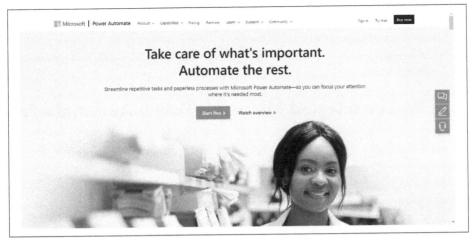

Figure 2-9. Signing up for a Power Automate Free trial

2. Enter your work or school email address and click the "Start free" button (see Figure 2-10). This will take you to a page with a three-step wizard for creating your free Power Automate account.

You can sign up for Power Automate Free using any email address, but only work or school accounts can enable the premium features of Power Automate in a trial.

Figure 2-10. Starting a Power Automate Free trial

3. Click "Sign in" and sign in with your work or school account and password (see Figure 2-11). This will take you to a screen showing your work or school account and your default region.

Figure 2-11. Signing in using your work or school account

4. Click "Get started" to start your free account (see Figure 2-12). This will take you to a confirmation screen.

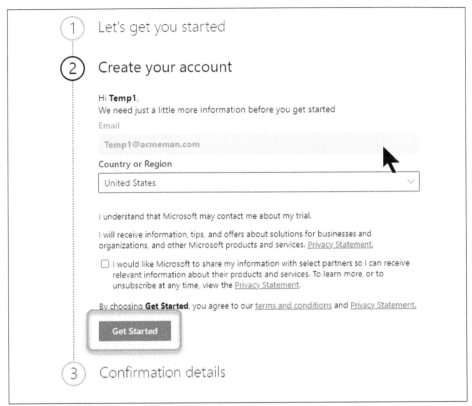

Figure 2-12. Setting up your Power Automate Free account and getting started

5. Click "Get started" to confirm that you want a Power Automate Free account (see Figure 2-13). This will take you to the Power Automate website.

Figure 2-13. Confirming your account

6. Click "Get started" one last time to accept the region you entered in the wizard (see Figure 2-14). You will now see the home page of the Power Automate website. On the Home page, select the Templates tab in the lefthand toolbar.

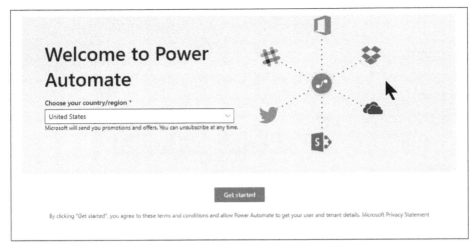

Figure 2-14. Setting environment region

7. Type "Copy documents" in the search box and click the "Copy files from one OneDrive for Business account or folder to another" template card to create a new flow (see Figure 2-15).

Figure 2-15. Creating a template flow

8. Sign in to authorize the OneDrive Connections (if necessary) and click Continue (see Figure 2-16).

Figure 2-16. Authorizing connections

9. Type a slash (/) in the Folder and Folder Path fields of the trigger and the action. Click Save in the upper-left corner to save the completed flow. Click the arrow next to the flow name in the upper-left corner (see Figure 2-17). This will return you to the flow's description.

Figure 2-17. Saving a flow

10. Click Edit in the Owners box on the right side of the screen (see Figure 2-18). This is where you would go to share the flow with other users.

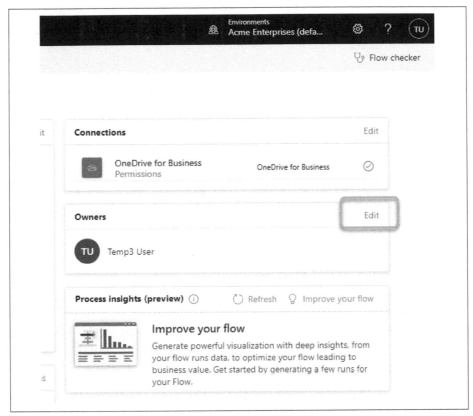

Figure 2-18. Sharing a flow

11. Sharing a flow with another user when using the Power Automate Free license will prompt you to start a trial. Click "Start trial" (see Figure 2-19).

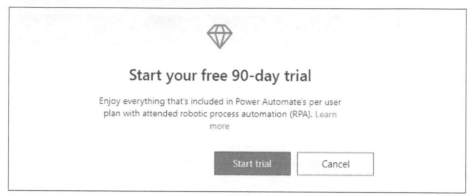

Figure 2-19. Starting Power Automate trial

12. Click the Gear menu and show "My plans."

Power Apps Developer Plan

Free Power Automate trial licenses provide an easy way to learn Power Automate without incurring additional cost. But the time limits often make it difficult to learn enough before the trial runs out. Activating a Power Apps Developer Plan provides a different free option for learning Power Automate that is not timeboxed. As I mentioned earlier in this chapter, the Power Apps Developer Plan has some limitations. But most of these limitations will not affect you as you begin to learn Power Automate. This is the license plan I would recommend for anyone who wants to learn Power Automate.

 To sign up for a Power Apps Developer Plan, you will need a work or school account that logs in to either Microsoft 365 or Dynamics 365. A free Microsoft account will not be enough.

There are two ways to obtain a Power Apps Developer Plan. If your organization already uses the Power Platform, you can get a Developer Plan by having your administrators create a new Developer environment for you. You can also sign up directly on the Power Apps Developer Plan website.

Exercise 2-2. Signing up for a Power Apps Developer Plan

To sign up for a Power Apps Developer Plan with a work or school account, follow these steps:

1. Open a web browser and navigate to the Power Apps Developer Plan (*https://oreil.ly/FSbx5*). You will see the website shown in Figure 2-20.

Figure 2-20. Power Apps Developer Plan sign-up page

2. Select "Try free" in the upper-right corner of the website. That will take you to the wizard shown in Figure 2-21.

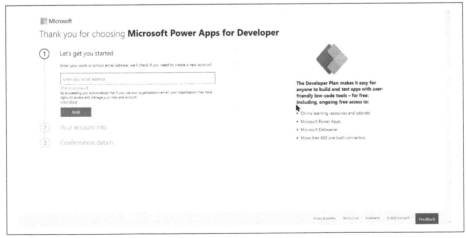

Figure 2-21. Developer Plan sign-up step 1

3. Enter your work or school email address and click Next. You will be asked to confirm your account information.

 A credit card is not required to sign up for a Power Apps Developer Plan.

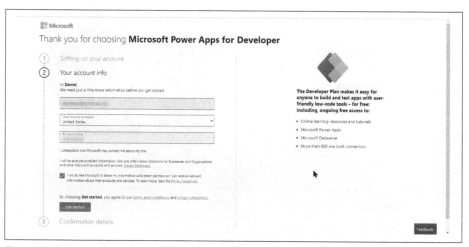

Figure 2-22. Developer Plan sign-up step 2

4. Fill in your account information and select whether Microsoft can share your email information with partners or not. Then click "Get started."

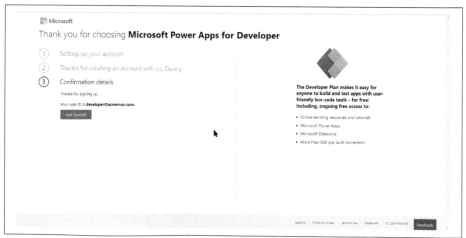

Figure 2-23. Developer Plan confirmation

5. You've now successfully signed up for a Power Apps Developer Plan. Clicking "Get started" will navigate you to the Power Apps Designer. To log in and create Power Automate flows, follow the steps in Exercise 2-3.

Exercise 2-3. Logging in to Power Automate

Power Automate uses a web-based design studio. To log in, you'll need your work or school email address and password. Follow these steps to log in to the Power Automate Design Studio website:

1. If you aren't already there, navigate to *https://make.powerautomate.com*. Then sign in with your work or school account (see Figure 2-24).

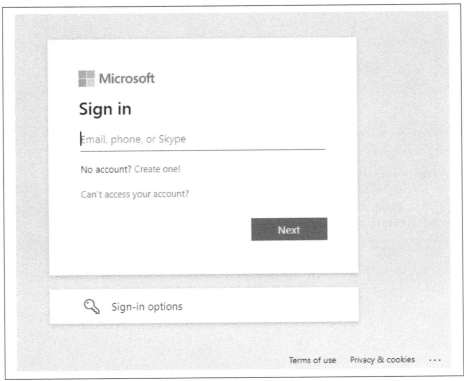

Figure 2-24. Work or school account login

2. Type in the password for your work or school account (see Figure 2-25).

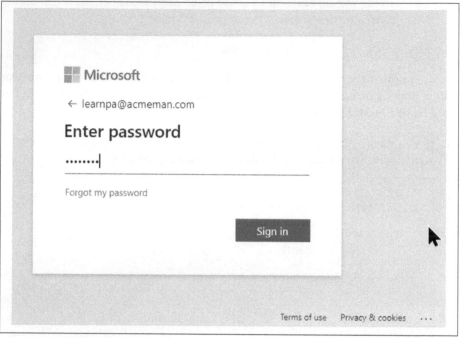

Figure 2-25. Password prompt

3. Click Yes to minimize the number of times you will be asked to provide your user information again (see Figure 2-26).

Figure 2-26. ""Stay signed in" prompt

4. If you signed up for the Power Apps Developer Plan, use the Environments drop-down in the upper-right corner to select your developer environment. This is the only environment where your Developer Plan license will let you access premium features. Your developer's environment will be named using your user's name followed by the word *environment*. In Figure 2-27, you can see me selecting my developer environment.

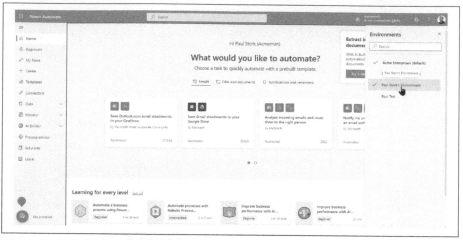

Figure 2-27. Selecting the developer environment

Summary

In this chapter, you learned the necessary background information to start using Power Automate. We reviewed the following:

- The different licenses required to run flows
- How to sign up for a Power Automate Free or Power Apps Developer Plan
- How to log in to the Power Automate Designer website
- The building blocks used to create flows
- The different types of flows and simple examples of each

We've now covered all the necessary background material to create your first flow. I've listed the various licenses available and what each one covers. You can choose any plan that fits your business needs, but if you're not sure which one to start with and are looking to learn Power Automate, the Power Apps Developer Plan license is a good starting point and will provide sufficient access for you to get the most out of this book. In this chapter, I explained how to sign up for the Developer Plan and explained how it will give you free access to all the Power Automate features you need while you are learning to use the product.

Now that we've covered the background material, it's time to create your first Power Automate flow. In the next chapter, I'll show you three different ways to create a flow. Hands-on exercises are included so you can learn by doing.

CHAPTER 3

Building Your First Flow

Now that you have all that foundational knowledge, it's time to start building your first flows. I'll start off by showing you how to build a completely functional flow using a prebuilt template. Then, I'll cover how to construct a flow from scratch when there is no template that matches what you want to do. Finally, I'll review how to design a workflow using Microsoft Visio and then import that into Power Automate. By the end of this chapter, you'll know how to assemble triggers and actions to create Power Automate flows. Then, in Chapter 4, we'll fill in the details of the triggers and actions with dynamic content to create fully functional flows.

How to Use Templates

The easiest way to build a fully functional flow is to use a prebuilt template. Power Automate includes a large list of templates to fit a variety of scenarios. You can search for a template or browse them by categories to find a template that matches what you need to accomplish. Figure 3-1 shows the Templates tab in the Power Automate website with the "All templates" category selected. The Templates tab can be used to browse or search for a template to match your scenario. You can also use a Search box at the top of the page or a drop-down on the right to select how the templates are sorted.

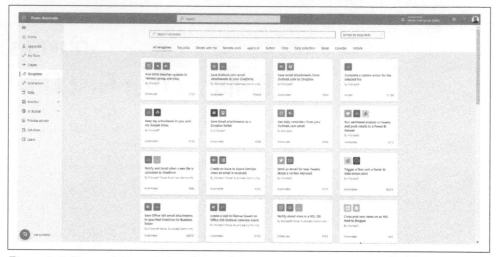

Figure 3-1. Power Automate templates tab

When you start with a template, the trigger, actions, and the logical flow are already done for you. You can just pick the flow and provide a few details if necessary, and the flow is ready to run. For example, you might want a flow that will check the weather forecast. If you search the templates for the term *weather* you will find a flow with the following specifications:

- The flow is triggered manually.
- It uses the MSN Weather service.
- It returns the weather forecast for your current location.
- Output reports the temperature based on your personal regional settings.
- Output is sent via a push notification.

Your search will show you a template called "Get today's weather forecast for my current location," as shown in Figure 3-2. You don't need to provide any information to complete the flow. It uses your regional settings and the location of your device as input to return the weather forecast.

Figure 3-2. Getting today's weather template

Using Flow Templates

The hardest part of using a template to build a flow is finding a template that fits the exact scenario you want to accomplish. Templates are organized into categories like Top picks, Remote work, Approval, Button, Data collection, and more. You can browse or search a particular category to find what you want. You can also sort each category by the template's popularity, name, or publish date (see Figure 3-3). Each template in the list is displayed as a card that shows the following:

- The trigger and connections used in the flow
- A descriptive title
- Who created the template

- The type of flow that the template will create
- How many flows have been created using this template

Get today's weather forecast for
my current location
By Microsoft

Instant   352807

Figure 3-3. Template description card

Let's take a closer look at each of these elements. The "Get today's weather forecast for my current location" template uses a manual trigger and two connectors. We know this because the blue icon with a finger pushing the button is the manual trigger and the other two icons are the connectors for MSN Weather and Notifications. After you work with Power Automate for a while, you will get to know many of the icons used to represent connectors and triggers. You can also see that Microsoft created the template, that it creates an instant cloud flow, and that it is very popular with over 35,000 flows created using the template.

In addition to the information displayed on each card, there is also a brief description of what the template does. This description is only visible when you access a specific card, but the text is included in the search engine that populates your results. For example, if you search for "weather pushed to mobile devices," you'll see three template cards including the one in Figure 3-3. This card is included because the description reads "With a single button tap get today's weather forecast pushed to your mobile devices." The search is selecting templates based on all the information displayed on the card as well as the description.

Now that you understand the information that is presented on the template description cards, finding the right template is just a matter of matching what you are trying to do with that information. This can be done by either browsing through the template card list or by searching to narrow down the list of cards to review.

Once you have identified the template you want to use, creating a flow from it is relatively easy. Let's try a simple example. Here's the scenario: in your organization, employees upload monthly status reports to a specific SharePoint document library. When a status report is uploaded, the employee's manager should be informed and have a chance to review the report and either approve or reject it. If you search on "approve a file" in the Approvals category, you will see the seven template cards that relate to different approval scenarios (see Figure 3-4).

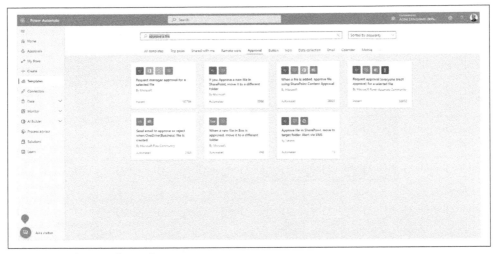

Figure 3-4. Approval templates

After reviewing the flow specs, we see that none of the templates are exactly what we want, but the closest match is the first template in the list: "Request manager approval for a selected file."

Exercise 3-1. Creating a flow from a template

Let's walk through how to create a flow using an existing template and review how it works. Then, in the next section, we'll look at how to modify the flow to fit our scenario more closely. To get started, complete the following steps:

1. Log in to *https://make.powerautomate.com*, and select the Templates tab in the navigation bar on the left.

2. Select the Approval tab along the top and type "approve a file" in the search bar.

3. Click on the template named "Request manager approval for a selected file."

4. Wait for the list of connections to show on the bottom of the page. You should see green check marks next to each connection, as shown in Figure 3-5.

Figure 3-5. Template description card

5. Once all connections have been authenticated, click Continue.

6. The flow designer appears (see Figure 3-6). The template has added and configured a trigger and all the actions necessary. All you need to do is select the Site Address and Library Name for the SharePoint site where the files will be uploaded. We'll discuss what to do if you don't see the site and library in the dropdowns in Chapter 4.

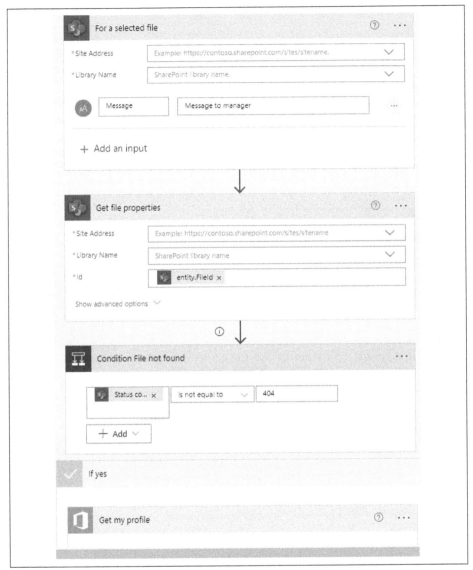

Figure 3-6. Template in flow editor

7. Click Save in the upper-right corner to save your completed flow.

Exercise 3-2. Modifying a templated flow

The flow you completed in the previous example is close to the scenario I described, but it's not an exact match. Templates don't always provide a perfect match for the scenario you have in mind. You may have to modify them to change a trigger, add actions, or remove some actions. That is the case with the scenario I presented in the previous section. There is one major thing about the template that doesn't match our scenario. In our scenario, the flow is to be triggered automatically when a file is uploaded. But in the template we've used, the flow is triggered manually after a file is selected. To match the scenario exactly, you will need to change the trigger from a manual trigger to an automatic trigger.

 Making changes to the triggers and actions in a flow may require that other actions, or the logic of the flow itself, be changed.

Complete the following steps to modify your existing templated flow to match the scenario we discussed:

1. Remove the existing "For a selected file" trigger by clicking the ellipsis (…) menu in the upper-right corner of the trigger and selecting Delete (see Figure 3-7). Click OK on the confirmation dialog.

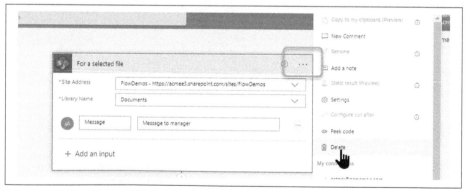

Figure 3-7. Deleting existing trigger

2. Type "file created" in the Search box of the trigger dialog and select the "When a file is created (properties only)" trigger, as shown in Figure 3-8. Select the Site Address and document Library Name from the drop-downs, just as you did in the original template.

Figure 3-8. Adding a new trigger

We've now changed the flow so it triggers automatically, whenever a file is uploaded to the document library. But we aren't done yet. That one change will have a cascading effect through the rest of the flow. Changing the trigger will remove some data elements that were used to configure later actions in the template. It will also change the security context that the flow will run under. These factors require us to make the following additional changes to the flow:

- Add the ID of the file used to trigger the flow to the "Get file properties" action, since the ID in the original trigger no longer exists.

- Remove the "Get my profile" action, since the flow no longer runs in the security context of a person who started it.

- Change the User Principal Name (UPN) field in the "Get manager" action to "Modified by email," since you want to send the file to the manager of the person who uploaded the file.

- Change the To field in both Email actions to "Modified by email" so the emailed results go to the person who uploaded the file.

Let's step through each of these changes. For now, just make the changes as described. I'll explain more in Chapter 4 about exactly how to make these changes.

1. Place your cursor in the blank Id field of the "Get file properties" action. Type `first(triggerBody()?['value'])?['ID']` into the Expression tab of the Dynamic content dialog and click OK, as shown in Figure 3-9.

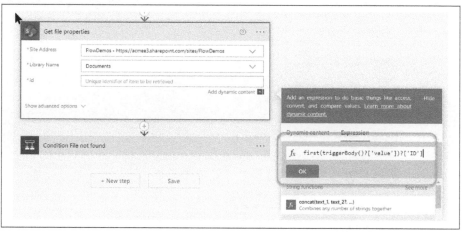

Figure 3-9. Adding file Id from trigger

You can use the Expression tab of the Dynamic content dialog to enter functions and JSON representations of dynamic content values. We'll discuss JSON more fully in Chapter 4.

2. Expand the "Condition File not found" action to display the rest of the flow. Remove the existing "Get my profile" action by clicking on the ellipsis (…) menu in the upper-right corner of the action and selecting Delete. Click OK on the confirmation (see Figure 3-10).

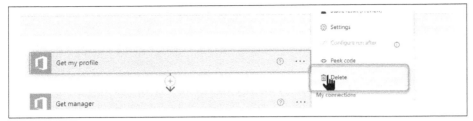

Figure 3-10. Deleting "Get my profile" action

3. Place your cursor in the blank User (UPN) field of the "Get manager" action. Select the "Modified by Email" entry from the Dynamic content dialog in the "Get file properties" section (see Figure 3-11).

Figure 3-11. Informing requestor of approval if modified by email

 In most organizations, a user's email address is the same as their UPN. If this is not true in your organization, you need to add steps to search for the user using their email or Display-Name to retrieve their UPN.

4. Expand the Condition below the "Start an approval" action on the right side of the screen. Expand each of the Email actions under the "If yes" and "If no" outcomes of the condition. Place your cursor in the To field of each email and insert "Modified By Email" from the Dynamic content dialog. You can either scroll down to find the "Get file properties" section or type "Email" in the Search Dynamic content box (see Figure 3-12).

Figure 3-12. Adding email address

5. Change the name of the flow in the upper-right corner to "Request manager approval modified." Click Save to save your modified template.

You can see how making one change to a templated flow can cascade into multiple additional changes that need to be made. So, if you don't find exactly the template to fit your scenario, is it worth it to use templates? Even if you can't find exactly what you need in a template, templates can provide valuable examples of how to perform certain sets of actions. Although you had to make changes to this templated flow to get it to fit our scenario, there were major sections dealing with the approval and how to respond to the approval that didn't need to be changed. Understanding the patterns of actions used by templates can be useful when you start building your own flows, even if you don't start with a template.

Using Templates as a Learning Experience

In the previous section, you had to enter some custom JSON code into one of the actions to be able to access one of the values from the trigger you added. That was because the new trigger provided the ID of the file or files created as an array. The custom code you entered retrieved the first record of the array using the `first()` function. Then it accessed the ID property of that record.

But if you work with that same trigger today, you'll find that it triggers for each individual file and doesn't use an array anymore. This is a good example of one of the problems with using prebuilt templates. Prebuilt templates use triggers and actions at a particular point in time. These triggers and actions may change as Microsoft rolls out updates to Power Automate or the connectors. Another good example of this is the use of the "Start an approval" action in the flow. This action is no longer available anywhere other than in templates because it has been superseded by a new action called "Start and wait for an approval." The new approval action has slightly different outputs than the original.

 Prebuilt templates are a snapshot of the triggers and actions that existed when they were made. So, over time, triggers and actions in older templates may not work the way you expect them to. This can cause a lot of confusion if you are working with a templated flow but referencing current online documentation because they may not match.

These changes may also break existing flows built from the templates. If they do break, you need to understand what the template does to be able to modify it and get it working again. Many people use templates like prebuilt opaque code. They simply create a flow from a template, fill in a few values, and expect it to work. When and if it breaks, they have no idea how it works and can't fix it.

This does not mean that you shouldn't use templates. They can be very useful tools and save you a great deal of work. But they are not a substitute for understanding how Power Automate works. In fact, they are just the opposite. They are examples of what Microsoft's developers and other knowledgeable makers have built. They can supply you with patterns that you can use when building your own flows from scratch. So, yes, you should continue to use templates when building flows, but take the time to understand what the trigger and each action is doing. That will help with your overall learning and also make it easier to fix them when they break. Almost all templates will inevitably break at some point.

Creating a New Cloud Flow

There are several reasons why you might build a flow from scratch. There may be no template that matches your scenario or the template may use older, deprecated actions that should be replaced. For example, the template you modified in the last section used a deprecated form of the trigger and approval action. Your flow will be much more stable and reliable if you aren't using old, deprecated triggers and actions. In this section, you'll build a cloud flow from scratch using the same scenario we discussed in the last section.

Starting with a Blank Flow

The first step when building a flow is to choose what type of flow it will be. I covered the different types of flows available in Chapter 2. In our case, the flow will run in the cloud so it will be a cloud flow. The specific type of cloud flow is determined by the trigger used. For our scenario, we want to use an automated trigger so the flow runs each time a file is uploaded. Depending on our exact scenario, there are other options available. You could use a recurrence trigger that runs once a day and gets all the status reports submitted in the last 24 hours, but that would make it more difficult for a manager to approve one file and reject another. You could also use the "For a selected file" manual trigger in the template, but that would require an extra step for employees. They would have to upload the file and then select it and start the flow manually. Each type of trigger has different advantages and disadvantages. For our scenario, the automated trigger fits best.

Exercise 3-3. Create a new cloud flow

To create a new automated cloud flow from scratch, do the following:

1. Navigate to *https://make.powerautomate.com* and click on the My flows tab. Select "Automated cloud flow" from the "+ New flow" drop-down (see Figure 3-13). This will open a dialog box where you can input a title and choose a trigger.

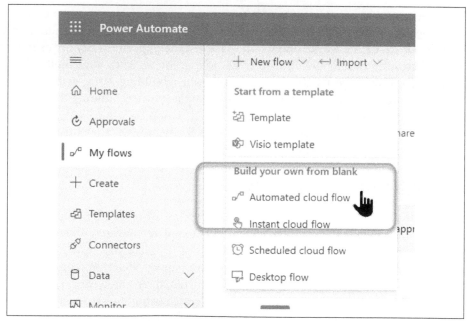

Figure 3-13. Creating new automated cloud flow

2. In the "Build an automated cloud flow" dialog box, type "Request Manager approval for a status report" in the Flow name field. Type "file created" in the "Search all triggers" field. Select the "When a file is created (properties only)"

trigger for SharePoint. Click Create to create the new automated flow. The flow design screen will appear (see Figure 3-14).

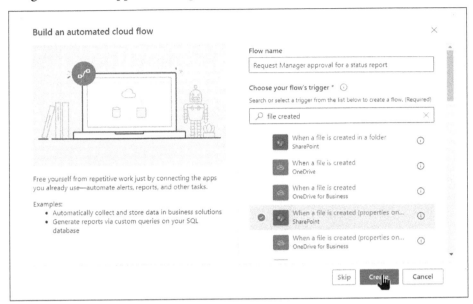

Figure 3-14. Setting title and picking trigger

3. Select the Site Address and Library Name for the SharePoint site where the files will be uploaded, just like you did when adding the trigger to modify the templated flow (see Figure 3-15).

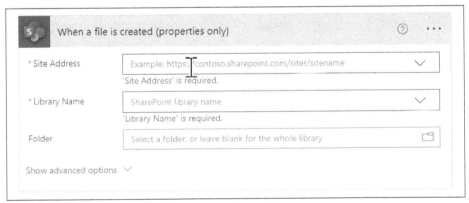

Figure 3-15. Selecting Site Address and Library Name

You've now created your base flow and configured your trigger. But you can't save it yet. To save a flow, it must contain a trigger and at least one action. Since you haven't added any actions yet, you can't save your work.

Now you can begin adding actions to your flow to accomplish the automation in our scenario. It's a good idea at this point to think through our scenario and create a list of what needs to happen and in what order the steps need to occur. This will provide the basic plan of what you need to add to the flow. You may need to add more actions than you think of at this point, but that's OK. This will give you a good overall plan of how the workflow must proceed. For our scenario, the basic steps are as follows:

1. Identify the manager of the person uploading the status report.

2. Send an Approval request to that manager.

3. If the report is approved, let the original requestor know. If not, ask them to revise the report and resubmit it.

Now you can start translating those basic steps into specific Power Automate actions:

1. Click "+New step" below the trigger you've already added. Type "manager" into the Search connectors and actions field in the "Choose an operation" dialog box. Select "Get manager (V2)" from the filtered list of actions (see Figure 3-16).

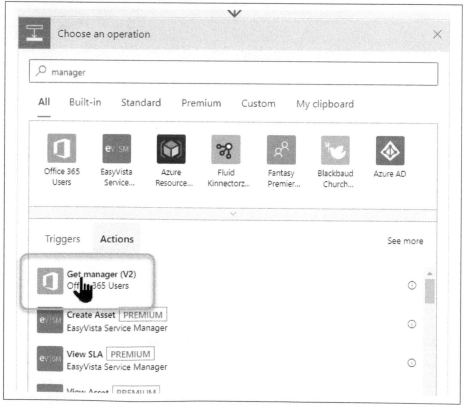

Figure 3-16. Adding "Get manager" action

2. Place your cursor in the blank User (UPN) field of the "Get manager" action. Select the "Modified By Email" entry from the Dynamic content dialog in the "When a file is created (properties only)" section (see Figure 3-17).

Figure 3-17. Inserting "Modified By Email"

3. Click "+New step" below the "Get manager" action you just added. Type "approval" into the Search connectors and actions field in the "Choose an operation" dialog box. Select "Start and wait for an approval" from the filtered list of actions (see Figure 3-18).

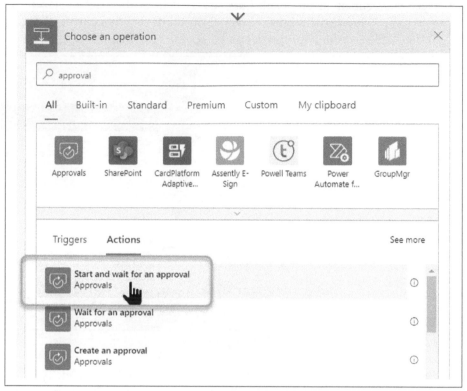

Figure 3-18. Adding "Start and wait for an approval"

"Start and wait for an approval" is a synchronous action that will send an approval and wait for all responses before proceeding. "Create an approval" and "Wait for an approval" are two halves of an asynchronous approval. The first creates the approval, but the flow doesn't pause to wait for responses until the "Wait for an approval" action is processed.

4. Since you have only one manager per user, select "Approve/Reject – First to respond" from the "Approval type" drop-down. This will configure the approval so it will be completed when one person approves or rejects the document (see Figure 3-19).

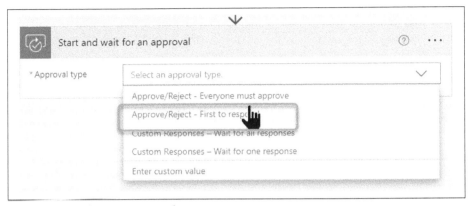

Figure 3-19. Selecting approval type

Fields marked with a red asterisk next to their names are required and must be filled in. Other fields are optional but may provide useful information.

5. Now you can fill in the rest of the information needed to create the approval and send it to the manager. You need to configure the fields in the action with the following information:

    • Type suitable text into the Title field, something like "Status Report Approval."

    • Insert Mail from the "Get Manager (v2)" section of the Dynamic content dialog into the "Assigned to" field.

    • Type a brief request in the Details field, something like "Please approve this status report." You'll learn how to format the Details field using markdown language and add additional dynamic content in future chapters (see Figure 3-20).

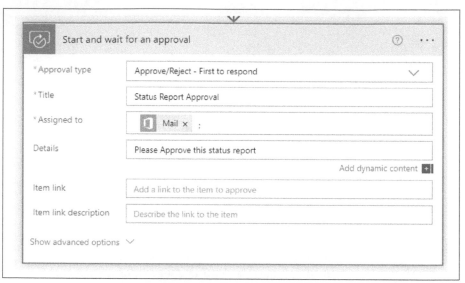

Figure 3-20. Completed Approval action

When the flow reaches the "Start and wait for an approval" action, it will pause until either the flow times out or the manager assigned to the approval responds. You'll want the flow to do different things depending on the decision made by the approver. To do that, you'll use a Condition action.

6. Click "+New step" below the "Start and wait for an approval" action you just added. Select Condition from the list of actions (see Figure 3-21).

Figure 3-21. Inserting Condition action

Condition actions evaluate one or more logical statements. If the evaluation is true, then the "If yes" branch of the flow is executed. If the evaluation is false, then the "If no" branch is executed. In your flow, you want to check whether the status report was approved or not. You can do that by using the Outcome entry in the dynamic content returned by the Approval action (see Figure 3-22).

7. Place your cursor in the Choose a value field of the Condition action. Select the Outcome entry from the Dynamic content dialog in the "Start and wait for an approval" section. Select "does not contain" from the center operation drop-down, and type "Reject" in the righthand Choose a value field.

Figure 3-22. Configuring Condition action

The Outcome entry normally contains a comma-delimited list of the responses submitted by all the approvers. So, if there were three approvers who all approved, then the Outcome would contain "Approve, Approve, Approve." However, if any of the approvers reject the document, then the Approval will stop accumulating responses. So, if the fourth of five approvers rejects the document, then the Outcome will contain "Approve, Approve, Approve, Reject." As a result, it's usually best to do a condition where "Outcome does not contain Reject."

The "Condition" action provides two branches for continuing the flow: one if the condition is true and one if it is false. For our scenario, you want to send an email in either case, but each email will have a different subject and body. To do that, you'll add an Email action to each branch of the condition and configure the action appropriately.

8. Click "Add an action" inside the "If yes" branch of the condition. Type "Email" into the Search connectors and actions field in the "Choose an operation" dialog box. Select "Send an email (v2)" from the filtered list of actions (see Figure 3-23).

Figure 3-23. "Send an email" action

9. Now you can fill in the rest of the information needed to email the result of the approval back to the person who originally uploaded the document. You need to configure the fields in the action with the following information:

- Click "Add dynamic content" just below the To field. Select the "Modified by Email" entry from the Dynamic content dialog in the "When a file is created" section.

- Type suitable text into the Subject field, something like "Status Report Approved."

- Type suitable text into the Body field, something like "Your manager approved your status report." You'll learn how to use the formatting controls or HTML to format the body of the email in future chapters (see Figure 3-24).

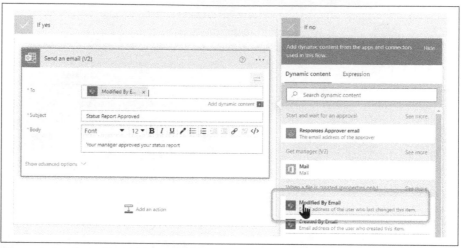

Figure 3-24. Completing email fields

10. Repeat steps 8–9 in the "If no" side of the box with an appropriate Subject and Body.

11. Click Save to save your flow.

Creating a Flow from a Description

One of the newer ways to create a flow is by describing what you want—in everyday language—to an AI engine. Power Automate then uses AI to interpret your description and provides you with a customized flow that you can use to build out your workflow. Since this is a new feature and still in preview, there are some limitations. First, it currently only supports the English language. Second, it will work best with flows that depend on Microsoft products and connectors. For example, approving a file that has been uploaded to SharePoint will be more easily recognized than approving a file uploaded to Google Drive. Additional language support and better support for non-Microsoft connectors will be added as the feature matures.

Exercise 3-4. Create a flow using AI

In this example, you'll describe our scenario and review the flow that Microsoft's AI builds for you:

1. Navigate to *https://make.powerautomate.com* and click the My flows tab. Select "Describe it to design it (preview)" from the "+ New flow" drop-down. This will open a three-step wizard where you can describe your flow (see Figure 3-25).

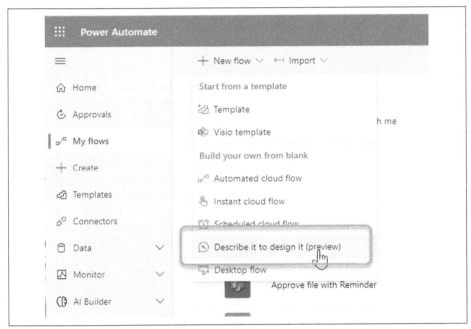

Figure 3-25. Describing flow to design it

2. On the first page of the wizard, type the following short description of what you want the flow to do into the text box under "Describe your flow in everyday words:"

    When a status report document is uploaded, the employee's manager should be informed, have a chance to review the report, and either approve or reject it.

    The wizard will also provide some alternate suggestions based on what you type. Click the arrow next to your entry to proceed (see Figure 3-26).

Figure 3-26. Describing your flow

3. After you submit your description, the wizard will show you a suggested flow. You can accept this flow or click "Show a different suggestion" at the bottom of the page to see a different suggested flow. Click Next to accept this suggestion and move to the next page (see Figure 3-27).

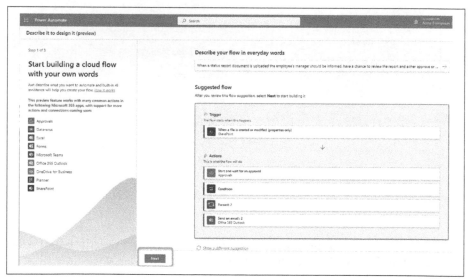

Figure 3-27. Accepting suggested flow

4. On the second page of the wizard, you will review the connections needed in the suggested flow. If any connections are not already authenticated, then provide appropriate authentication information. Click Next to move to the final page (see Figure 3-28).

Figure 3-28. Reviewing connections

5. On the last page of the wizard, you have the option to fill in fields used in the flow's actions. Dynamic content won't be available at this point so you can only use static entries. It's usually best to wait until the flow is created before you fill in this information. Click "Create flow" to create the flow (see Figure 3-29).

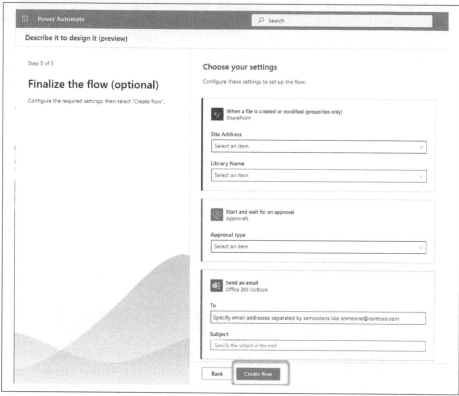

Figure 3-29. Creating the flow

6. The suggested flow is now created in the Power Automate design studio (see Figure 3-30). You can now finish filling in the fields used in your actions with either static entries or dynamic content, just like any other flow. If you want to save this flow, fill in all the required entries and click Save.

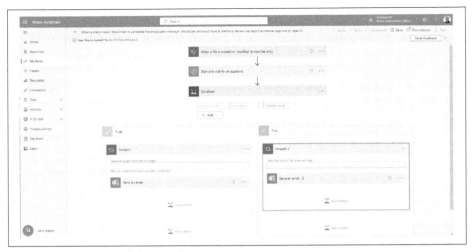

Figure 3-30. Suggested flow in designer

You can see from this example that there is still a lot of work to be done after the AI builds the suggested flow. So, this method won't make building flows a lot faster. But if you can describe what you want to build yet don't know how to start, this can be an excellent tool to get a flow started.

Design a Flow with Visio

In the previous section, I recommended that you make an ordered list of what the flow is supposed to do before you start adding an action to a flow. Planning like this is always a good idea. Having a solid understanding of what you are trying to do, and the order in which you need to do it, will save you from having to do a lot of restructuring later. Restructuring a flow can be a very time-consuming process.

Planning what a flow will do can be as simple as making a list of steps, as you did when building a flow in the previous section. Microsoft also provides a formal tool that can make this easier. You can use Visio to create a visual flowchart of what a flow is supposed to accomplish. You could do the same thing in the Power Automate flow designer, but that will require filling out a lot of additional details in the actions. Using Visio, you can design how the actions flow without filling in the specific details of the actions. After creating the action flowchart in Visio, you can export it as a template. You can then import that template into Power Automate to create a basic flow. You can then edit the flow to add the specific details required in each action. Visualizing a flow using Visio can be particularly useful if you are creating a flow for a client or collaborating with a group of people.

Prerequisites

Creating Power Automate templates with Visio requires a specific version of the Visio desktop application. The Visio desktop application must be the Office 365 version with a Plan 2 license (see Figure 3-31). Visio 2021 or previous standalone versions won't work. The less expensive Office 365 Visio Plan 1 license does not include Power Automate integration. If you don't have a Visio Plan 2 license, you can get a 30-day trial from the Visio plans and pricing website (*https://oreil.ly/M_JaO*) to try it out. Click "Try free" and follow the prompts. An existing Office 365 work or school account is required.

Figure 3-31. Sign-up page for Visio trial

In addition to having a Visio Plan 2 license, it's also important that you have some experience working with Visio as an application.

Design a Workflow in Visio

You can start designing a Power Automate flow using Visio either on the Power Automate website or directly in the Visio desktop application. Work through the following exercise to build a small Visio flowchart and import it into Power Apps.

Exercise 3-5. Create a BPMN flowchart in Visio

In this example, you'll create a Business Process Modeling Notation (BPMN) in Visio. You will then map triggers and actions onto the Visio shapes and export the flow to Power Automate. From there, you'll be able to fill in the final details.

BPMN is an industry standard method used by business analysts to visualize a business process.

1. Open your Visio desktop application. In the lower-left corner, click Account. Look at the Product Information to make sure that you have Microsoft Visio Plan 2. You should see something similar to the screenshot shown in Figure 3-32.

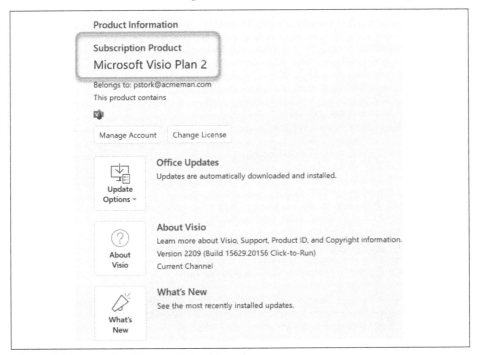

Figure 3-32. Opening Visio and checking plan

2. On the left sidebar, click New. Type "BPMN" in the "Search for online templates" text box. Click "BPMN Diagram" in the list of templates that is displayed (see Figure 3-33).

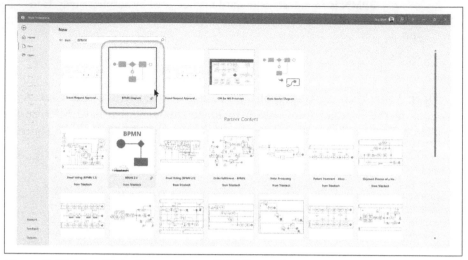

Figure 3-33. New Visio diagram from BPMN template

3. Click Create in the pop-up dialog that appears (see Figure 3-34).

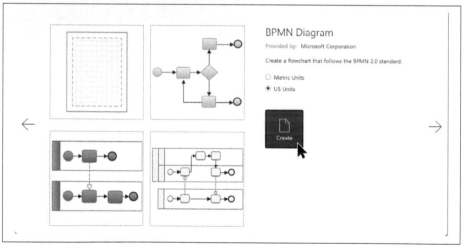

Figure 3-34. BPMN Diagram dialog

This will open the BPMN Basic Shapes stencil and create a blank Visio drawing. You are now ready to begin creating your BPMN flow.

4. Select the Start Event shape from the BPMN Basic Shapes stencil on the left side of the screen and drag it out onto the blank drawing. Your screen should now look like the screenshot in Figure 3-35.

Figure 3-35. Starting Event shape in Visio

5. Hover your mouse over the Start Event you just added. You will see four blue arrows radiating from the Start Event shape. Move your mouse over the blue arrow to the right of the Start Event and select the rectangle at the bottom of the dialog (see Figure 3-36). This will insert a Task connected to the Start Event.

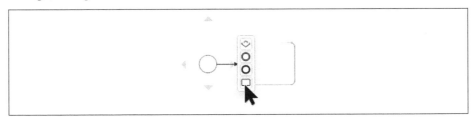

Figure 3-36. Adding a Task

6. Hover over the Task you inserted and repeat the procedure to add a second task inline after the first. Your drawing should now look like the screenshot in Figure 3-37.

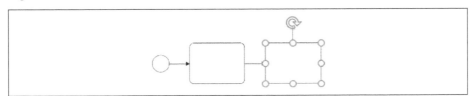

Figure 3-37. Adding a second Task

7. Repeat the process to add a Gateway (diamond shape) from the dialog and two more Tasks, one above and one below the diamond. Your drawing should now look like the screenshot in Figure 3-38.

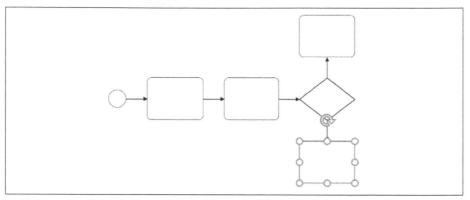

Figure 3-38. Building a Visio approval flow drawing

8. Double-click on the Start Event. Type "File is created" to label the first task in the flow. Double-click on the rest of the shapes and add labels to them also. Your drawing should now look like the screenshot in Figure 3-39.

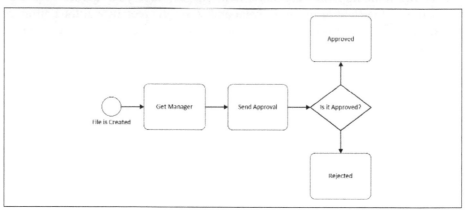

Figure 3-39. Visio approval flow drawing with labels

The drawing in its current form would be a valuable aid if you are collaborating with a group or trying to document a flow. But the flowchart is still lacking Power Automate–specific information. The next step in designing a flow using Visio is to map specific triggers and actions onto the shapes you've created. Once that mapping is completed, we'll be able to export the drawing to create the basics of a flow in Power Automate.

Exercise 3-6. Preparing the Visio template for export

1. Select the Process tab and click Export (see Figure 3-40). This will open a panel where you can associate each shape with a specific trigger or action in Power Automate.

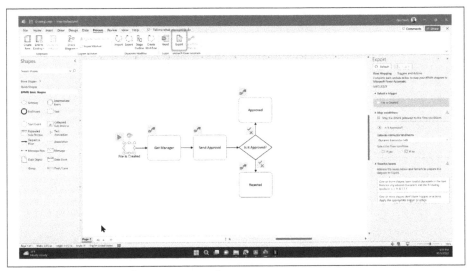

Figure 3-40. Mapping flow triggers and actions

2. Select the Start Event in the drawing. Click on the Trigger and Actions tab in the Export panel to the right. Select "SharePoint - When a file is created (properties only)" from the list of triggers in the panel (see Figure 3-41).

Figure 3-41. Choosing a trigger

3. Select the Get Manager shape in the drawing. Type "Office" in the Search box in the Export panel, and select the Office 365 Users connector from the Filter by Connectors list. Scroll down and select the "Office 365 Users – Get manager (V2)" action from the Actions list (see Figure 3-42).

Figure 3-42. Choosing an action

4. Click the arrow in the Search box to clear the previous search. Select the Send Approval shape in the drawing. Type "Approval" in the Search box in the Export panel and select "Approvals – Start and wait for an approval" action from the Actions list (see Figure 3-43).

Figure 3-43. Mapping an Approval action

5. Select the Approved and Rejected tasks and map each of them to an "Office 365 Outlook – Send an email (v2)" action. Click Refresh when you are done (see Figure 3-44).

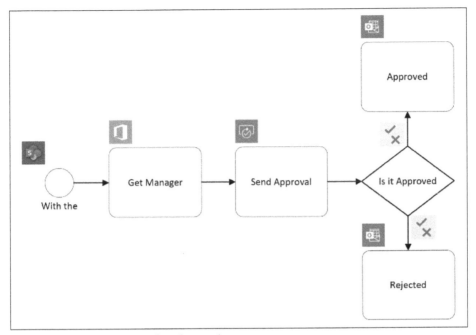

Figure 3-44. Mapping results of a condition

6. Select the icons with the checkmark and the "X" and position them above and below the "Is it Approved" gateway. Click the "If yes" radio button in the Map conditions box (see Figure 3-45).

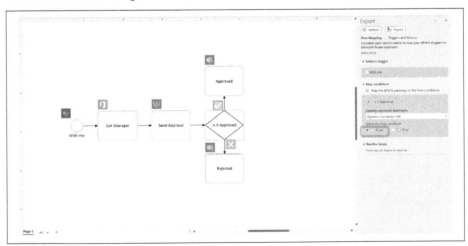

Figure 3-45. Choosing Yes and No branches

The Export panel now shows that there are no issues to resolve. The Export button is now activated so we can Export the flow and fill in the details in Power Automate.

Exercise 3-7. Export your workflow to Power Automate

1. Select the Export button in the Export panel to export your workflow diagram to Power Automate. This will open a dialog box where you can name your flow. Wait for the connectors to be authenticated and click "Create flow" (see Figure 3-46).

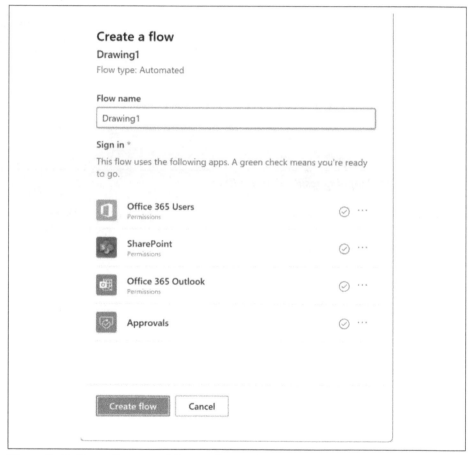

Figure 3-46. Exporting a workflow to Power Automate

2. Once the flow is exported to Power Automate, you will see a success report dialog similar to the one in Figure 3-47. Click Done to close the dialog.

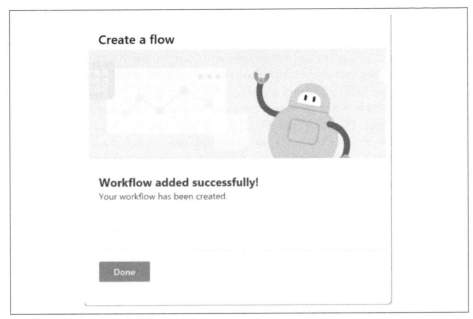

Create a flow

Workflow added successfully!
Your workflow has been created.

Done

Figure 3-47. Flow added dialog

3. In the Power Automate website, click on the My flows tab. Sign in if you aren't already authenticated to the website. You will see a flow called "Drawing 1," or whatever name you gave it when you exported the drawing. Click on the pencil icon to Edit the imported flow. Your screen should now look something like Figure 3-48.

Figure 3-48. Imported flow

4. You can now fill in the details of the flow the way you did in Exercise 3-3.

Summary

In this chapter, you learned four different ways to create a new cloud flow. First, you can use a prebuilt template to create a flow and then modify it to fit the exact scenario that you need. You can also build a flow manually, from scratch, starting with a specific trigger and adding actions to accomplish your goal. You can also have an AI engine design the flow for you based on a typed description. Finally, you can design a workflow in Visio, then map the Visio shapes to a specific Power Automate trigger and actions. Once the mapping is complete, you can import the Visio flowchart into Power Automate and finish the configuration of the trigger and actions there.

I've shown you how to build flows, but I haven't spent much time explaining the details. That's about to change. In the next chapter, we'll dig into the details you need to know to work with triggers and actions. Of course, we won't have enough space to cover every trigger and action available in all 600+ connectors. But you will gain insight into using dynamic content to configure the fields in different actions. You'll learn about the difficulties that often arise when working with dynamic content and how to use JSON to work around those limitations. You'll learn how to use functions to process and transform dynamic content to produce the values you need. Finally, you'll understand the different settings available on the context menu that you can use to modify the way that the trigger or actions work in a flow.

CHAPTER 4

Working with Triggers and Actions

In Chapter 3, you learned how to create new flows four different ways. Because you first need to understand how to create a flow before diving into the details, I didn't spend a lot of time explaining how the triggers and actions were being used or discussing how to fill them in. In this chapter, I will focus on helping you understand how to work with triggers and actions to create flows. I'll explain how to find a trigger or action that will do what you want and how to use dynamic content to configure them at runtime. You'll also learn how to use functions to transform the dynamic content into the specific values that you need and how to reference the dynamic content directly using JavaScript Object Notation (JSON). Finally, I'll review how to modify the settings of some of the triggers and actions to change the way they operate in specific circumstances. By the end of this chapter, you'll be able to create flows that you can begin to use to automate business processes in your organization.

Triggers, Actions, and Connectors

Triggers and actions are the primary building blocks in Power Automate. Each trigger or action represents an API that can be used to interact with a specific data source. Triggers and actions are both defined and contained in connectors.

Finding the Right Connector

At the time of writing, there are more than 645 connectors, with more being added every quarter. Many of the connectors are created by Microsoft. Others are created by third-party software vendors. For example, Oracle has created a connector that can be used to access an Oracle database. Some connectors are also created by independent developers and then verified by Microsoft. If you can't find a connector for the data source you want to use, you can create your own custom connector.

Creating custom connectors is an advanced topic and beyond the scope of this book. You can read more about custom connectors for Power Automate in the documentation (*https://oreil.ly/q9-IS*).

With hundreds of connectors to choose from, one of the problems you will face is finding the connector that you want to use so you can access its triggers and actions. To make this easier, Power Automate provides a categorized search dialog that you can use to find a specific connector. Once you find a connector you are interested in, you can drill down to the documentation to get specific details about what that connector contains.

Exercise 4-1. Exploring connectors

In this example, we will browse through the list of available connectors to find the Dataverse database connector and look at the documentation provided.

1. Log in to *https://make.powerautomate.com* and select the Connectors tab in the navigation bar on the left. This will bring up a list of all the connectors available for Power Automate. You can use the drop-down on the right to limit the list to only include standard or premium connectors. Figure 4-1 shows the connector list filtered to show only standard connectors.

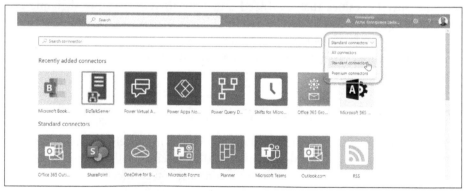

Figure 4-1. Filtering the connector list

2. Change the drop-down back to All Connectors and type "Dataverse" in the Search connector text box at the top of the page. You should now see two Dataverse connectors, one current and one legacy. Hovering your mouse over a connector will display a tooltip that shows the full name of the connector. As shown in Figure 4-2, both connectors display a green PREMIUM label that identifies that these are premium connectors that require additional licensing, as discussed in Chapter 2.

Figure 4-2. Searching for a connector

3. Select the green Microsoft Dataverse connector. This will bring up a page of information about the current Microsoft Dataverse connector, as shown in Figure 4-3. The page contains the following:

   - A brief description of the connector
   - A link to additional documentation
   - A list of the triggers contained in the connector
   - A list of templates used by the connector

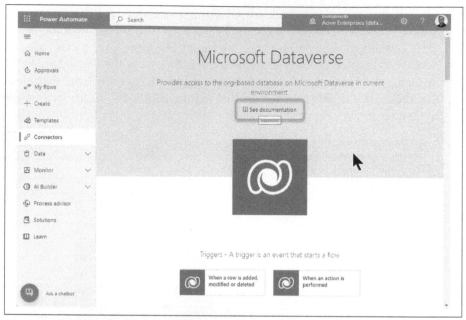

Figure 4-3. Dataverse description page

4. Select the "See documentation" link. This will take you to the connector documentation in Microsoft's connector reference list, as shown in Figure 4-4. The documentation will provide detailed information about the connector, including a list of all the triggers and actions contained in the connector.

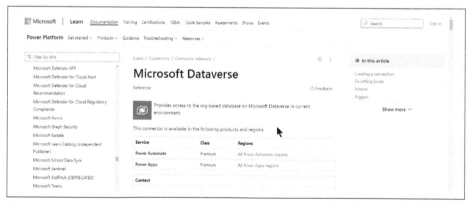

Figure 4-4. Dataverse documentation page

5. Click on the Actions link in the upper-right corner of the page. This will take you to a list of the Actions contained in the Dataverse connector, as shown in Figure 4-5. This list describes each action available in the Dataverse connector.

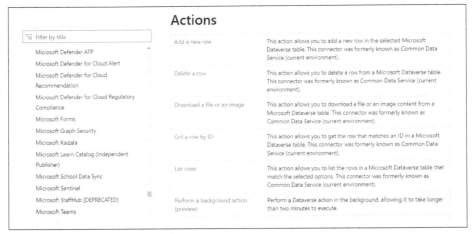

Figure 4-5. Dataverse actions list

6. Select the "List rows" action from the list. This will display information about that specific action, including a list of input parameters and values returned by the action (see Figure 4-6). The data type of the parameter and whether it's required or not is critical when trying to fill out the fields in a trigger or action.

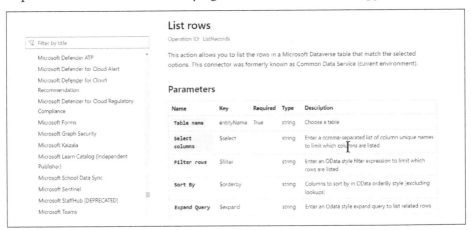

Figure 4-6. "List rows" action documentation

7. Spend some time looking at other connectors and their documentation. Then, I'll show you how to use them in a specific flow.

Choosing a Trigger

Triggers represent the events that you will use to start your flow. They also provide the first set of data that your flow can use to complete your business process. Triggers can be automated, manual (instant), or scheduled (recurrence). The trigger you choose to start your flow will have a number of effects on your flow:

- It will determine what user security context the flow runs under.
- It will provide input parameters for your flow.
- It will determine when your flow will run.

In almost every case, a flow will have only one trigger and it's the first item in the flow. The designer will let you add more than one trigger, but this will normally prevent your flow from running. Because triggers determine the security context for the flow and provide input parameters, having two different triggers in the same flow will cause a problem. For example, an automated trigger, like when an item is created, will run using your security account and have information about the item that was created. But a manual trigger will run in the context of the person who starts it and will only contain parameters that they provide. Recurrence triggers provide yet a third case because they run in your security context but provide little in the way of input parameters. Choosing the right trigger is always an important design decision.

This doesn't mean that the first trigger you choose locks you in. You can select a trigger when you create a flow or add it in the designer later. You can also change a trigger after you've started designing a flow by deleting the existing trigger and adding a new one.

 Deleting a trigger and replacing it will remove any references to dynamic content provided by the old trigger. As a result, removing and replacing a trigger can be a labor-intensive operation after a flow has been developed.

Let's try a simple scenario for the next few examples: You receive an email once a month from your accountant with an Excel spreadsheet containing an itemized list of your business expenses for the last month. You would like to save that spreadsheet with a descriptive filename to a folder in your OneDrive for Business site.

Exercise 4-2. Choosing a Trigger

1. Log in to *https://make.powerautomate.com*, and select the "My flows" tab in the navigation bar on the left. Select "Automated cloud flow" from the drop-down.

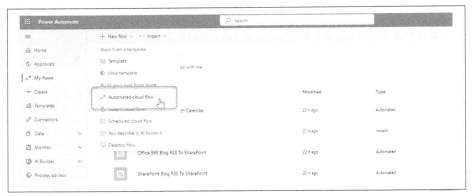

Figure 4-7. Creating an automated flow

2. In the "Build an automated cloud flow" dialog box, type "Upload Monthly Expense report" as your flow name and search for Outlook in the search box. Select "When a new email arrives (V3)" from the Office 365 Outlook connector (see Figure 4-7). Click Create to create your flow using that name and trigger. Clicking Skip will let you name your flow and pick a trigger in the designer.

Figure 4-8. Naming flow and choosing trigger

The trigger you chose is preconfigured to watch all the incoming email in your Office 365 email inbox. Since you only get one spreadsheet a month, you will be wasting a lot of flow runs looking for the expense spreadsheet. So, you'll want to find a way to limit how often the flow will run. One way to do that is by adding filters to the trigger that will keep it from starting too often.

3. Select "Show advanced options" to display fields that you can use for filtering. To test your results, you'll use your own email address in place of the accountant's email in this example. Type your Office 365 email address in the From field. Select it from the people picker dialog that displays below the field (see Figure 4-9). Change the Only with Attachments drop-down at the bottom to Yes. Now the trigger will only fire if the email is from you and contains an attachment.

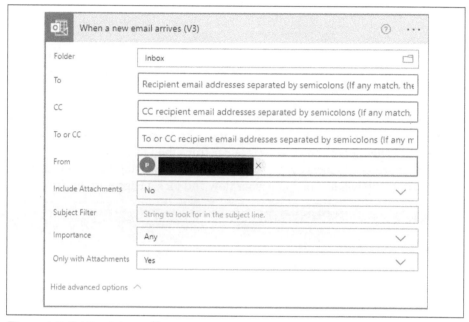

Figure 4-9. Setting trigger filters

But what if you get multiple emails each month from your accountant and all have files attached? You would still end up with more flow runs than you want. There is an alternate trigger that will only start when you flag an email in your mailbox. Using that trigger, you can choose which emails to run the flow on. To change the trigger, do the following:

4. Open the ellipsis (…) menu in the upper-right corner of the trigger and Select Delete. Click OK in the dialog to confirm the deletion (see Figure 4-10).

Figure 4-10. Deleting existing trigger

5. Type "Outlook" in the Search connectors and triggers search box. Select "When an email is flagged (V4) (preview)" trigger from the list (see Figure 4-11).

Figure 4-11. Adding an "When an email is flagged" trigger

6. Set the From and Only with Attachments fields in Advanced options the same way you did in step 3. Now the flow will only trigger when you flag an email in your mailbox that arrived from your accountant and that contains an attachment (see Figure 4-12).

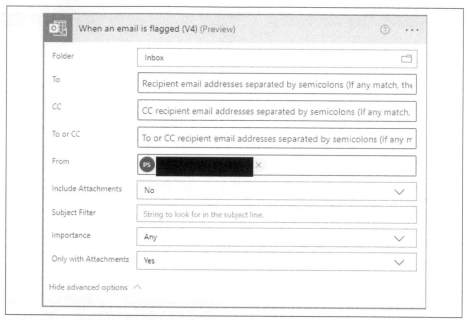

Figure 4-12. Completed trigger

You won't be able to save the flow yet because it only contains a trigger. For a flow to accomplish anything, it must have a trigger and at least one action. We'll look at adding actions next.

Adding Actions

Actions are the building blocks that you use to enhance and manipulate information in your flow to accomplish your business purpose. They implement the logic of your business process. Adding actions uses the same dialog that we used to add a new trigger to the designer after we deleted the previous trigger. In this next example, we'll add actions to complete the flow for our scenario.

Exercise 4-3. Adding additional actions

1. Click "+ New step" just below the trigger that we added in the previous example. This will open the "Choose an operation" dialog (see Figure 4-13).

Figure 4-13. Adding an action step

2. Type "get attachment" in the search box, and select the "Get Attachment (V2)" action from the Office 365 Outlook connector (see Figure 4-14).

Figure 4-14. Adding "Get Attachment" step

3. Click "+ New step" just below the Get Attachment action that you just added. Type "create file" in the Search box, and select the "Create file" action from the OneDrive for Business connector. Your flow should now look like Figure 4-15.

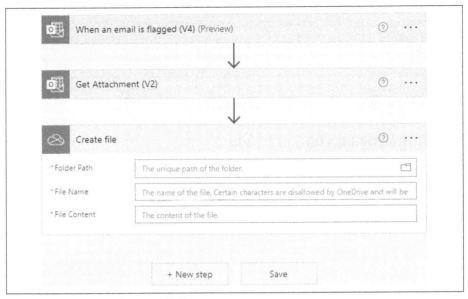

Figure 4-15. Adding "Create file" step

Your basic flow is now complete, but you still can't save it because the details of the actions have not been filled in. The actions need information to accomplish their tasks, so you need to provide the details just like you did for the trigger fields earlier in this chapter. Triggers are usually configured using static values because they are the first thing in the flow. But later actions can be filled in using static values, variables, or content derived from the trigger or previous actions in the flow. When we use anything other than static values, we are using what Power Automate calls *dynamic content*.

Adding Dynamic Content

Dynamic content can hold several distinct types of data, such as the following:

- An individual value with a specific data type
- An object that has properties containing either simple or complex values
- An array of values, objects, or other arrays

No matter what it holds, dynamic content represents the input and output values from the trigger or other previous steps. As a flow progresses, the amount of dynamic content grows. That means that you can use output from previous actions to configure additional actions. For example, you might retrieve information about a person's manager using the "Get manager" action in the Office 365 Users connector. Once you have the manager, you can send an email to them using the email address that was retrieved as a property of the manager object value.

Selecting Dynamic Content to Add

To configure a trigger or action with dynamic content, just place your cursor in the field where you want to use the dynamic content. That will automatically open the "Add dynamic content" dialog. The dialog, as shown in Figure 4-16, has two tabs: Dynamic content and Expression. We'll examine the Expression tab in the next section.

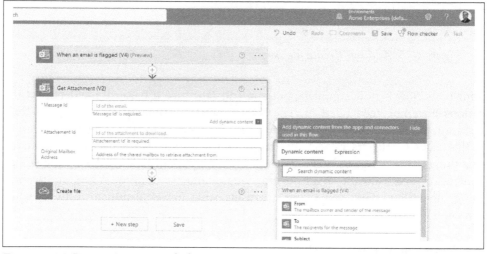

Figure 4-16. Dynamic content dialog

On some computers, the dynamic content dialog box won't be displayed when you want to fill in a field in an action. This is caused by the screen resolution and available whitespace next to the actions in the designer. If enough whitespace does not exist, the dynamic content will be shown in an abbreviated list below the field, as shown in Figure 4-17. If the content you want is not displayed in the short list, you can click the "See more" link. Changing the size of the window or resolution of the monitor to increase the whitespace available will return the normal dynamic content dialog.

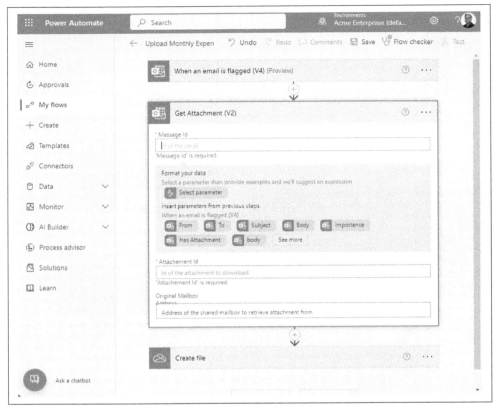

Figure 4-17. No dynamic content dialog

The Dynamic content tab shows a list of the dynamic content grouped by the trigger or action that it came from.

Exercise 4-4. Configuring actions with dynamic content

In this example, we'll complete the flow we started earlier by adding dynamic content entries to the fields in the actions.

1. Click on the "Get Attachment (V2)" action to expand it and view the fields. Select the Message Id field to enter the Message Id of the email to get the attachment from. This will open the Add dynamic content dialog. Type "id" in the Search dynamic content box. This will filter the list of dynamic content available to make it easier to find the Message Id value. Click on Message Id under the "When an email is flagged (V4)" grouping (see Figure 4-18). This will insert the Message Id of the email flagged in the trigger.

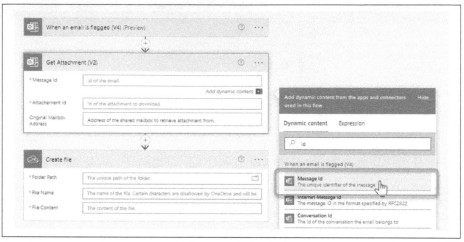

Figure 4-18. Inserting Message Id dynamic content

Fields with a red asterisk (*) in front of their names are required fields. Dynamic or static values must be supplied for those entries. Fields without the asterisk are optional and can be left blank in most circumstances.

2. Select the Attachment Id field in the "Get Attachment (V2)" action. Filter the dynamic content on Id again and select Attachments > Attachment Id to insert it. An "Apply to Each" loop will be added around the "Get Attachment (V2)" action since there may be more than one attachment that needs to be processed (see Figure 4-19).

Figure 4-19. Adding Attachment Id

 When you access a value that is contained in an array, Power Automate will automatically enclose the action where you used the dynamic content in an "Apply to Each" loop. The loop will reference the array, and the dynamic content will reference the value inside the array.

3. Select the "Create file" action and drag it inside the "Apply to each" loop to make sure that we create one file for each attachment (see Figure 4-20). Select the "Create file" action to expand it.

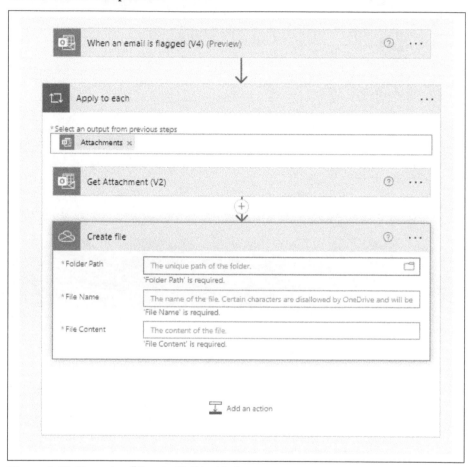

Figure 4-20. Dragging "Create file" inside loop

4. Click on the folder icon inside the Folder Path field. Use the navigation arrows in the dialog to drill down to the folder where you want to store the file (see Figure 4-21).

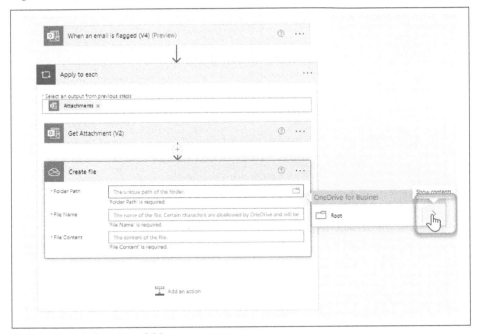

Figure 4-21. Selecting a folder

5. Select the "File Name" field in the "Create file" action. Filter the dynamic content on Name, and select Name under the "Get Attachment (v2)" action group to insert it. Select the "File Content" field and insert the Content Bytes under the "Get Attachment (v2)" action group (see Figure 4-22).

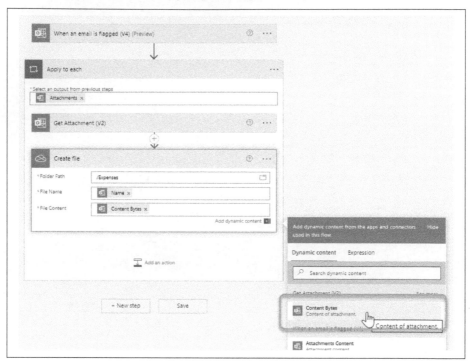

Figure 4-22. Selecting File Name and File Content

 Inserting dynamic content from the wrong action can lead to unexpected results. For example, in the previous step, if you had picked Attachment Content from the trigger, you would end up with an empty file because the loop is based on a different array, so the Attachment Content is null at that point in the flow.

Now that you've filled in all the required fields in the trigger and actions, you can save and test your flow.

6. To save the flow to the cloud, select the Save link in the upper-right corner of the designer (see Figure 4-23).

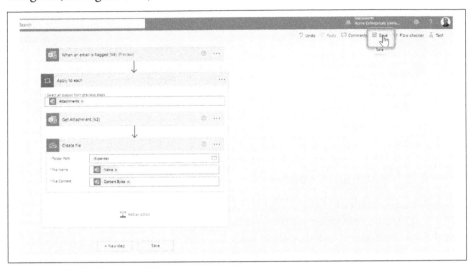

Figure 4-23. Saving your flow

7. To test whether your flow runs successfully or not, select the Test link in the upper-right corner of the designer. Select the Manually radio button that appears. Click the Test button. This will put your flow in Test mode (see Figure 4-24).

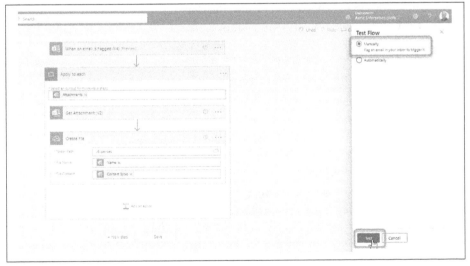

Figure 4-24. Testing a flow

8. Send an email to yourself that contains an attachment. After the email arrives, flag it to start the flow. After the flow runs, you will see whether it was successful

or not. Each action will show a green circle with a checkmark if the flow succeeded. You can also check the folder in OneDrive for Business to see if the file(s) were saved successfully (see Figure 4-25).

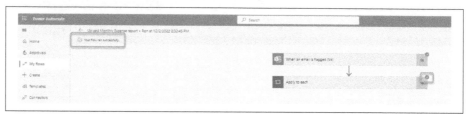

Figure 4-25. Checking a flow run

Where Is My Dynamic Content?

Since dynamic content is produced by almost every action in a flow, the list can get quite long. In the previous example, we used the Search box to filter the list so that we could find the content we wanted to add. If you can find the entry you want, adding dynamic content to a field in an action is a straightforward process. But there are some circumstances where it becomes much more difficult because the dynamic content you want doesn't show up in the dialog. There are a few reasons why the dynamic content might not show in the dialog when you try to add it.

First, the dynamic content may not be available at this point in the flow. Dynamic content is generated by outputs of actions and the trigger. If a certain action hasn't run yet in a flow, then it makes sense that the dynamic content for that action can't be added until after the action runs. Dynamic content may also be in a different scope than the current action. For example, you can't add dynamic content from inside a loop to an action outside the loop. Each iteration of the loop will have a specific value that is only in scope while you are inside the loop.

But the most troublesome reason why dynamic content doesn't show in the dialog is because of aggressive filtering by the dynamic content dialog. The content may not be the right data type for the field you are populating. For example, let's say you are in a field designed for a date, and the value you want to add is a string. You'll see another example of this filtering when we start working with functions in the next section.

If you don't see some dynamic content in the dialog, that doesn't necessarily mean it's not available. One way to fix this problem is to add the dynamic content you want to a Compose and then use the output of the Compose in the action where it's not showing. I'll show you some other ways to access the dynamic content you need without using a Compose—by using functions and JSON notation. Let's look first at JSON notation and then see how we can use that in functions to manipulate the dynamic content in our flow.

Using JSON

JavaScript Object Notation (JSON) is a language-independent data interchange format. Like Extensible Markup Language (XML), it provides a way to transport data between applications formatted as a string. Power Automate can work with both XML and JSON, but JSON is the format used internally to pass inputs and outputs from one action to another. When you look at the run history of a flow to troubleshoot it, you will see that many of the flow actions have inputs and outputs that contain JSON. You can also use JSON to access dynamic content that doesn't appear due to over-filtering in the dynamic content dialog. Understanding JSON is a critical skill to write and troubleshoot flows.

Understanding JSON Syntax

JSON syntax uses special characters to encapsulate specific types of data. Arrays are surrounded by square brackets, objects are marked with curly braces, and properties within objects are displayed as key-value pairs. Individual arrays, objects, and properties are separated by commas. Together these elements create a data hierarchy that can be understood by almost any modern application. Figure 4-26 displays a simple JSON array of people. Each person has a name, an age, and a birthdate.

```
[
    {
      "Name": "John Doe",
      "Age": 49,
      "Birthdate": "1973-10-16"
    },
    {
      "Name": "Mary Stevens",
      "Age": 35,
      "Birthdate": "1987-1-23"
    },
    {
      "Name": "Sam Adams",
      "Age": 55,
      "Birthdate": "1967-5-11"
    }
]
```

Figure 4-26. Sample JSON array

Flows reference data items in JSON using a particular syntax. If the array in Figure 4-26 was passed in as the output of a particular trigger, then you could reference Mary Stevens's age as the following:

```
outputs('People_Array')[1]?['Age']
```

Each part of this line specifies something in the array:

- `outputs('People_Array')` references the JSON output of a Compose action called "People Array."

- `[1]` references the second item in the array. Arrays use a zero-based index in JSON.

- `?['Age']` references the Age property of the object. The ? specifies that the property may be null, which means it may be missing from the values.

Using this kind of syntax means that you can reference almost any value used by the flow directly. But getting the reference right can be challenging for an inexperienced developer. There are a few various places that you can look in a flow to find the JSON reference you want.

Looking Up JSON Syntax

The first place you can look to find the syntax used in JSON is to hover your mouse over any entry in a field. When you do, a tooltip will be displayed that shows what the JSON syntax is for that value. Figure 4-27 shows the JSON reference for a ResponseId field that is output by a "When a new response is submitted" trigger in the Microsoft forms connector.

Figure 4-27. JSON syntax tooltip

The one problem with using the tooltip approach is that you can't copy the value. If you want to use that value in another field, you'll need to type it in yourself. But there is another way that you can access the JSON syntax of a field to copy and paste it somewhere later in your flow. If you select the ellipsis menu on an action, you will see an entry called Peek code. Not all actions have a Peek code option, but those that do will show you a read-only JSON representation of the entire action. You can highlight

JSON input values in this view to copy and paste them elsewhere in your flow. Figure 4-28 shows the Peek code view for the action shown in Figure 4-27. You can see the highlighted `response_id` parameter. You can use Ctrl + C to copy that syntax for use elsewhere.

```
'Get response details' (code view)

 1  {
 2      "inputs": {
 3          "host": {
 4              "connectionName": "shared_microsoftforms",
 5              "operationId": "GetFormResponseById",
 6              "apiId": "/providers/Microsoft.PowerApps/apis/shared_microso
 7          },
 8          "parameters": {
 9              "form_id": "oMo2_6VV1U-6-u2FhIF4UwiVvC0KRg5Ig95WB3_VoJ9UNU8z
10              "response_id": "@triggerOutputs()?['body/resourceData/respon
11          },
12          "authentication": "@parameters('$authentication')"
13      },
14      "metadata": {
15          "operationMetadataId": "bbc01c9f-ca73-4948-84df-2689d2ced1dd"
16
17  }
```

Done

Figure 4-28. Peek code view

 When using the Peek code view, make sure you remove the @ sign from the front of the JSON you copy. JSON values referenced inside a flow start with an @ sign, but it should not be included when you reference them in the designer.

Parsing JSON

JSON stores values, arrays, and objects in string format. But just having the string doesn't always mean that you can reference the values inside using JSON. For example, if the JSON values are returned by something like a Representational State Transfer (REST) call to a web service, then the flow will only see them as a string value, not as JSON. To access the values stored in the JSON string, we need to parse the string to apply a schema. To do this, we use an action in Power Automate called Parse JSON.

Exercise 4-5. Using the Parse JSON action

In this example, we'll create a flow to parse and use one of the sample values from the array in Figure 4-26.

1. Log in to *https://make.powerautomate.com*, and create a new instant cloud flow that uses the "Manually trigger a flow" trigger (see Figure 4-29). Name the flow "Parse JSON sample."

Figure 4-29. Creating Parse JSON sample flow

2. Click "+ New step" to add an "Initialize variable" action. Name the variable var JSON, and select String from the drop-down as the variable type. Type the JSON string from Figure 4-26 into the Value field of the "Initialize variable" action (see Figure 4-30).

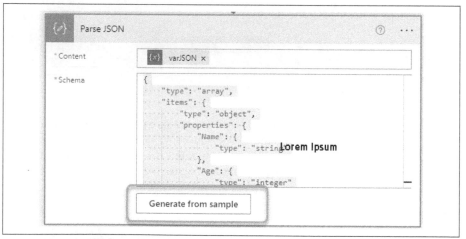

Figure 4-30. Initializing a string variable

3. Click "+ New step" to add a Compose action. Click inside the Inputs field to display the Dynamic content dialog. Select the Expression tab and type **variables ('varJSON')[1]?['Age']** into the function (fx) text box (see Figure 4-31). Click OK to insert the value.

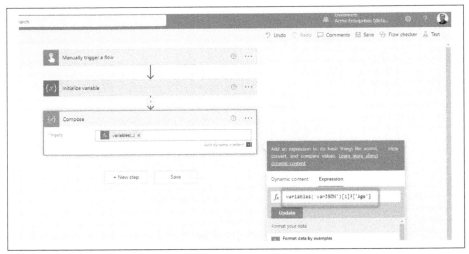

Figure 4-31. Viewing JSON property in Compose

4. Save and test your flow. The flow will fail because the variable is viewed as a string rather than JSON at this point (see Figure 4-32). We need to parse the string as JSON before we can access the fields inside.

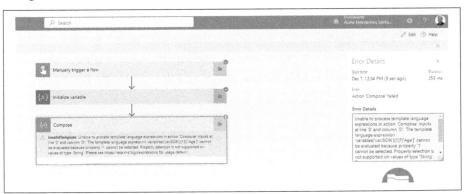

Figure 4-32. Flow test fails

5. Use the ellipsis menu to delete the Compose action. Click "+ New step" to add a Parse JSON action. Click your mouse inside the Content field to display the Dynamic content dialog. Select varJSON under the Variables section to add it to the Content field. Copy the JSON in the Value field of the "Initialize variable" action using Ctrl + A to highlight it and Ctrl + C to copy it. Click the "Generate from sample" button in the Parse JSON action and paste the JSON into the dialog (see Figure 4-33). Click the Done button to close the dialog.

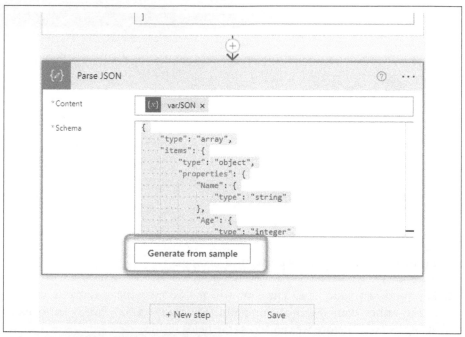

Figure 4-33. Filling in Parse JSON action

6. Click "+ New step" to add a Compose action. Click inside the Inputs field to display the Dynamic content dialog. Select the Expression tab and type **body('Parse_JSON')[1]?['Age']** into the fx text box (see Figure 4-34). Click OK to insert the value.

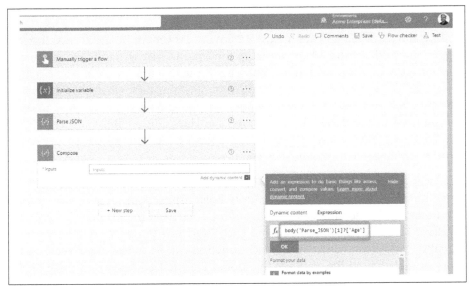

Figure 4-34. Inserting JSON expression

7. Save and test your flow. You should have no errors and see the value 35 in the outputs of the Compose (see Figure 4-35).

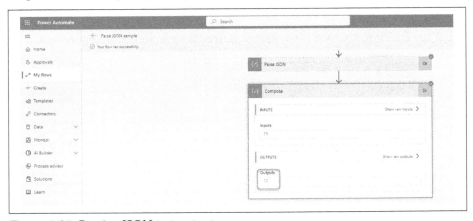

Figure 4-35. Parsing JSON test output

Now that you know how Power Automate passes information from one action to the next and you can access it directly using JSON, it's time to look at how you can use functions to manipulate that content.

Working with Expressions

Getting started when you are building a flow in Power Automate is easy. Just select a trigger and add actions. Then configure the actions with dynamic content produced by the trigger or previous actions. But what if the dynamic content isn't exactly what you need? For example, the trigger returns a date and time when the record was last modified, but you need to know whether that date and time is more than 60 days ago. So, you need to calculate today's date minus 60 days. Power Automate has a full set of functions that you can use to complete complex calculations and operations to transform dynamic content into the data you need.

In Power Automate, these functions are called *expressions*. Power Automate uses the same functions that are available in Azure Logic Apps. You can find a list of available functions in the documentation (*https://oreil.ly/TXjBY*). This website provides an excellent source of information about each function's parameters and outputs. Individual links to documentation for each function can be found organized by category or as an alphabetical list of all the functions. This makes it easy to browse the lists to find details about any specific function.

These functions can be used inside a Power Automate action field to do things like convert a date to Universal Time Code, calculate mathematical formulas, combine strings to create a specific result, and much more. For example, since the equals operator in a Condition action is case sensitive, you might want to convert the dynamic content on both sides to lowercase to get a case-insensitive match. You can do that using the function toLower(<<dynamic content>>) as shown in Figure 4-36.

Figure 4-36. Using toLower() *in a Condition*

Many of these inline functions are also available as Power Automate actions. For example, convertTimeZone() will provide the same output as the Convert Time Zone action in the built-in Date Time connector. Using an inline function in place of an action can decrease the number of steps required in your flow. However, nesting multiple functions together can make your flow more difficult to troubleshoot by increasing the complexity of the fields in an action. I recommend that beginners start out using more actions and then replace them with inline functions as they become more proficient.

Understanding Function Syntax

Figure 4-37 shows the documentation for the toLower() function shown earlier. From the documentation, we can see that toLower() requires a single parameter of type string and returns that string in all lowercase letters. The documentation also provides an overall description of what the function does, as well as an example.

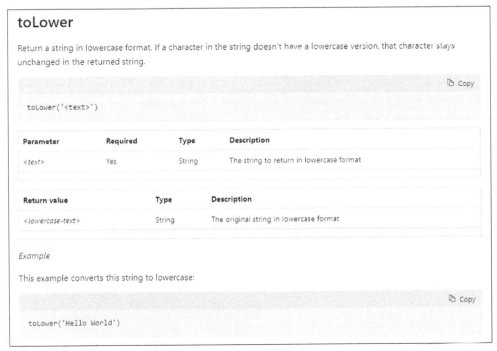

Figure 4-37. *toLower() function documentation*

Adding Dynamic Content to an Expression

Functions should be added to fields in Power Automate actions using the Expressions tab in the Dynamic content dialog. But typing an expression alone directly into the field won't work. The function will be considered a text entry, and the expression won't be evaluated. IntelliSense is a tool that can assist you when entering expressions through the Expressions tab. When you begin typing an expression in the Expressions tab, a list of potential expressions will be shown. You can complete your entry by choosing from the list, as shown in Figure 4-38.

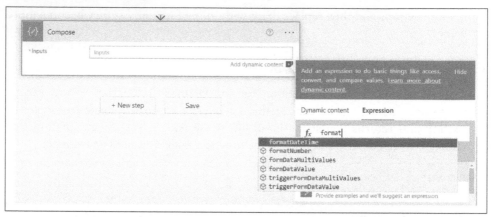

Figure 4-38. Expressions list

After entering the name of an expression, IntelliSense will also display a pop-up with an explanation of the function's syntax, as shown in Figure 4-39.

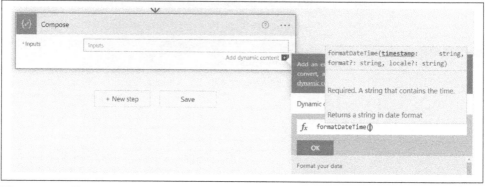

Figure 4-39. Function syntax in Expressions tab

Expression parameters can be entered either as static entries or JSON references to other dynamic content. String parameters are entered surrounded by single quotes. Trying to use double quotes when entering parameters is a common error when getting started with Power Automate flows. This will result in an error when you try to save the function, notifying you that the expression is invalid.

Dynamic content can be entered as a parameter by switching to the Dynamic content tab in the dialog and picking the value you want to add. However, because of aggressive filtering, the dynamic content you want won't be displayed in the list when you want to use it in an expression. If you know the JSON syntax for the value, you can enter it directly in the Expression tab. You did this in Example 3-2 in the previous chapter, to access the ID of the first record in a filtered array of records. Entering JSON directly won't change the data type requirements for the parameters, but it will help you overcome the aggressive filtering done by the Dynamic content tab.

Exercise 4-6. Using the Dynamic content Expression tab

In this example, we will send an email when a new row is added to the Dataverse Contacts table. We'll need to use a few different functions to retrieve and format the information for the email.

1. Log in to *https://make.powerautomate.com*, and create a new automated cloud flow that uses the "When a row is added, modified, or deleted" trigger from the Dataverse connector (see Figure 4-40). Name the flow "Writing Expressions."

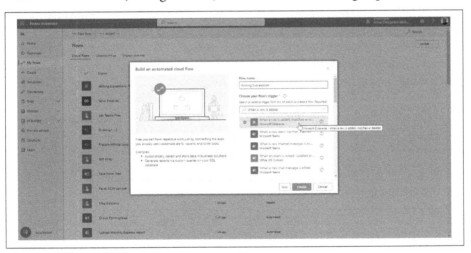

Figure 4-40. Creating Writing Expressions flow

2. Select the Change type to be Added so the flow only triggers when new rows are added. Select the Contacts table from the Table name drop-down, and select Organization to be the Scope, so any record added to the Contacts table will trigger the flow (see Figure 4-41).

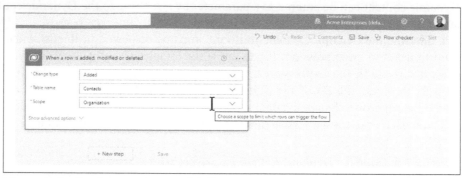

Figure 4-41. Configuring "Row Added" trigger

We want to include the name of the Company that the new contact is associated with and the time when the row was added. Dataverse returns a globally unique identifier (GUID) for the Company, so we'll need to look up the Company in the Accounts table. Since company is optional, we'll need to use a `Coalesce()` expression to check if the GUID is null before doing the lookup.

3. Click "+ New step" to add a "List rows" action from the Dataverse connector. Select the Accounts table in the Table name field. Click on the "Show advanced options" link to expand the advanced options. Type "accountid eq" in the "Filter rows" field. Select the Expression tab of the Dynamic content dialog. Type **coalesce(** in the fx text box. Place your cursor inside the parentheses and switch to the "Dynamic content" tab. Select the Company Name Value dynamic content. Add the following after the dynamic content you just added: **,guid().** This will supply a random GUID if the Company Name field is null. The text box should now contain this :

```
coalesce(triggerOutputs()?['body/_parentcustomerid_value'],guid())
```

Click Update to insert the expression into the "Filter rows" field (see Figure 4-42).

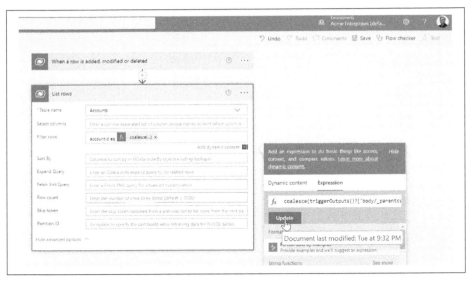

Figure 4-42. Coalesce() expression

4. Click "+ New step" to add a "Send an email (v2)" action. Type your email address in the To field. Type "A new Contact was added" in the Subject field. Type "A new Contact was added at" followed by a space in the Body field. The Dynamic content dialog will be displayed. Select the Expression tab in the dialog (see Figure 4-43).

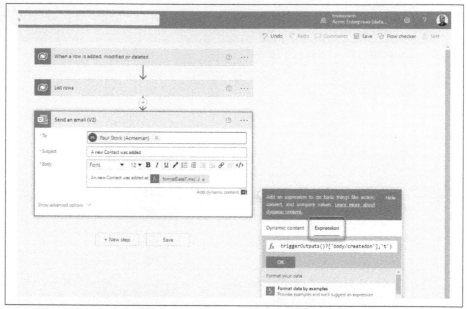

Figure 4-43. The Expression tab

5. Begin typing "format" in the fx text box. Select the `formatDateTime` function from the list and add parentheses after it if necessary (see Figure 4-44).

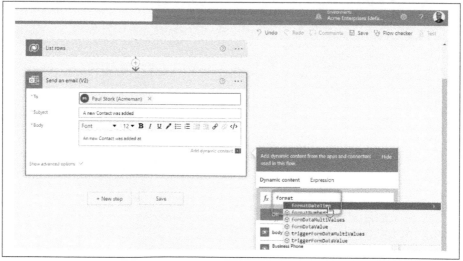

Figure 4-44. Selecting an expression

6. Place your cursor inside the parentheses and switch back to the Dynamic content tab. Select Description from the dynamic content in the trigger group. In the resulting expression, change body/description to body/createdon. Add a comma and 't' just before the closing parentheses. The text box should now contain this:

```
formatDateTime(triggerOutputs()?['body/createdon'],'t')
```

Click OK to insert the expression into the email body (see Figure 4-45).

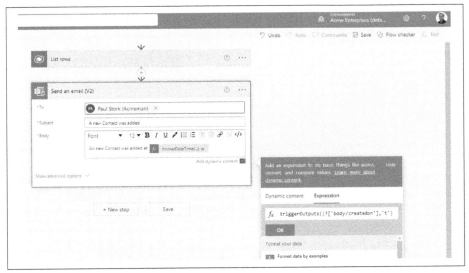

Figure 4-45. Formatting the Createdon time

Createdon cannot be selected directly as dynamic content when using a function because the Dynamic content dialog aggressively filters the available values and thinks that it's the wrong data type for the function. However, by using JSON notation, we can access the value directly.

7. Type **for** after the FormatDateTime() function in the Body of the email. Type **first()** into the fx text box in the Expressions tab. Select the "Dynamic content" tab and insert the value Dynamic content from the List rows section. This will get the first row of the output from the "List rows" action we added previously. What we really want is the Name field from that first row. But that isn't available. Move to the end of the first() function and type **?['Name']** after the close of the function. The text box should now contain the folloing:

```
first(outputs('List_rows')?['body/value'])?['Name']
```

Click Update to insert the expression into the email body (see Figure 4-46).

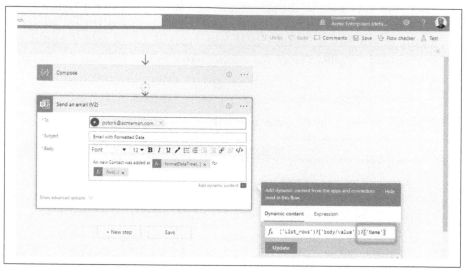

Figure 4-46. Using `first()` *to get Company Name*

8. Click Test in the upper-right corner and select the Manually radio button. Click the Test button at the bottom of the panel. Select Tables from the Data drop-down on the left side of the screen. Open the Account table and select Edit from the Edit drop-down menu. Select "+ New row" to add a new row to the table. Type "Acme Manufacturing" as the Account Name (see Figure 4-47). Click the Back link on the menu.

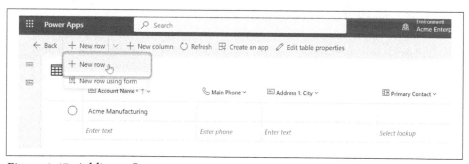

Figure 4-47. Adding a Company in Dataverse

9. Select Tables from the Data drop-down on the left side of the screen. Open the Contact table and select Edit from the Edit drop-down menu. Click "+New row" from the "+New row" drop-down to add a new Contact to the table (see Figure 4-48). Type the following values into the form:

- First Name: John
- Last Name: Doe

- Account Name: Acme Manufacturing

Click Save & Close. Click Done.

Figure 4-48. Adding a New Contact

10. Adding a New Contact record should trigger the flow within a few minutes. Return to Power Automate and review the flow for errors (see Figure 4-49).

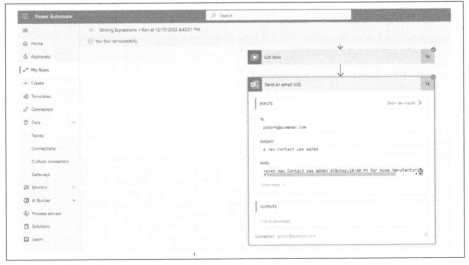

Figure 4-49. Reviewing flow history

Format Data by Examples

One of the most common uses for expressions in Power Automate is to apply a custom format to dynamic content. For example, you may want to take a date-time value that is written in ISO 8601 format and add it to an email in a format that is more familiar to your user. Power Automate makes this easy by supplying a "Format data by examples" entry in the Expressions tab. When you select that entry, a wizard will walk you through the process, asking for several things. First, it will ask you to pick the dynamic content field you want to format. Next, it will ask for one or more sample values and the output you would like for each. Once you have supplied those, it will provide you with a suggested expression to achieve that result. You can then test the expression and insert it into the field in the designer. You will be warned that you can't get back to the "Format data by examples" wizard once you've inserted the value.

"Format data by examples" will only work on a single value at a time. You can't use it to format arrays or multiple selections. But it does provide an easy way to obtain a specific output without needing to be completely familiar with all the functions available.

Exercise 4-7. Formatting a date

In this example, you'll modify the email sent by the flow you created in Exercise 4-6 to include the date and time that the row was created. You'll format the date and time the way you would like to see it presented.

1. Log in to *https://make.powerautomate.com*, and click on the flow titled "Writing Expressions" in your My flows list. Click on the Edit link at the top of the flow detail pane (see Figure 4-50).

Figure 4-50. Editing existing flow

2. Expand the "Send an email (V2)" action and delete the `formatDateTime` expression by clicking on the "x" (see Figure 4-51).

Figure 4-51. Removing existing `FormatDateTime` expression

3. With the input cursor where the `formatDateTime` expression used to be, click on the Expression tab and select "Format data by examples" from the list of expressions (see Figure 4-52).

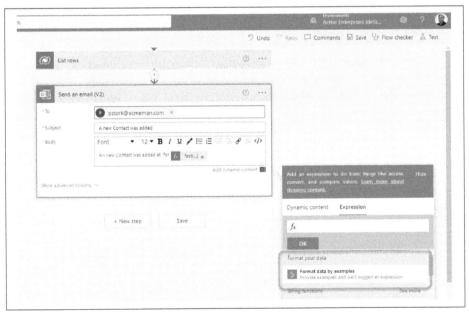

Figure 4-52. Starting "Format data by examples" wizard

4. Type "Created" into the Search box, and select Created On from the "When a row is added, modified or deleted" trigger (see Figure 4-53).

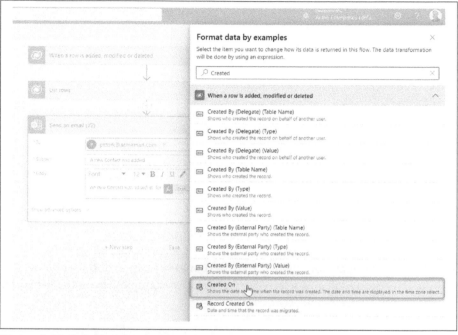

Figure 4-53. Selecting dynamic content

5. Type a typical ISO 8601–formatted date-time value like "2022-12-28T 10:00:00.000Z," into the Example value field. Type the date-time format you would like to see in the Desired output field (see Figure 4-54). Click "Get expression."

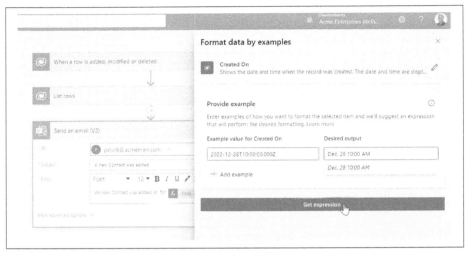

Figure 4-54. Getting expression

6. Click Apply to insert the expression generated by the wizard into the email. A warning will appear stating that you will not be able to go back to the wizard after inserting the expression. This means any edits to the expression will need to be made manually. Click "Got it" to close the dialog (see Figure 4-55).

Figure 4-55. Inserting expression

7. Save and test the modified flow by adding a New Contact record. This should trigger the flow within a few minutes. Return to Power Automate and review the flow for errors (see Figure 4-56).

Figure 4-56. Reviewing flow history

If you know what you want your data value to look like but aren't sure how to build a function to format the content, try using "Format data by examples." It should at least give you some ideas on how to do it even if your first attempt isn't perfect.

Using the Action Ellipsis (…) Menu

When building flows, you will usually configure your actions by using dynamic content and functions. But there are times when just manipulating the values supplied to fields in an action is not enough. In those cases, you will use the ellipsis (…) menu of the action or trigger to do additional configuration. Figure 4-57 shows a typical ellipsis menu.

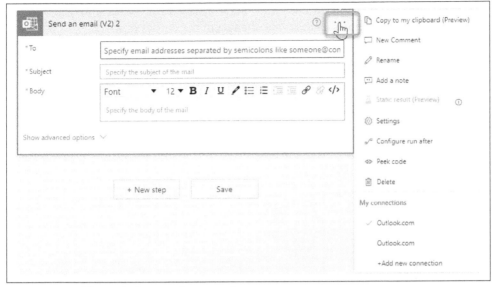

Figure 4-57. Ellipsis (…) menu for an action

The options available depend on the action or trigger itself. However, there are several entries that are common to most actions and triggers. Following are the common entries found on most ellipsis menus:

- Copy to my clipboard
- New Comment
- Rename
- Add a note
- Static result (Preview)
- Settings
- Run after
- Peek code
- Delete
- My connections

I'll go over each of these menu entries at some point in the book. Some of them, like "Static result (Preview)" and "Run after" will be covered in Chapter 7 when I cover troubleshooting. I'll also dedicate a section to the Settings menu entry later in this chapter since it contains a variety of additional choices. You have already been introduced to some options, like Peek code and Delete, earlier in the book. You saw how to use Peek code to look up and copy the JSON syntax for a value, and you've used Delete in a couple examples. Let's review the rest of the entries now.

Copying Actions

The Copy entry on the ellipsis (…) menu can be used to copy a formatted action to your computer's clipboard. Then, when you add an action you can use the My clipboard tab, as shown in Figure 4-58, to paste a copy of the action into the designer. The My clipboard tab will show all the actions you've copied since you logged in to the designer.

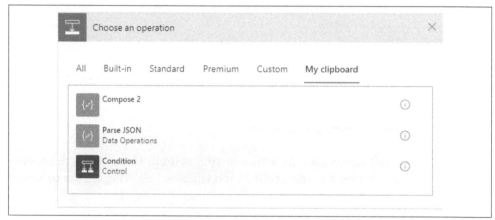

Figure 4-58. Pasting actions from My clipboard

 Copying triggers isn't currently supported, so the Copy entry is grayed out on the Trigger menu.

You can even copy actions between two different flows by copying the actions you want, closing that flow, and opening the other one in the same Power Automate tab. You must use the same tab because the clipboard is specified in your current web session. If you open a different browser and log in again, you'll get a different clipboard. When I showed you how to use Peek code earlier in this chapter, you saw that the action and its configuration is stored in JSON code. What you are copying when you use the "Copy to my clipboard" entry is that JSON configuration. Pasting that JSON in as a new action creates a copy of the action in a new location. Because it is using JSON references, the copy/paste may not work correctly if some of the references are not in scope when pasting the action in a new location. For example, if you copy an action inside an "Apply to each" loop and then try to paste it outside the loop, it won't have access to values generated inside the loop. The paste will work, but an error will occur when you try to save the flow.

Renaming Actions and Triggers

Actions must have unique names within the flow and are limited to no more than 80 characters in length. When you add additional actions in a flow, a number is automatically added to the default name. For example, the second Compose you add to a flow will be named "Compose 2," and the third would be "Compose 3." This will satisfy the requirement that all action names must be unique. But it will make the logic of your flow hard to follow.

Using the Rename entry on the ellipsis menu, you can supply your own specific name to the action. If you only have one "List rows" action in a flow, it's probably clear what it does. But if you have multiple Initialize Variable or Compose actions, it may be harder to remember what each of them is used for. Providing a meaningful name for each action can be time-consuming, but it should be done for actions that occur more than once in a flow.

Renaming an action after you have used dynamic content produced by that action in other actions may break those dynamic content JSON references. So, it's a good idea to rename actions as you add them to the designer.

Renaming actions to give them more meaning will help you keep track of what your flow is doing. But adding marginal comments and notes to document your flow is also important. There are two entries on the ellipsis menu that can be used for this kind of documentation.

Adding Comments

The Comments link is best used when collaborating with other users to develop a flow. Using Comments, you can add marginal comments to the right side of the flow designer for a specific action. You can even @mention another user in the context of a comment. Doing that will add their name to the comment and send the comment to them by email. Users can also reply to a comment to create a comment thread. Each action in a flow can have multiple comment threads. The number of comment threads in an action or trigger are displayed in an indicator within the action card.

The Comments panel can be toggled open or closed using the Comments link at the top of the designer screen. Figure 4-59 shows a typical comment thread in a flow. Comment threads can be deleted or simply marked as resolved and left in the finished flow.

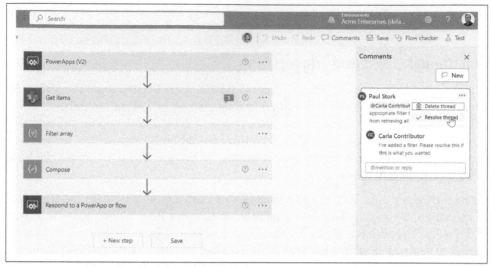

Figure 4-59. Comment thread in a flow

Adding Notes

Notes can also be added inline to each action and trigger in a flow. As shown in Figure 4-60, notes appear below the action header and above any fields that need to be filled in. One common use of the note field is to store the JSON source for functions used in the action so that they are easily visible without hovering over them to get a tooltip or loading them into the Expressions tab.

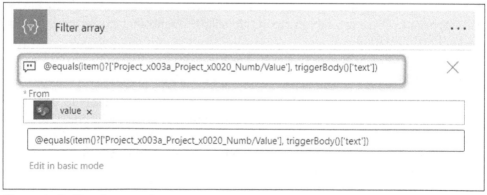

Figure 4-60. Note in an action

Adding a New Connection

Connections are created automatically when you add an action to a flow. But there are times when you want to create a new connection or switch which connection an action is using. The ellipsis menu will display a list of existing connections that you can use with a specific action, and there is an "+Add new connection" link that can be used to create new connections. If your flow is stored in a solution, then you will also see connection references listed.

 Connections are displayed using the name of the account used in the connection. This name cannot be changed. This can make it difficult to differentiate between various connections in the ellipsis menu. Connection references can be given more descriptive names.

Changing Action Settings

Each of the ellipsis menu settings I've discussed so far focuses on one thing. But there is also a Settings menu entry that provides access to a variety of settings. These settings can vary from action to action, but in this section I'll cover the common settings available on most actions. Figure 4-61 shows a typical Settings panel for an action.

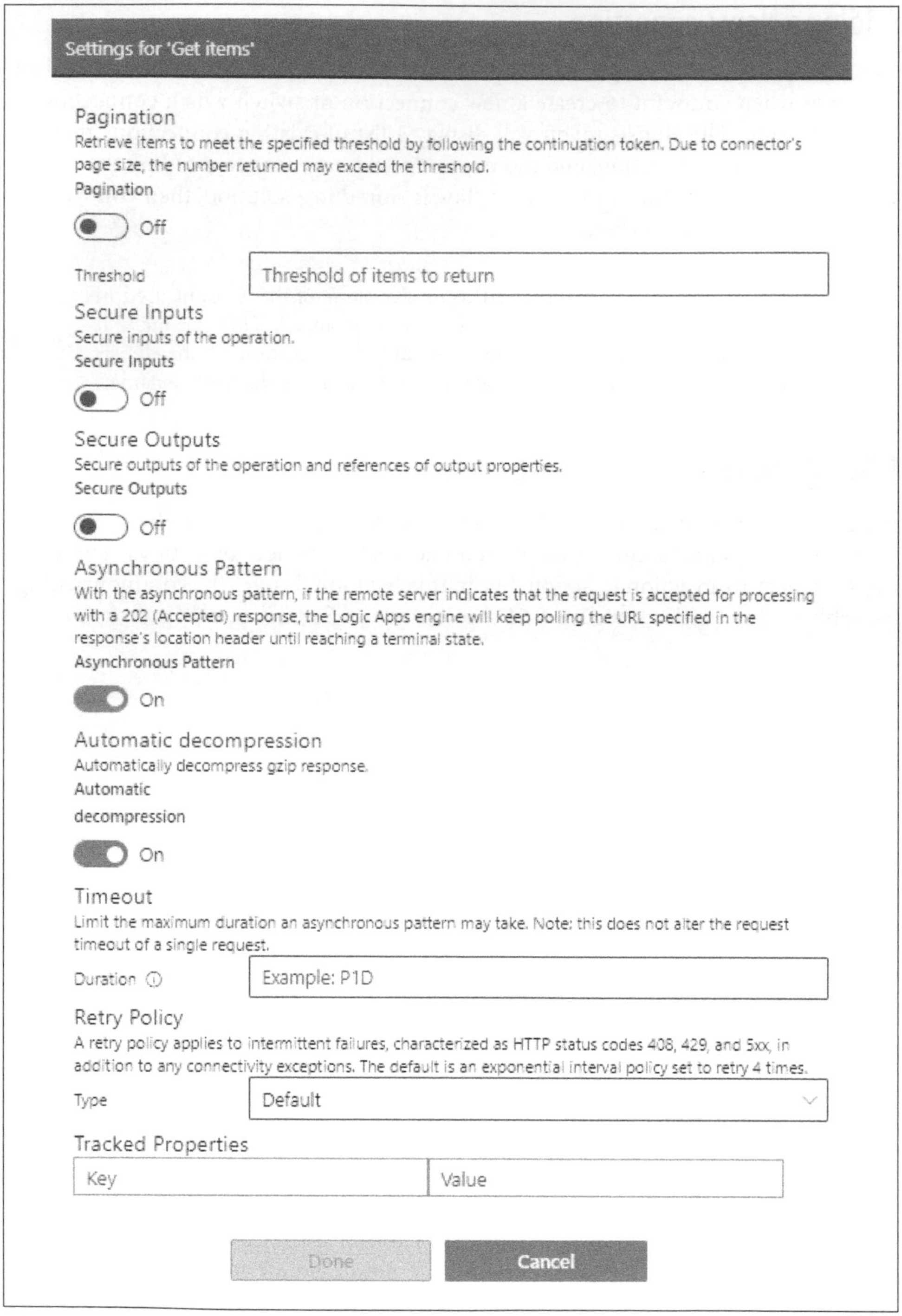

Settings for 'Get items'

Pagination

Retrieve items to meet the specified threshold by following the continuation token. Due to connector's page size, the number returned may exceed the threshold.

Pagination

(●) Off

Threshold	Threshold of items to return

Secure Inputs

Secure inputs of the operation.

Secure Inputs

(●) Off

Secure Outputs

Secure outputs of the operation and references of output properties.

Secure Outputs

(●) Off

Asynchronous Pattern

With the asynchronous pattern, if the remote server indicates that the request is accepted for processing with a 202 (Accepted) response, the Logic Apps engine will keep polling the URL specified in the response's location header until reaching a terminal state.

Asynchronous Pattern

(●) On

Automatic decompression

Automatically decompress gzip response.

Automatic

decompression

(●) On

Timeout

Limit the maximum duration an asynchronous pattern may take. Note: this does not alter the request timeout of a single request.

Duration ⓘ	Example: P1D

Retry Policy

A retry policy applies to intermittent failures, characterized as HTTP status codes 408, 429, and 5xx, in addition to any connectivity exceptions. The default is an exponential interval policy set to retry 4 times.

Type	Default ⌄

Tracked Properties

Key	Value

[Done]   [Cancel]

Figure 4-61. Settings panel

Following are explanations for most of the common settings you will find on the Settings panel.

Pagination

Actions that retrieve an array of records will default to retrieving the first 100 records. If you want to retrieve more than that, you will need to enable the Pagination feature on the Settings menu. Once Pagination is enabled using the toggle, you can set a threshold for the maximum number of items that will be retrieved. The action will then continue to retrieve records in batches until it reaches the maximum threshold value.

You need to be careful when enabling Pagination because it can have a significant impact on the performance of your flow. You also need to be aware that there are limits on how large an array you can process using loops, depending on your license level. These limits range from a low of 5,000 items to a high of 100,000.

Secure Inputs and Secure Outputs

Input and output parameters for your flow are always passed using HTTPS encryption. But they will show in the flow run history. So, if your flow actions use confidential data, you should enable the Secure Inputs and Outputs features in the action's Settings. This will hide the inputs and outputs in the flow run history.

Asynchronous Pattern

The normal return status code for most APIs is 200. But some connector actions will return a 202 status code, which means they have accepted the task but haven't completed it. The Asynchronous Pattern feature is enabled on actions by default. This tells the action to continue to poll the server until the action times out or receives a valid HTTP status termination code. It should not be disabled unless you know that the API doesn't use a 202 status code.

Automatic Decompression

JSON responses are normally returned in a compressed state to minimize their size. Automatic Decompression is also enabled by default. This setting will decompress a GZIP response sent by a connector API. It shouldn't be disabled unless you know the connector sends a raw JSON response.

Timeout

Running flows will time out after 30 days, but occasionally it's helpful to time out an individual action. As we discussed, most actions will run in an Asynchronous mode—they continue to check the server until it completes the request. Using the

Timeout setting, you can set a timeout for a specific action. The duration is set using an ISO 8601 duration. For example, setting the timeout of a "Start and wait for an Approval" action to P29DT12H will automatically time out an approval before the whole flow times out at 30 days. You can then relaunch the flow to create a new approval that will be good for another 30 days.

 ISO 8601 is an international standard that defines how to state a date and time or a duration as text. The duration format is as follows, where (n) is replaced by a number:

P(n)Y(n)M(n)DT(n)H(n)M(n)S

- P is the duration designator and is always placed at the beginning of the duration.
- Y is the year designator and is not used in Power Automate.
- M is the month designator and is not used in Power Automate.
- D is the day designator that follows the value for the number of days.
- T is the time designator that precedes the time components.
- H is the hour designator that follows the value for the number of hours.
- M is the minute designator that follows the value for the number of minutes.
- S is the second designator that follows the value for the number of seconds.

Retry Policy

Actions don't always succeed the first time the API is called. The server may be down, or the service may be too busy to take more requests. To adjust for that, there are four different Retry Policy types:

Default
An exponential interval policy set to retry four times.

None
Do not retry an API call that fails.

Fixed Interval
Count establishes the number of times to retry the call, and Interval sets the amount of time to wait between tries.

Exponential Interval
> Count establishes the number of times to retry the call, and Interval sets the maximum amount of time to wait for the first retry; successive retries will occur on a decreasing interval.

Tracked Properties

Tracked Properties can be used to store a particular key-value pair with a particular action. The value does not show in either the Input or Output of the action but can be retrieved in a later action using the `actions()` function. For example, if you create a Tracked Property called "My Tracked Property" in the Dataverse List Rows in Table action, you could retrieve the value of that property later in the flow with `actions(List Rows in Table)?['TrackedProperties']?['My Tracked Property']`. Tracked Properties let you store data that can then be retrieved in other steps of your flow. This may be more efficient than depending on dynamic content that must be processed each time it is used.

Trigger Settings

There are also a few settings that are specific to triggers. In addition to the settings already covered, these settings include the following:

- Split On
- Custom Tracking ID
- Concurrency Control
- Trigger Conditions

Figure 4-62 shows a typical Settings dialog for a trigger.

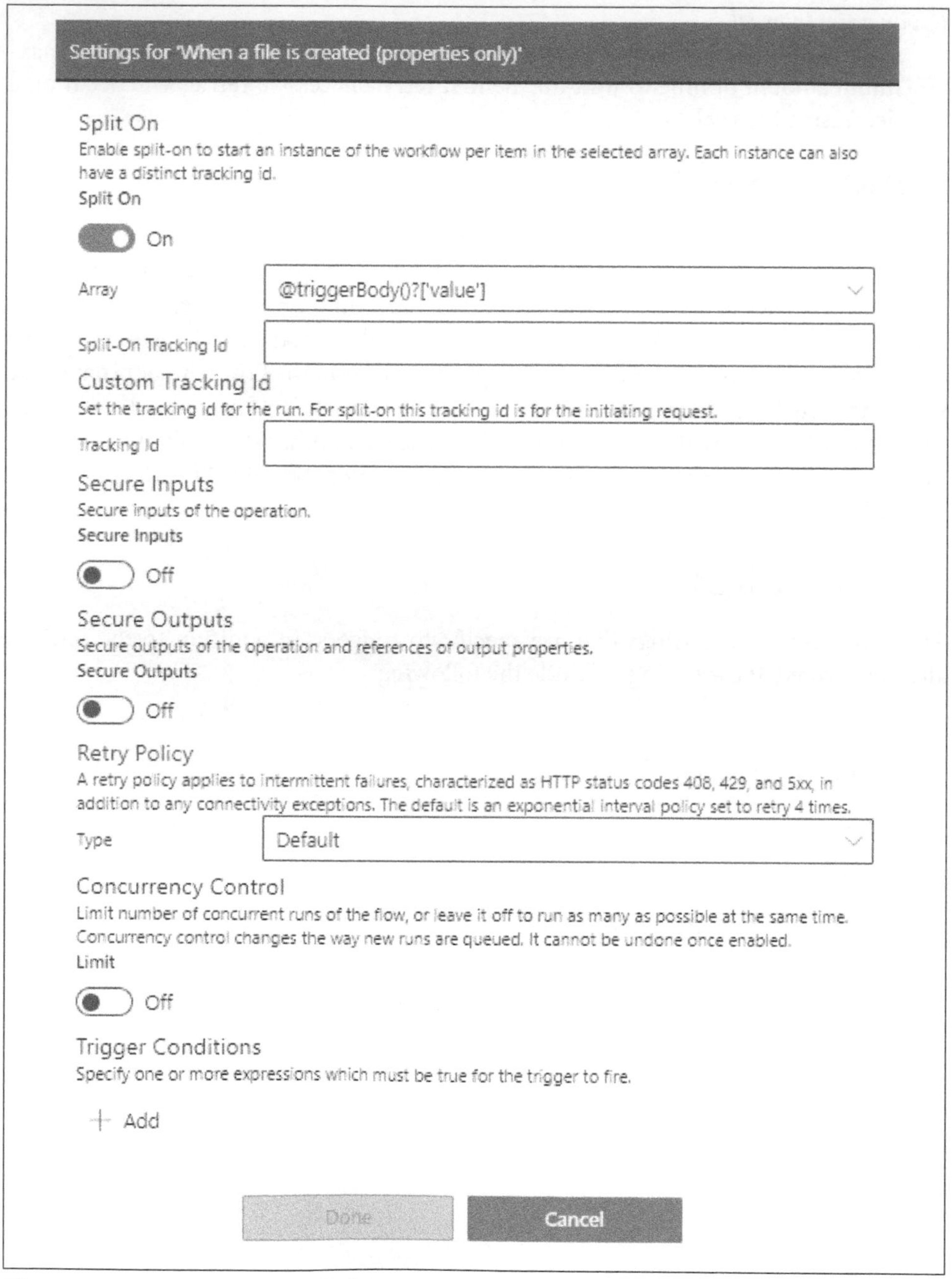

Settings for 'When a file is created (properties only)'

Split On

Enable split-on to start an instance of the workflow per item in the selected array. Each instance can also have a distinct tracking id.

Split On

⬤◯ On

Array

@triggerBody()?['value']

Split-On Tracking Id

Custom Tracking Id

Set the tracking id for the run. For split-on this tracking id is for the initiating request.

Tracking Id

Secure Inputs

Secure inputs of the operation.

Secure Inputs

◉◯ Off

Secure Outputs

Secure outputs of the operation and references of output properties.

Secure Outputs

◉◯ Off

Retry Policy

A retry policy applies to intermittent failures, characterized as HTTP status codes 408, 429, and 5xx, in addition to any connectivity exceptions. The default is an exponential interval policy set to retry 4 times.

Type

Default

Concurrency Control

Limit number of concurrent runs of the flow, or leave it off to run as many as possible at the same time. Concurrency control changes the way new runs are queued. It cannot be undone once enabled.

Limit

◉◯ Off

Trigger Conditions

Specify one or more expressions which must be true for the trigger to fire.

+ Add

Done   Cancel

Figure 4-62. Trigger Settings dialog

Split On

Triggering events can often happen simultaneously. For example, when multiple users fill in a Microsoft form, they may submit forms at the same time. So, most triggers are designed to allow inclusion of one or more items in the data passed as part of the trigger. There is a trigger option called Split On that can be used to break this collection of data apart and start one flow instance for each item. Split On is enabled by default. Once enabled, select for each new instance which item level in the array is used. Turning off the Split On option lets you work with all the items triggered at the same time in one flow.

The Split On tracking ID lets you specify a value of the original item that will be used as a unique index to differentiate between the flow runs. This is related to the Custom Tracking ID, which we'll cover next.

Custom Tracking ID

The Custom Tracking ID is a feature that was created for Azure Logic Apps. It's still present in Power Automate because it is built on the foundation of Azure Logic Apps. Although you can set a Custom Tracking ID in the trigger settings, there is no way to view this value in Power Automate.

Controlling Concurrency

In most cases where Split On is enabled, Power Automate will generate as many instances of a flow as necessary to process the items in the incoming array of data. Each instance of the flow will be added to a queue and run one after another as each previous instance finishes. This guarantees that the flow instances run completely independent from each other. This is the default condition when the Concurrency control is disabled.

But running the flows one at a time can slow things down. So, an optional setting lets you tell Power Automate to run up to 100 flow instances in parallel threads. To do this, you enable the Concurrency Control toggle to On and set the Degree of Parallelism slider to the number of parallel threads you want to enable. The minimum is 1, which is the same as disabling Concurrency. The maximum is 100. If you have more than 100 items to process, then it will process the first 100 in parallel and start a new thread as each thread finishes. Enabling concurrency can significantly improve performance of flows if they have no interdependencies.

Implementing Trigger Conditions

Trigger Conditions let you specify conditions that must be met before your flow will trigger. For example, you may have an approval flow that shouldn't run until all data entry is completed and the item is submitted for approval. If you are using a "When an item is modified" trigger, it will start on any modification. By adding a Trigger Condition, you can specify that the flow will only start when the item has been modified and a specific column value has been set to "Submit for Approval." Trigger Conditions let you fine-tune when your flow will run instead of testing for specific values after the flow is triggered. Trigger Conditions are often used to prevent infinite loops that occur when using a "When an item is modified" trigger and then making a modification inside the flow—this will normally trigger the flow again.

Exercise 4-8. Preventing infinite loops with Trigger Conditions

In this example, we'll create a flow that triggers when a SharePoint item is created or modified. To keep the flow from triggering in an infinite loop, we'll add a Trigger Condition to keep the flow from triggering again when an update is made by the flow.

1. Log in to your SharePoint online tenant and create a custom list called "Trigger Condition Demo." Add a "Multiple lines of text" column to the list called Updates. Under "More options," enable "Append changes to existing text" (see Figure 4-63). Add a Choice column called "Status." Set the three choices to Pending, Started, and Completed. Click the Save button.

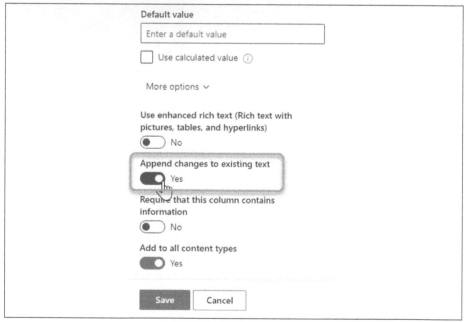

Figure 4-63. SharePoint updating column settings

2. Log in to *https://make.powerautomate.com,* and create a new automated cloud flow that uses the "When an item is created or modified" trigger (see Figure 4-64). Name the flow "Prevent Infinite Loop."

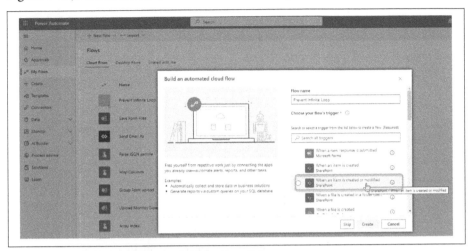

Figure 4-64. Creating "Prevent Infinite Loop" flow

3. Select the Site Address for the SharePoint site where you created the list in step 1. Select Trigger Condition Demo from the List Name drop-down (see Figure 4-65).

Figure 4-65. Configuring trigger

4. Click "+ New step" to add a Delay action from the built-in Schedule connector. Configure the Delay to wait for one minute. The delay is added to simulate work that the flow may be doing (see Figure 4-66).

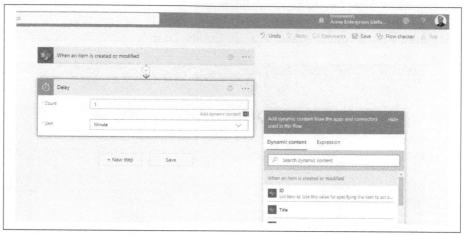

Figure 4-66. Configuring delay

 If an update comes immediately after the flow triggers, it may not cause the flow to re-trigger. But in many scenarios, for example, approvals, the updates don't come until later. This will typically cause the flow to re-trigger.

5. Click "+ New step" to add an "Update item" action from the SharePoint connector. Configure the action to use the same Site Address and List Name as the trigger. Insert the ID and Title dynamic content from the trigger into the ID and Title fields. Type `Concat('Updated ' '', formatDateTime(Utc Now(),'hh:mm'))` into the Expression tab and insert it into the Updates field (see Figure 4-67). Select Completed in the Status Value field.

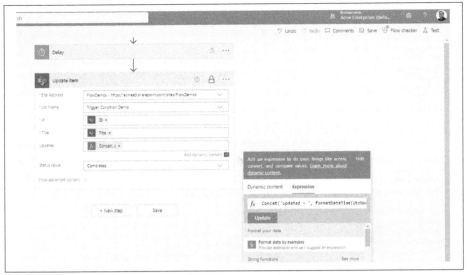

Figure 4-67. Adding "Update item" action

6. Save the flow and test it manually after starting the Test "Add a new item" to the Trigger Condition Demo list.

> Testing an automated flow still requires that you complete the action that will trigger the flow. If the flow is not in Test mode, it can take up to five minutes before the flow triggers.

7. Wait five minutes and then "Turn off" the flow from the flow description screen to keep it from starting additional runs (see Figure 4-68).

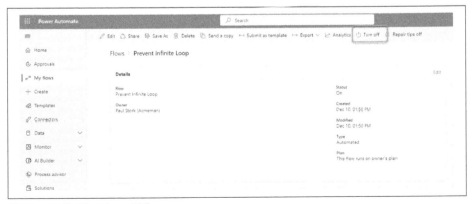

Figure 4-68. Turning off flow

If you look at the 28-day run history, you will see that the flow has run multiple times even though we only triggered it once. To fix this, we will add a Trigger Condition that will keep the flow from re-triggering when the flow makes the update.

8. Click "+ New step" and add a Filter Array action. Skip the From field for now. Add the Status Value dynamic content from the trigger to the left "Choose a value" field. Type "Completed" in the right side of the condition, and set the operation in the middle to "is not equal to." Click "Edit in advanced mode" in the action. You should see the expression as shown in Figure 4-69. Copy the formula that is revealed. This is the expression that will need to be true for the trigger to fire. Select the whole line and copy it to the clipboard using Ctrl + C. Once you have copied it, delete the "Filter array" action.

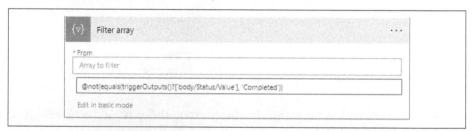

Figure 4-69. Trigger Condition expression using "Filter array"

9. Open Settings on the ellipsis menu. Click the plus sign (+) under Trigger Conditions and paste the expression you copied into the field using Ctrl + V (see Figure 4-70). Repeat the testing you did in steps 5 and 6. This time, there should be only one flow run.

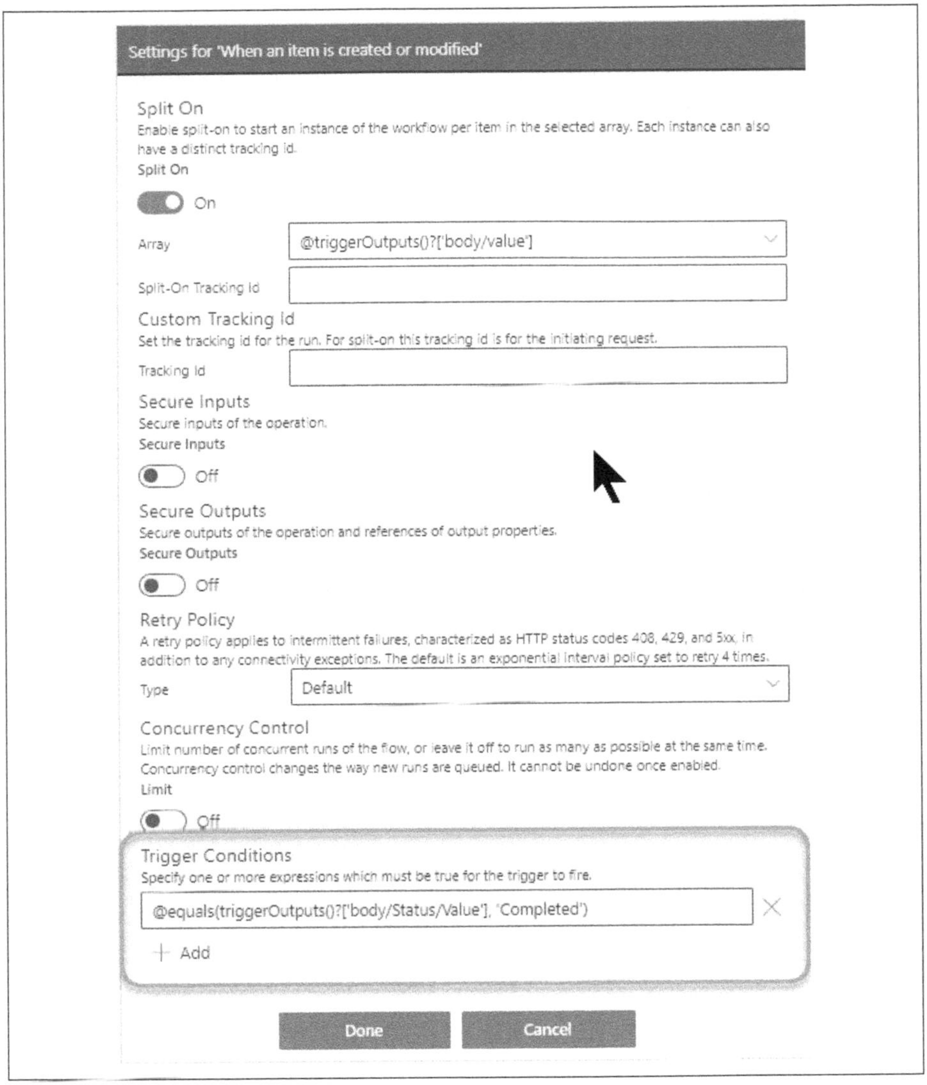

Figure 4-70. Adding Trigger Condition

Summary

In this chapter, you learned how to fill out the action fields in your flow using either static or dynamic content. You also learned how to manipulate those dynamic content values using function expressions. Finally, you looked through all the common advanced settings on the ellipsis menu that you can use to adjust the way that triggers and actions behave. I don't have enough space in this book to show you how to use all the functions. But I did show you where to find detailed information on all the available functions. You'll learn more about individual functions as you find use for them in your flows. You will continue to use a lot of the common functions as you progress through the book, but you'll need to rely on Microsoft's documentation to learn how to use some specific functions in the future.

So far, most of the flows we've built or examined are constructed in a single straight line of actions. But in the real world, things are seldom that simple. In the next chapter, we'll look at how to choose different courses of action depending on the dynamic content values produced by the flow. I'll also show you how to split your flow so it can run multiple concurrent branches simultaneously. Finally, I'll show you how to loop through an array of values to do the same actions on each value. Once you are done, you'll have all the basic tools you need to begin transforming business processes into Power Automate flows.

CHAPTER 5

Implementing Logic

In Chapter 4, you learned how to add and configure triggers and actions in a flow. You now know how to create a flow from scratch with a trigger and add actions to it that do things in a sequence. But not all business processes can be accomplished using that kind of sequential logic. What if a flow needs to do something different depending on the data it discovers? What if you need to do more than one thing at a time? Or what if you need to process multiple rows of data? In this chapter, you'll learn how to build a flow that adapts to the data it is processing by implementing a logical flow. I'll explain how Condition and Switch actions can be used to travel down different paths by evaluating the values of data in the flow. I'll show you how to use looping actions to do the same set of steps on multiple rows of data in an array. Finally, I'll cover how to split your flow into multiple parallel branches so it can do several different things simultaneously. By the end of the chapter, you'll have all the tools you need to begin building complex flows that automate real-world business processes in your organization.

The Control Connector

Six actions may be used to change the logical path followed by a Power Automate flow. These actions are all found in the built-in Control connector:

- Condition
- Apply to each
- Do until
- Scope
- Switch
- Terminate

I'll detail how to use the Scope and Terminate actions in Chapter 7 when I discuss troubleshooting. But here is a quick overview of those two actions:

The Scope action
> This is a container that can host a sequential string of actions. One of its major benefits is that it can be expanded or contracted to show or hide the list of actions it contains. This can be used to make the overall logical flow easier to read at a high level by dividing your flow into manageable chunks. Scopes can also be used to aggregate error messages, which is why we'll discuss them when I cover troubleshooting.

The Terminate action
> This can be used to end a flow immediately, at any point. This can be useful if you need to stop a flow before it would normally complete its work due to an error condition. Because it is used primarily to control the logic of a flow when an error arises, I'll wait to discuss this action when I cover troubleshooting.

Controlling Actions with Conditions

The most common logic action used in Power Automate flows is the Condition action. A Condition action is essentially an If/Then statement. In its simplest form, a Condition action has a lefthand field, a righthand field, and an operator in between. The fields can be filled in with either dynamic content, an expression, or a static value.

 There is also an If() function that can be used inside a field if you just want to return a value based on whether a formula evaluates to true or false. This can simplify your flow by eliminating unnecessary condition actions.

The operator in between the fields is then used to determine whether the condition is true or false. The list of available operators changes depending on the data type of the values being compared. For example, if you are comparing two numbers, the available operators will be: is equal to, is not equal to, is greater than, is greater than or equal to, is less than, or is less than or equal to. But, if comparing two strings it will be: contains, does not contain, is equal to, is not equal to, is greater than, is greater than or equal to, is less than, is less than or equal to, starts with, does not start with, ends with, or does not end with. One common problem with Condition actions is trying to compare two values that are not the same type.

If the value of the condition evaluates as true, then one set of actions is executed. If it's false, then another parallel set of actions is executed.

Be careful of case sensitivity when comparing values. Conditions are case sensitive and will return false if an unexpected case is used. Use expressions to generate null, false, and true values for the right-side field of a condition.

Complex conditions are possible by grouping logical conditions together and specifying that they all must be true (And operator) or that only one needs to be true (Or operator). Grouping conditions is a very powerful feature but often leads to unanticipated results. Complex logical conditions are often difficult to articulate and may require a lot of work.

Exercise 5-1. Setting approval status

In this example, you will use a condition to evaluate whether a document was approved or rejected by a group of people. If it was approved, you will record the approval status in the metadata of the document. If it was rejected, you will record the status and send an email back to the original author informing them of the rejection.

1. Create an automated cloud flow titled "Approve file submission" using the "When a file is created (properties only)" trigger. Choose a SharePoint site from the Site Address drop-down and Documents from the Library Name drop-down (see Figure 5-1).

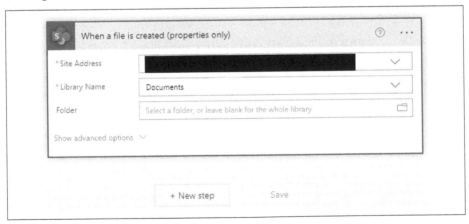

Figure 5-1. Creating approval flow

2. Add a "Get manager (V2)" action to the flow and insert the Modified By Email dynamic content into the User (UPN) field (see Figure 5-2).

The "Get manager (V2)" action will retrieve the email of the user who uploads the file from Azure Active Directory (AAD) if your organization has specified the reporting structure of users in AAD. When a file is uploaded, the "Created By" and "Modified By" user is the same.

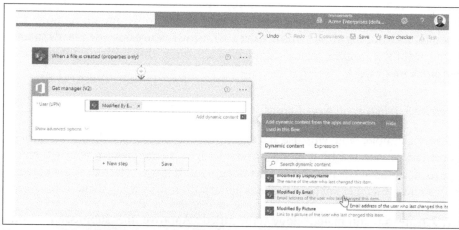

Figure 5-2. Get manager

3. Add a "Start and wait for an approval" action. Select "Approve/Reject – Everyone must approve" as the Approval type. Type "Sample Approval with Condition" as the Title. Insert the Mail dynamic content output by the "Get manager" action into the Assigned to field. Type your email address after the semicolon following the Mail dynamic content in the Assigned to field (see Figure 5-3).

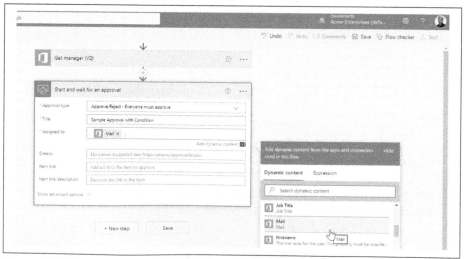

Figure 5-3. "Start and wait for an approval" action

4. Add a Condition action and set the lefthand value equal to Outcome. Set the righthand value to Reject, and set the operator in the middle to "does not contain." The Outcome dynamic content will accumulate the responses of each approver as a comma, delimited string until either all the approvers respond or one of the approvers rejects the item (see Figure 5-4). We then test to see if the item was approved by checking to see if Outcome contains the response Reject. If it does, the item was not approved. If it doesn't, then the item was approved.

 Most of the dynamic content returned by an approval is contained in collections, but Outcome provides a single string value that summarizes whether the item was approved or rejected. This lets you check the response to an approval without using a loop.

Figure 5-4. Checking approval Outcome

5. Add an "Update file properties" action to the Yes side of the condition. Select in the Site Address and Library Name you used for the trigger. Set the remaining properties as follows:

   - Id: ID dynamic content from the trigger
   - Title: File name with extension dynamic content from the trigger followed by " - Approved"

   Add an "Update file properties" action to the No side of the condition. Select in the Site Address and Library Name you used for the trigger. Set the remaining properties as follows:

   - Id: ID dynamic content from the trigger
   - Title: File name with extension dynamic content from the trigger followed by " - Rejected"

Add a "Send an email (V2)" action to the No side of the condition. Set the remaining properties as follows:

- To: Modified By Email dynamic content from the trigger
- Subject: Type "File Rejected"
- Body: Type "Your file was Rejected." Insert File name with extension dynamic content between "file" and "was" (see Figure 5-5).

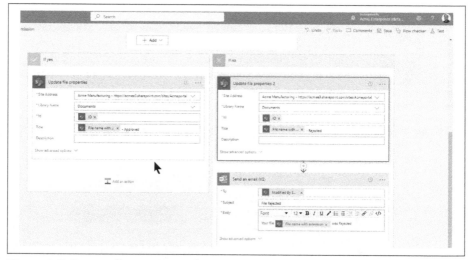

Figure 5-5. Responding to approval

6. You can now Save and Test your flow by uploading a document. To easily test the flow, change the email addresses used in step 3 to your own email address. Otherwise, your manager will get the request to approve your test document.

Using Switches

Conditions can only be used to send a flow down one of two branches, but a Switch can be used to send a flow down one of 26 branches. When you add a Switch to a flow, you get one box labeled Switch, a second box labeled Case, and a third box labeled Default (see Figure 5-6).

Figure 5-6. Switch action

The On field in the Switch is filled in with dynamic content or an expression that resolves to a single value. The Equals field in the Case box is then set to a static value. The branch in that Case will be followed if the value in the Switch is equal to the value in the Case. Up to 24 additional Case boxes can be added using the plus (+) sign between the last Case and the Default case. The Default branch is used if the value in the Switch doesn't match any of the Case values. You can nest additional switches in the Default branch to extend the Switch to another 25 Cases and a Default case.

> Power Automate actions can only be nested eight levels deep. This limits how many If/Then conditions you can chain together to evaluate complex logic. The best way to handle this is by summarizing the result from your nested conditions as a string. Then, you can start your logic again at level one using a Switch action to add additional levels.

Unlike Conditions, Switches can only evaluate specific values, not ranges. So, if you need to handle a range of values, you need to use one Case in the Switch for each potential value in the range. Switch-Case values are also case sensitive and can't be null, so functions like `Coalesce()` and `Upper()` are often used in the Switch to get a predictable value to compare to the Case. The last thing to understand about Switches is that, unlike the Condition action, there is no `Switch()` function that can be used in place of the action.

Exercise 5-2. Reacting to the day of the week

In this example, you will use a Switch to evaluate a specific date and postpone action until Monday morning if the date falls on a weekend day. This flow would normally be part of a larger flow, but we will keep it short and focus on the workings of the Switch. I'm sure you'll see how this pattern could be used in a bigger flow to pause a flow for a couple days to finish its work during the work week.

1. Create an instant cloud flow titled "Wait for Monday" using the "Manually trigger a flow" trigger. Expand the trigger and add an Input of type Date called InputDate (see Figure 5-7).

Figure 5-7. Manual trigger with input

2. Add an "Initialize variable" action to the flow. Type varDate in the Name field and Select String from the Type field (see Figure 5-8).

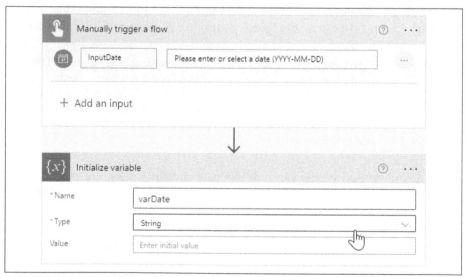

Figure 5-8. Initializing a variable

3. Add a Switch action to the flow. Insert the following expression into the On field of the Switch (see Figure 5-9). This will return a three-letter abbreviation for the day of the week, with the date formatted as follows:

```
formatDateTime(coalesce(triggerBody()['date'],utcNow()),'ddd')
```

Coalesce() is often used in Switches to substitute a non-null value in case the value being evaluated is null.

Figure 5-9. Adding a Switch

4. Type "Sun" into the Equals field of the Case. Add an additional Case for Sat (see Figure 5-10). You can use the Default case for the other days: Mon, Tue, Wed, Thu, and Fri.

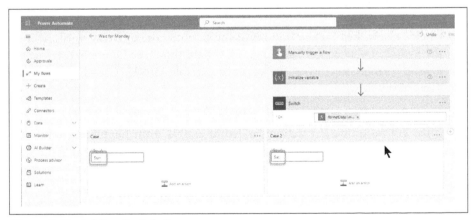

Figure 5-10. Adding Switch Cases

5. Add a "Set variable" action to each Case and the Default case. Use the actions to set the value of the `varDate` variable you initialized at the top of the flow (see Figure 5-11). Use the following formulas:

- Sun case: `addDays(triggerBody()['date'],1)`

- Sat case: `addDays(triggerBody()['date'],2)`

- Default case: InputDate dynamic content

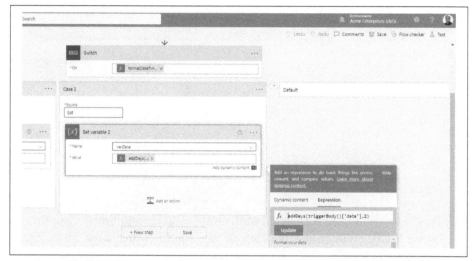

Figure 5-11. Building Case branches

6. Click "+New Step" at the bottom of the flow to add a "Delay until" action after the Switch. Delay actions require a UTC date-time (see Figure 5-12). Use the following formula to convert the `varDate` variable into UTC and insert it into the Timestamp field:

```
convertToUtc(variables('varDate'),'Central Standard Time')
```

This will postpone any actions added after this from happening until the date stored in the `varDate` variable is reached. You can replace Central Standard Time with the time zone name found in this list of Time Zone IDs (*https://oreil.ly/ Bv3br*) for your time zone.

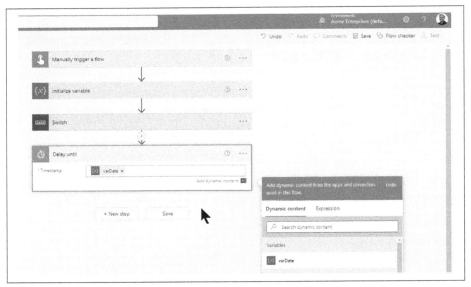

Figure 5-12. "Delay until" action

7. You can now Save and Test your flow. Use the calendar icon in the input box to pick a previous date. The flow should run to completion. If the date you picked was a Saturday or Sunday, the Delay until should be set for the following Monday. Otherwise, it should be set for the date entered (see Figure 5-13).

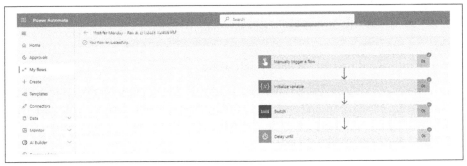

Figure 5-13. Successful delay

Calling Child Flows

So far in this chapter, I've shown you two ways to run different sections of code inline based on a logical condition or a specific value. But what if you want to run the same set of actions multiple times within a flow without duplicating the actions? To do that, you can add the actions to a separate flow and then call that Child flow from different places in your main flow.

Child flows can be almost anything, but they do have certain requirements. First, they must be built inside a solution. Normally, the flow invoking the Child flow is also built in the same solution. Second, the Child flow must use either a manual, Power Apps, or "When an HTTP request is received" trigger.

 The "When an HTTP request is received" trigger requires a premium license. The manual and Power Apps triggers are both included in the standard license.

Another feature of a Child flow is that it can use Input and Output parameters. Input parameters must be one of the following simple data types:

Text
> a string

Yes/No
> a Boolean

File
> a string containing a filename and a JSON representation of the file *contentBytes*

Email
> a string containing an email address

Number
> an integer or a floating point number

Date
> a string containing an ISO 8601 date-time

The Type specifications for parameters is mostly for documentation purposes. None of the string-based parameters are strongly typed. For example, you can pass any string as a Date or Email value, but you'll receive an error when you try to use the value as a Date or Email if it's not valid.

 To transfer an array of values to a Child flow, use the Text parameter and pass the array as a JSON string. Then, parse the JSON array in the Child flow to gain access to the full array.

There are two ways to return output to a Parent flow from a child. You can use the "Respond to a Power App or flow" action, which returns one or more of the same data types as the manual trigger. Or you can use the Response action from the Request connector. The Response action can return a complex body consisting of

JSON. You also specify the JSON schema that will be applied to the JSON when it is received. Using the Response action, you can return a full array of complex data objects, but the Response action does require a premium license.

Exercise 5-3. Calling a Child flow

In this example, you will create a Child flow that calculates the result of a simple math problem. You'll pass in two number parameters and divide the first number by the second. Then, you'll return the result to the Parent flow.

1. Log in to *https://make.powerautomate.com*, and select the Solutions tab in the navigation bar on the left. This will bring up a list of all the solution packages available in Power Automate. Click on the "+ New solution" link in the menu bar. This will open a panel on the right side of the screen, as shown in Figure 5-14. Type "Call a Child Flow" as the Display name of the Solution and select the CDS Default Publisher from the Publisher drop-down. Click the Create button to create your new solution (see Figure 5-14).

Figure 5-14. Creating a solution

2. Create a new instant flow using the +New > Automation > Cloud flow menus. Type "Divide Numbers" as the Flow name and select a Manual trigger (see Figure 5-15).

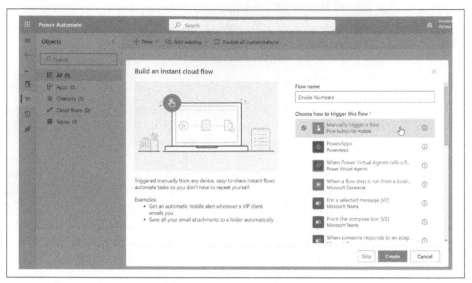

Figure 5-15. Creating a Child flow

3. Expand the trigger and add two number inputs named Divisor and Dividend (see Figure 5-16).

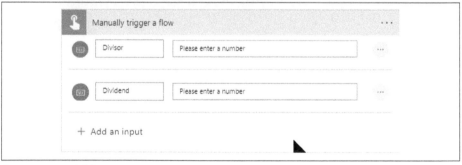

Figure 5-16. Adding trigger inputs

4. Add a Compose action. Set its Inputs field to the following expression:

    ```
    div(triggerBody()['number_1'],triggerBody()['number'])
    ```

    `triggerBody()['number_1']` is the Dividend input field, and `triggerBody()['number']` is the Divisor input field (see Figure 5-17).

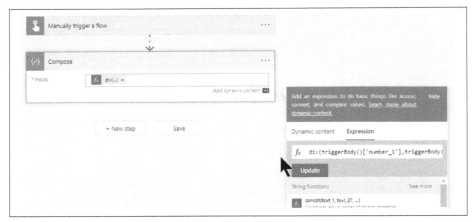

Figure 5-17. Calculating result

5. Add a "Respond to a PowerApp or flow" action. Add a Number output called Result and set it to the Outputs of the Compose action (see Figure 5-18). Save and Exit the flow designer to go back to the Solution screen.

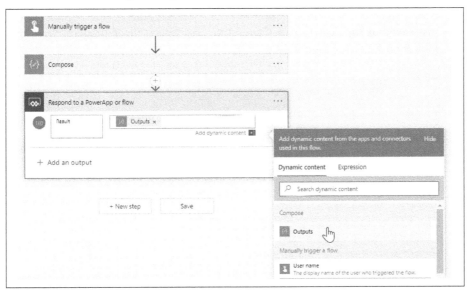

Figure 5-18. Responding to calling flow

6. Create a new instant flow using the +New > Automation > Cloud flow menus. Type "Invoke Child Flow" as the Flow name and select a Manual trigger (see Figure 5-19).

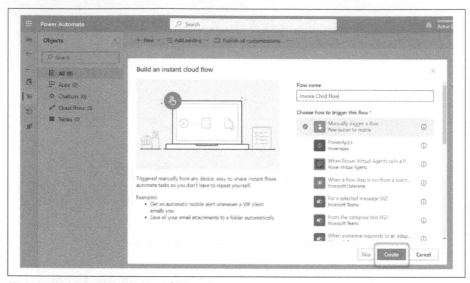

Figure 5-19. Creating Parent flow

7. Add a "Run a Child Flow" action to the flow. Select the Divide Numbers flow you just saved as the flow to run. Type "100" into the Divisor field and "10" into the Dividend field (see Figure 5-20).

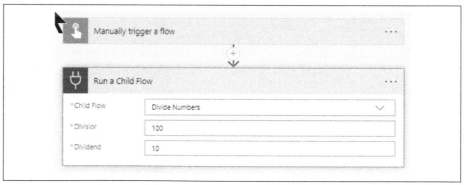

Figure 5-20. Running a Child flow

8. Save and Test the flow manually. You should see a result of 10 in the Outputs in the Parent flow (see Figure 5-21).

Figure 5-21. Child flow Output result

In the real world, Child flows are normally much more complex, but this example is a good demonstration of how to call a Child flow. To do this, we created a solution package, a Parent flow, and a Child flow. I'll explain more details about solution packages in Chapter 6.

Processing Arrays with "Apply to each" Loops

Running the same set of actions repeatedly doesn't always require using a Child flow. If you have an array of values that you want to process, you can use one of two types of looping actions. The most commonly used looping action in Power Automate is the "Apply to each" action. You can manually add an "Apply to each" action to a flow, but it is usually added by Power Automate when you try to use a value from an array in an action. For example, if you try to use the Modified by Email dynamic content from a list of SharePoint items to address an email, Power Automate will automatically add an "Apply to each" action around the "Send an email" action where you use the value. The "Apply to each" loop will then send one email for each entry in the list of items. Once the loop is created, you can add any number of additional actions inside the "Apply to each." But it's a good idea to keep the loop as short as possible to minimize the performance drain on your flow.

Depending on your license, there are limits to the maximum number of loops that you can execute. Standard and free licensed users in the low performance profile will be limited to 5,000 items. You can review the performance profiles and specific limits in Microsoft's online documentation (*https://oreil.ly/xAH0Z*).

You can enable Concurrency in the Settings menu of the "Apply to each" action. By default, each loop completes before the next loop executes. But you can enable Concurrency to have up to 50 loops running in parallel. Running loops in parallel will not preserve the order of the list in the results but can drastically improve the performance of the loop.

Another factor that will affect performance is the use of variables inside the loop. Whenever you set the value of a variable, all the other concurrent loops must stop processing to guarantee access to the variable. This can slow down concurrent processing. To get the best performance out of a loop, you should avoid variables and enable concurrency.

Exercise 5-4. Archiving email attachments to a SharePoint list

In this example, you will retrieve a set of attachments from an incoming email and save them as attachments to a SharePoint list item.

1. Log in to your SharePoint online tenant and create a custom list called "Email Attachment Archive Demo." Add a Date and time column to the list called "Received Date." Enable "Include Time" on the column. Click the Save button (see Figure 5-22).

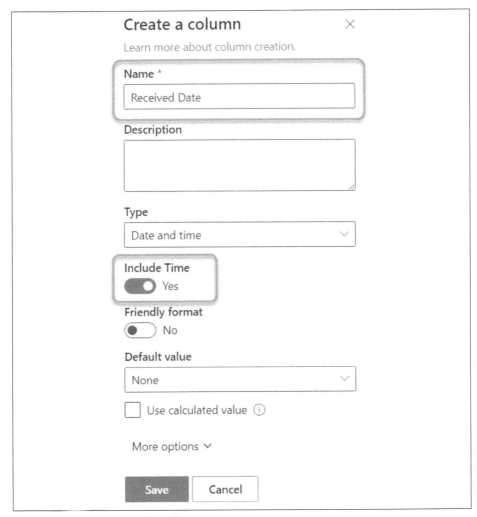

Figure 5-22. Creating archive list

2. Create an automated cloud flow and name it "Archive Email Attachment" using the "When a new email arrives (V3)" trigger from the Office 365 Outlook connector. Expand the trigger and click on "Show advanced options." Set Include Attachments to Yes, set Subject Filter to Test Archive, and Set Only with Attachments to Yes (see Figure 5-23).

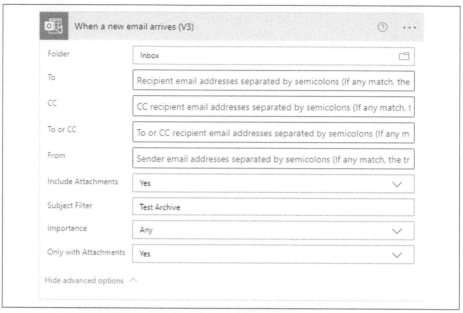

Figure 5-23. Email received trigger

3. Add a "Create item" action from the SharePoint connector. Set the Site Address and List Name to a list that allows attachments. Set the Title to the Subject dynamic content from the email trigger (see Figure 5-24).

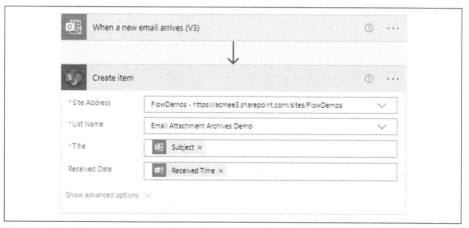

Figure 5-24. Creating a SharePoint item

4. Add an "Add attachment" action from the SharePoint connector. Set the Site Address and List Name to the list you used in step 2. Set the ID field to the ID dynamic content from the SharePoint "Create item" action. Set the File Name to

the Attachment Name and the File Content to Attachment Content from the trigger (see Figure 5-24). An "Apply to each" loop will be added around the "Add attachment" action to process the Attachments array.

Information about the attachments in the email is provided as an array of objects with the Attachment Name and Content being two of the object properties. When we use the Attachment Name, Power Automate automatically adds an "Apply to each" loop around the "Add attachment" action. The loop will be used to process properties from each attachment.

Figure 5-25. Adding attachment

5. Save the flow and use the arrow in the upper-right corner to navigate back to the flow detail page. Click the "Turn on" link to enable the flow (see Figure 5-26). (It was disabled because it was a copy of a previous flow.) Edit the flow again and Test the flow manually by sending an email with attachments to yourself with the Subject line "Test Archive." Wait until you receive the email. Then check the flow and the list to see if the attachments were added to a new item.

Figure 5-26. Turning on flow to run

This is just a basic example of how you can use an "Apply to each" loop in Power Automate. The specifics of your flow will depend on your requirements.

Using "Do until" Loops

"Apply to each" loops are easy to use, but they do have some limitations. One of the limitations is that the loop must process all the items in the list before it completes. There is no way to break out of the loop early if you find that you don't need to process the remaining items in a list. A "Do until" loop lets you repeat a set of actions until a certain condition is met. The loop continues to run until the specified condition is met. When the condition is met, the loop will exit and the flow will continue. So, if the condition is met before you process all the items in a list, the loop will complete without processing the additional items. For example, if you are creating a sum of all the records in a sorted list for one client, you don't need to keep processing after the client changes.

"Do until" loops also have a maximum iteration count just like "Apply to each" loops. But where "Apply to each" loops can iterate as many as 100,000 times depending on licensing, a "Do until" loop is always limited to no more than 5,000 iterations. Also, the actions within the "Do until" loop are always executed at least once even if the condition is true when the loop starts because the condition is checked at the end of the loop each time it is executed. If the condition evaluates to false, the set of actions is repeated and checked again at the end of the next loop.

A "Do until" loop can also be useful when you don't have a set of records to process. For example, let's say you need to keep checking a database until a record has been updated, or you need to keep checking a folder until a specific file is found. Once the condition is met, you can proceed with the rest of your flow.

Because "Do until" loops run until a specific condition is met, they do risk running as an infinite loop that will never complete. To prevent this, "Do until" loops contain two properties that limit how long they can run:

- Each loop has a default timeout set for one hour using an ISO 8601 duration.
- There is also a Count property that determines how many loops can be completed. If the timeout occurs or the loop count is reached before the loop condition is met, it will exit anyway.

Adding Parallel Branches

Up until now, we've looked at flows that proceed sequentially from one action to the next. In this chapter, we've reviewed several ways to redirect a flow down a different branch of actions or repeat a set of actions, but the flow still does one action at a time. Parallel branches in Power Automate allow users to run multiple actions at the same time, instead of one after the other in a sequential manner. This lets users streamline complex workflows and perform multiple tasks simultaneously, resulting in faster processing times and improved efficiency.

Parallel branches in Power Automate can be used to perform different actions simultaneously, such as sending emails, updating records in a database, or creating files in different systems. This provides users with greater control over the workflow, enabling them to tailor the automation process to their specific needs and requirements.

Care needs to be taken that the actions completed by each parallel branch are independent of each other. Otherwise, actions taken by one branch might interfere with actions executed by a parallel branch. For example, if two parallel branches try to update the same data item concurrently, one of the updates may get overwritten.

Parallel branches can be nested within one another, allowing for even more complex scenarios to be handled. You can also combine them with conditions and loops to control the flow of your actions. A combination of conditions, switches, loops, and parallel branches is essential for most complex business processes.

Exercise 5-5. Creating an approval reminder

In this example, we will use a "Do until" loop in a parallel branch to send out periodic reminders to approvers that an approval is still pending.

1. Make a copy of the flow you built in Exercise 5-1 using Save As in the ellipsis menu in the "My flows" list. Title the copy "Approve file with Reminder" (see Figure 5-27).

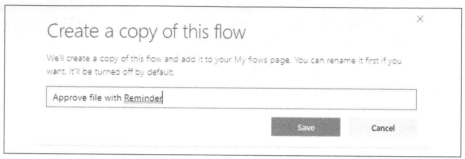

Figure 5-27. Copying existing flow

2. Edit the copy of the flow. Insert an "Initialize variable" action just above the "Start and wait for an Approval" action. Set the Name of the variable to varLoop Count, the Type to Integer, and the Value to 1. Delete the existing "Start and wait for an approval" action and replace it with two actions: "Create an approval" followed by "Wait for an approval" (see Figure 5-28). Set the "Create an approval" action as follows:

   a. Select "Approve/Reject – First to respond" as the Approval type.

   b. Type "Sample Approval with Reminder" as the Title.

   c. Type your email address in the Assigned to field.

   d. Fill in any other details you would like.

   Insert the Approval ID dynamic content from the "Create an approval" action into the Approval ID field in the "Wait for an Approval" action.

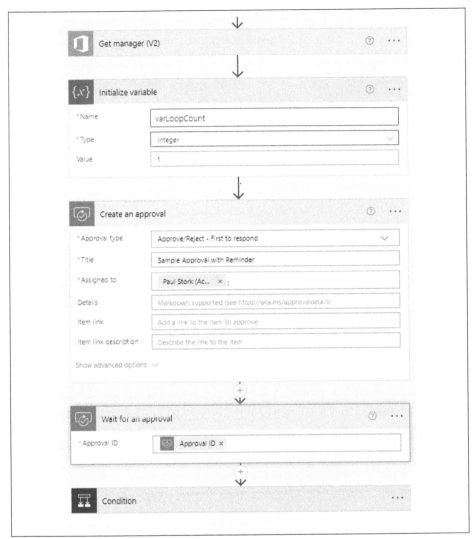

Figure 5-28. "Create an approval" and "Wait for an approval" actions

3. Using the plus (+) sign between the "Create an approval" and "Wait for an approval" actions, add a parallel branch to the flow (see Figure 5-29).

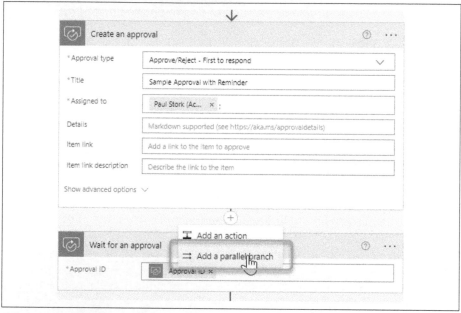

Figure 5-29. Adding a parallel branch

4. Add a "Do until" loop to the parallel branch. Set the left side of the condition to
   the varLoopCount variable, set the right side to 7, and set the operation to "is
   greater than or equal to."

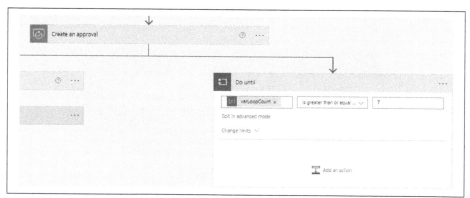

Figure 5-30. "Do until" loop in a parallel branch

Inside the loop, we'll set a short delay. Each time the delay cycles, we will increment the loop counter. If the loop counter reaches a certain level before the approval completes, a reminder email will be set and the loop counter will be reset to 1. If the approval completes, the loop counter will be set to a high number so that the loop will exit at the end of the next delay. For testing, we'll use a loop count of 6 and a delay of 10 seconds, for a total of 60 seconds. In a production environment, you'll use a longer delay, maybe an hour, and a higher count, like 24. With those values, a reminder would be sent once a day, but the flow would only wait a maximum of one hour after the approval is received before completing.

5. Inside the loop, add an "Increment variable" action. Select the varLoopCount variable and set the Value to 1 (see Figure 5-31).

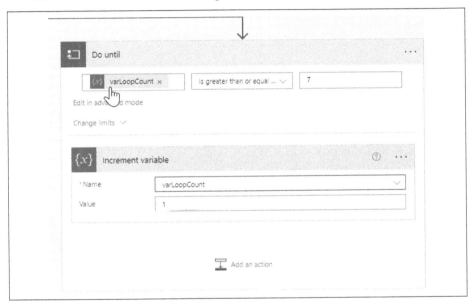

Figure 5-31. Increment loop counter

6. Add a Delay action. Set the Count to 10, and select Second as the Unit (see Figure 5-32).

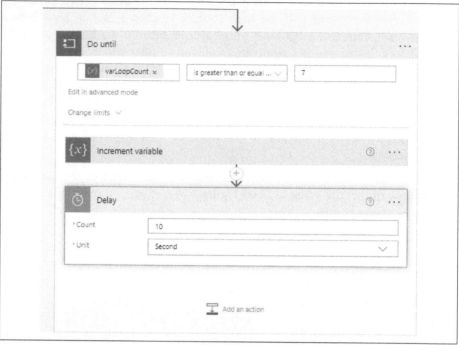

Figure 5-32. Delay action

7. Add a Condition below the Delay (see Figure 5-33). Set the left side of the condition to the varLoopCount variable, set the right side to 7, and set the operation to "is equal to."

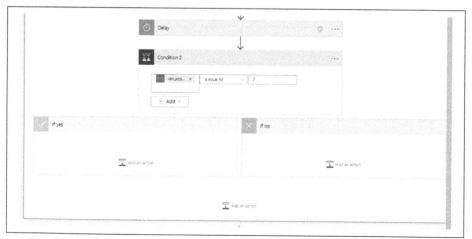

Figure 5-33. Adding a Condition

8. Add a"Send an Email (V2)" action to the If yes side of the Condition. Type your email address in the To field for testing. Type "Approval Reminder" in the Subject field, and Type "Please Review and respond to this approval" followed by the Respond link dynamic content from the "Create an approval" action (see Figure 5-34).

Figure 5-34. Sending reminder email

9. Add a "Set variable" action below the "Send an email" action. Select the varLoop Count variable in the Name drop-down and Set the Value to 1 (see Figure 5-35). This will restart the loop count back to its original value so another reminder will be sent when the loop count reaches 7.

Figure 5-35. Resetting the loop counter

10. Expand the condition in the other branch. Add Outcome back to the left side of the condition. (It was deleted when the original "Start and wait for approval" action was removed.) Add a "Set variable" action above the condition and below the "Wait for an approval" action. Select the `varLoopCount` variable in the Name drop-down and Set the Value to 10 (see Figure 5-36). This will stop the loop from sending any more reminders.

Figure 5-36. Setting loop counter to end reminder loop

11. Save the flow and use the arrow in the upper-right corner to navigate back to the flow detail page. Click the "Turn on" link to enable the flow. (It was disabled because it was a copy of a previous flow.) Edit the flow again and Test the flow manually by uploading a file. Wait a minute or two and check your email. You should have received both an approval email and a reminder. Respond to the approval and wait another minute for the flow to finish.

Summary

In this chapter, you learned how to create more complex flow logic using actions in the Controls connector. You saw how Conditions and Switches can be used to execute different sets of values depending on the result of an equation. You also learned to process arrays of data or wait for a specific condition to be met using different looping mechanisms. Finally, you discovered how a flow can execute multiple actions at the same time using parallel branches.

We've now covered all the basic skills you need to create and run Power Automate flows. In the next chapter, we'll look at how you can integrate Power Automate with the other applications in the Power Platform to create even more complex business applications.

CHAPTER 6

Integrating with Other
Power Platform Applications

Power Automate flows are a very powerful tool for automating manual business processes. But they do have some limitations. Cloud flows are triggered by an event, like a user pressing a button in the mobile app or modifying a record in a data source. But Power Automate alone doesn't provide much in the way of a user interface (UI) to interact with a flow at runtime. Some flow triggers can present a simple data entry panel to enter parameters at runtime, but there is no provision for formatting or styling such a panel—it is simply a list of the fields you specify in the flow trigger in the order that you add them. Similarly, while a flow is running, your options for interacting with a user are limited. The most common mechanism for interaction is email, which has limited capability for returning information to the flow.

Power Automate's limitations can be alleviated in many cases by integrating a Power Automate flow with one of the other Power Platform applications. In this chapter, I'll review what you need to know to integrate cloud flows with each of the other Power Platform applications.

As we discussed earlier in the book, Power Automate is one of five applications in the Microsoft Power Platform. The other Power Platform applications are as follows:

Power BI
  A tool to manipulate and visualize data to help make business decisions

Power Apps
  A low-code/no-code application for creating custom apps that leverage backend data sources

Power Pages
  A low-code/no-code application for building business websites

Power Virtual Agents
A low-code/no-code tool for building chatbots that engage employees or customers conversationally

One of the most common reasons for integrating a flow with another Power Platform application is to provide a UI to easily collect input parameters before running a flow. For example, you could use a Power App as a frontend to provide a user with an easy way to input information before invoking a flow. Using the Power App lets you configure the screen for easier input and allows you to use specialized controls like date pickers and toggle switches. This can make input easier and more efficient. After the input is complete, you can pass the information to a flow for processing.

Using Solutions

If you want to integrate Power Automate flows with any of the other Platform applications, the first thing you need to learn about is Solutions. Solutions are used to package applications, flows, Power Pages sites, Power BI reports, and bots. Integrating flows with other applications creates dependencies between the different components. Because this adds to the complexity of the applications involved, it's a best practice to separate development, testing, and production deployments. If you try to move a flow that is integrated with other applications, it will break the dependencies that the integration has created. The result is more work and refactoring after you move it to the new environment. Building out the applications, flows, and bots in Solutions lets you preserve those dependencies as you move the components.

Creating a New Solution

Creating a Solution is fairly straightforward. You only need to provide a Display name, a Publisher, and a starting Version number for the Solution. You also have the option to add a description and a configuration page. Most of the information you need is intuitive, but three items require a bit more explanation. Figure 6-1 shows the panel that is displayed to create a new Solution.

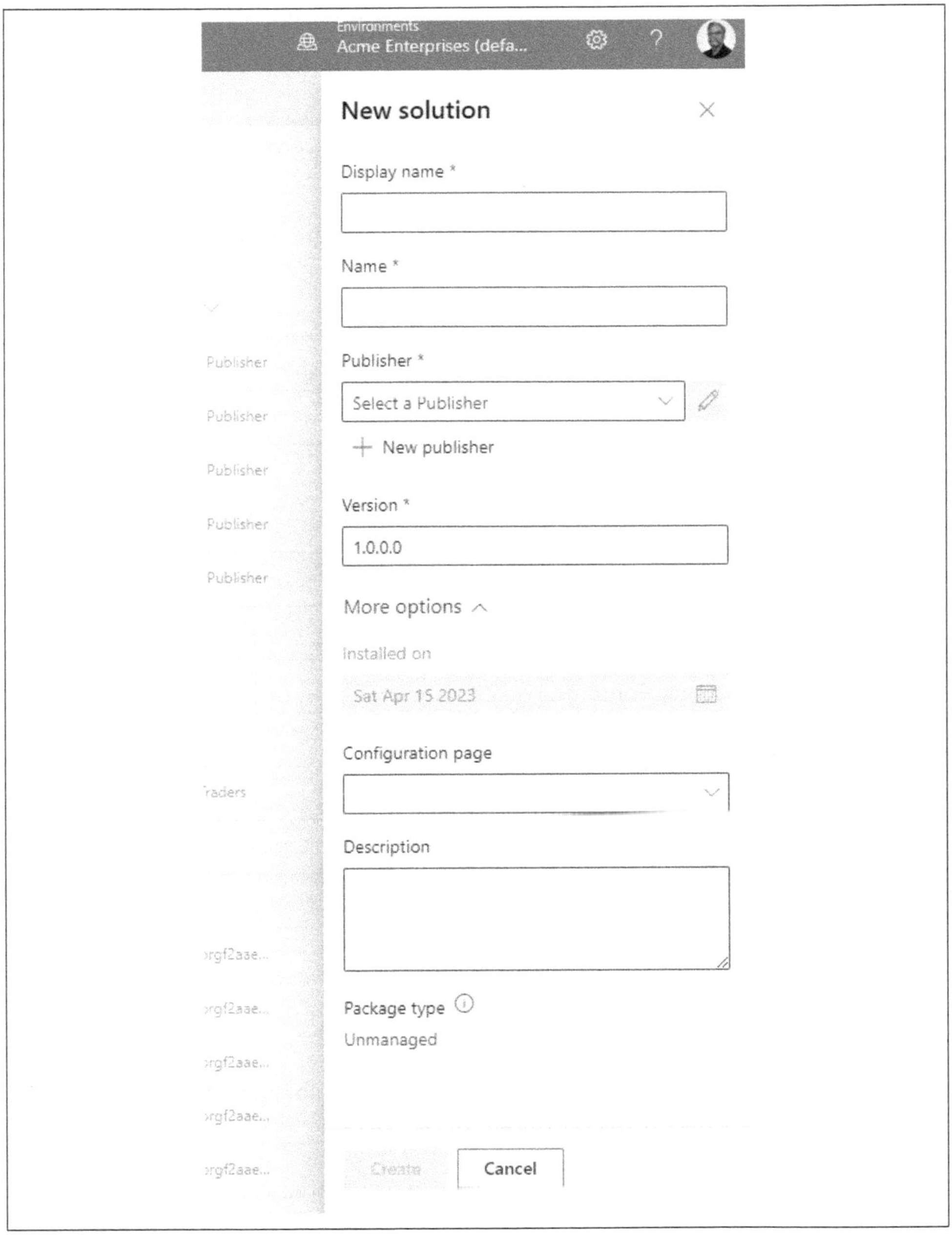

Figure 6-1. Creating a new Solution

The Publisher is the owner of the components in the Solution and identifies who developed them. But this ownership doesn't convey any security role. To let other users edit components, they need to be shared. For example, to let another user edit a flow, you need to share the flow with them and make them a co-owner. You can learn more about creating a Solution Publisher in the Power Platform documentation (*https://oreil.ly/6_lGc*).

The Version number defaults to 1.0.0.0. This four-digit versioning is typical for Microsoft and reflects the following:

- The first digit designates the major release number.
- The second digit designates a minor release (for example, new features added to a major release).
- The third number designates a revision, which is usually a fix for a previously implemented feature.
- The final number is the build number. This is incremented automatically each time the Solution is exported.

Configuration pages are most frequently used to display some light documentation or to require acceptance of a user agreement when a Solution is being imported.

Once you've created a new Solution, you can begin adding components to it.

Connection References

When you use a Connector action or trigger in Power Automate, you create a Connection. That Connection persists by creating an OAuth (Open Authorization) token to secure the Connection. The Connection stores the token but does not keep a copy of your credentials. In non-Solution-aware flows—or flows that aren't created inside a Solution—these Connections provide a static connection to the backend data source. A Connection has a read-only name that is the account that created it. This can make managing multiple Connections in different environments difficult.

A Connection Reference virtualizes Connections that you use in your flows. When you import the Solution to a new environment, you can change the underlying Connection without changing the Connection Reference in the flow itself. Using Connection References prevents the need to refactor the flow itself after import. Also, since Connection References have an editable Display name, tracking Connections across multiple environments is fairly easy. Multiple Connection References can point to the same Connection, and a flow can use different Connection References that point to the same Connection.

When you add an action to a Solution-aware flow, it will automatically create a Connection Reference that points to the Connection created. Or you can create Connection References manually inside the Solution and then use them when you add the action or trigger to the flow. Figure 6-2 shows the panel that is displayed when you create a Connection Reference manually. After selecting a Connector, you will be prompted to pick an existing Connection or create a new Connection.

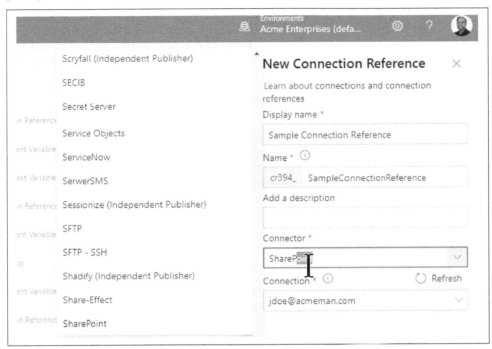

Figure 6-2. Creating a Connection Reference

Environment Variables

Another important components that you can create in a Solution are environment variables. They let you set specific configuration data when you import a Solution into a new environment. The environment variable is referenced as dynamic content when you build your flow, so changing the value of the variable when you import the flow to a new environment does not require you to make changes to the existing flow.

When you create an environment variable, you can choose one of six different data types:

Decimal number
> An integer or whole number

Text
> A simple string

JSON
> A string of JSON-formatted information

Yes/No
> A True or False value

Data Source
> A data source

Secret
> An encrypted value stored in an Azure Key Vault

Data Source environment variables are currently limited to Dataverse, SharePoint, and SAP ERP connectors. More connectors will be added in the future.

Environment variables can store both a default and a current value for each environment where a Solution is installed. If neither value exists when a Solution is imported, then you will be prompted to enter a value that will become the current value for that environment. Figure 6-3 shows the panel used to create a new environment variable.

Since environment variables are read-only in managed Solutions, it is critical that you remove the values before exporting. This is easily overlooked.

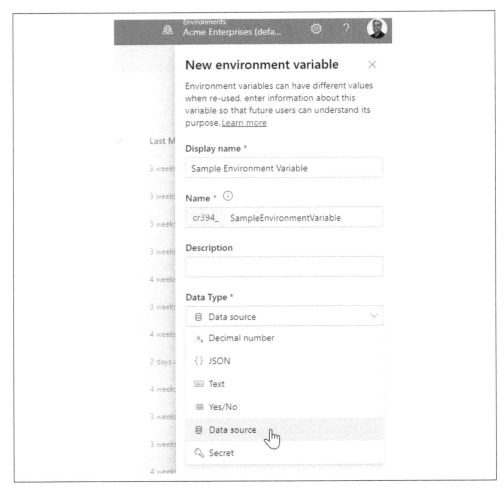

Figure 6-3. Creating an environment variable

Exercise 6-1. Creating a Solution

In this example, you will create a Solution and a simple flow that you can use later in this chapter.

1. Log in to *https://make.powerautomate.com*. Using the environment picker in the top-right menu, select one of your developer environments. Select the Solutions tab in the left sidebar. Click on the "+ New Solution" drop-down. Fill in the New Solution panel with the following information and click Create (see Figure 6-4):

   - Display name: Test Solution

   - Name: TestSolution

   - Publisher: CDS Default Publisher

   - Accept all other defaults

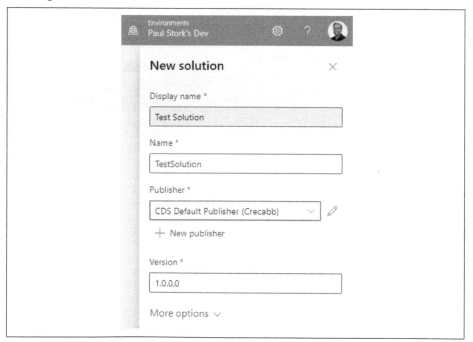

Figure 6-4. Creating a New Solution

2. In the Solution explorer, click the +New button to add an instant cloud flow to the Solution (see Figure 6-5). Name the Flow "Solution Demo Flow" and select the "Power Apps (V2)" trigger. Click Create.

Figure 6-5. Adding a cloud flow

Add a Compose action to the flow (see Figure 6-6). Use the Expressions tab to set the Input of the Compose to `formatDateTime(utcNow())`.

Save the flow. Use the arrow in the upper-left corner (next to the flow name) to return to the Solution explorer.

Figure 6-6. Updating and Saving the flow

You have now created a Solution and added one cloud flow to it.

Managed Versus Unmanaged Solutions

When you first create a Solution, it is unmanaged. When you export it, you have the option to create either a managed or unmanaged Solution. Unmanaged Solutions are fully editable, so they are normally used in development environments. Components in managed Solutions cannot be directly edited, so they are normally used when you import the Solution into a test or production environment. However, even in a production environment you can create an unmanaged Solution layer above the managed Solution and import components there to edit them. The edited components will be used in place of the ones in the managed Solution. However, adding an unmanaged layer to a managed Solution is not considered a best practice.

Exercise 6-2. Exporting and importing a Solution

In this example, you'll learn how to export the Solution containing your flow from the development environment where it was created. You'll also see how to publish your customizations so any changes you made to the flow will be included in the exported Solution. After completing the export, you'll learn how to import the managed Solution into a new environment where you can then run your flow.

1. Open the Solution you created in Example 6-1. Select the Overview tab. Click Export in the top menu to open the "Before you export" panel. Select the Publish button to commit all the changes you saved in your flow before you create your Solution export (see Figure 6-7). Once the Publish is complete, click Next.

Figure 6-7. Publishing changes

2. On the "Export this solution" panel, accept the Version number of 1.0.0.1 and select the Unmanaged radio button. Click the Export button (see Figure 6-8).

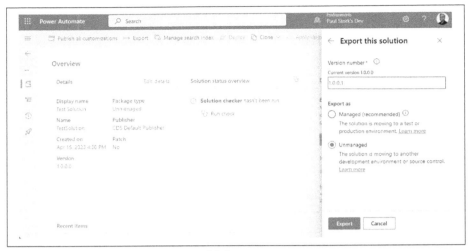

Figure 6-8. Exporting an unmanaged Solution

3. Wait a few minutes for the export ZIP file to be created. When the message bar turns green, click the Download button to download the Solution file (see Figure 6-9). The Solution file will now be in your Downloads folder.

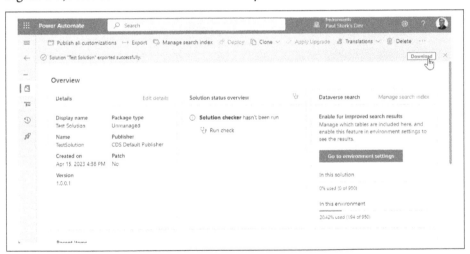

Figure 6-9. Downloading Solution file

4. Use the Environment drop-down to change to a different environment. Click the Import solution link on the top menu to open the "Import a solution" panel. Click the Browse button, navigate to your Downloads folder, and select the *Test-Solution_1_0_0_1.zip* file that you downloaded. Click Open to load the selected Solution file. Click the Next button (see Figure 6-10).

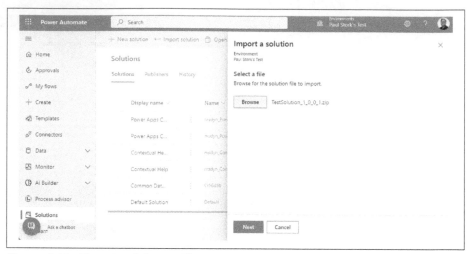

Figure 6-10. Choosing Solution file to import

5. Click the Import button to import the Solution into this environment (see Figure 6-11).

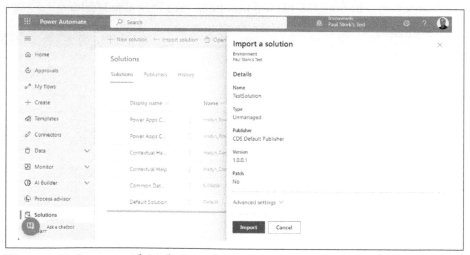

Figure 6-11. Importing the Solution

Wait a few minutes for the message bar at the top of the screen to turn green. Open the imported Solution to verify that your flow was imported (Figure 6-12).

Figure 6-12. Imported Solution

Minimizing Data Communications

Integrating a flow with other applications usually requires sending parameters from the other application to the flow and sending return values from the flow back to the invoking application. Depending on how much data is sent and how much bandwidth is available, this can be a time-consuming process. This is particularly true when working with mobile application clients. To guarantee the best performance, you should always minimize the amount of data transferred to the minimum required. Power Automate has three specific actions that are normally used to minimize the data being returned to an application like Power Apps:

Filter Array
> This action applies a specific condition to each row in an array and returns only the rows where the condition evaluates to True.

Data Select
> This action can be used to remap specific columns from an array into a new array. Calculations can also be applied to process column values during the remapping.

Parse JSON
> This action doesn't change the number of rows or columns returned but can be used to reinterpret an array that was processed by Filter Array or Data Select to make the column values available as dynamic content.

Power Apps

Power Automate flows are very good at processing large amounts of information, but their ability to interact directly with users is very limited. Power Apps on the other hand is all about creating an application with a UI. But since Power Apps is a declarative language, it can be difficult to use it to process large sets of data. In Power Apps, the closest thing to a loop is the ForAll() function. But ForAll() isn't really a loop since it simultaneously applies the formula to each item in the collection or table. This can make it difficult to work with large amounts of data. Power Apps also depends on delegable functions to deal with data sources over 2,000 items—this can cause issues. The solution to all these problems is to use Power Apps to create the UI in an application, but then call a flow to process the data. This integration lets both applications use their strongest features together.

Invoking a Flow from a Power App

To invoke a flow from a Power App, you need to do three things. First, you need to have a flow that uses one of the two Power Apps triggers. Second, you need to add the flow to the Power App using the Power Automate tab in the lefthand bar. Finally, once you've loaded the flow, you need to add a run function to a behavior property of a control, like OnSelect or OnVisible. All behavior properties in Power Apps start with "On."

 It is a best practice to use the newer Power Apps (V2) trigger whenever possible. The major difference is that you can define your input parameters in the trigger instead of defining them elsewhere in the flow by using the "Ask in Power Apps" dynamic content entry. Defining them in the trigger itself is better for documenting your flow and is also more stable. Power Apps and Templates still default to the older original trigger, but you should change this whenever possible.

Passing Input Parameters

The function you use to invoke the flow is the name of the flow, without spaces, followed by .run(). Inside the run function, you will be prompted to supply the input parameters. These parameters will be what you added to the flow, either in the V2 trigger or by adding the "Ask in Power Apps" dynamic content entry to fields in the flow for the original trigger.

Returning Values

There are two different actions you can add to the end of your flow to return values to your Power App. The first is the Respond to Power Apps action, which can be used to return a single object with one or more properties. Each property returned must be one of the following data types:

Text
    A simple string

Yes/No
    A True or False value

File
    A string containing a Base64-encoded file

Email
    A string containing an email address

Number
    An integer or floating point number

Date
    A string containing an ISO 8601–encoded date-time value

Properties cannot contain complex objects. Nor can you return an array of objects. The single object can then be loaded into a variable by adding the run command that invokes the flow to a Set() function.

The second action you can use to return values to the calling application is the HTTP Response Action. The body of this action can return a JSON-encoded array and schema. When the run command returns the array of values, you can capture it in a collection using either a ClearCollect() or Collect() function.

 The Respond to a Power App or a Flow action is standard, but the HTTP Response action is premium. Microsoft recently released a ParseJson() function for Power Apps that will let you return an array as a JSON string using the "Respond to a Power App or a Flow" action and convert it to a data table inside Power Apps. However, the values are more difficult to work with since they are untyped and must be converted to be used in Power Apps. The HTTP Response action is a better solution unless licensing concerns are an issue.

Exercise 6-3. Invoking a flow from a Power App

In this example, we will create a simple Power App where you can type in two numbers, press a button, and have a flow calculate the sum of the two numbers.

1. Navigate to the development environment where you created the Solution in Example 6-1. Open the Solution (see Figure 6-13).

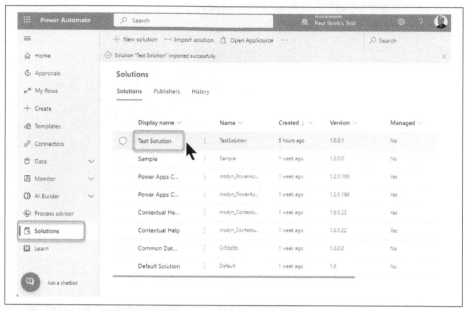

Figure 6-13. Opening existing Solution

2. Select Edit from the ellipsis context menu, next to the Solution Demo Flow you created in Example 6-1 (see Figure 6-14).

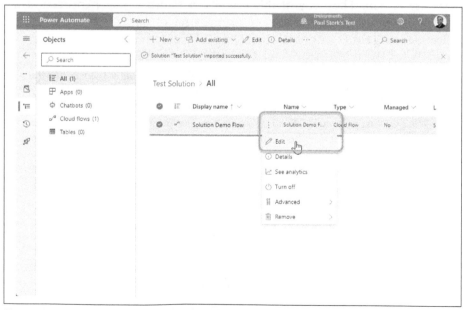

Figure 6-14. Opening Solution Demo Flow

3. Expand the trigger and select "+ Add an input" of type Number. Name the input "Number1." Add a second Number input called "Number2." These inputs will be used to pass two numbers to the flow to be added together (see Figure 6-15).

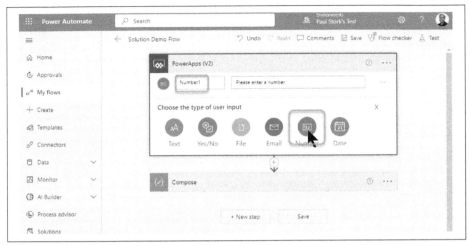

Figure 6-15. Adding trigger inputs

4. Delete the formula from the Compose action below the trigger (see Figure 6-16). Use the Expressions tab of the Dynamic content dialog to add the following function:

```
Add(triggerBody()['number'],triggerBody()['number_1'])
```

Figure 6-16. Adding input numbers together

5. Click the "+New step" button. Type "Power Apps" in the Search bar and select the Power Apps connector. Click on the "Respond to a PowerApp or flow" action to insert it into the flow (see Figure 6-17).

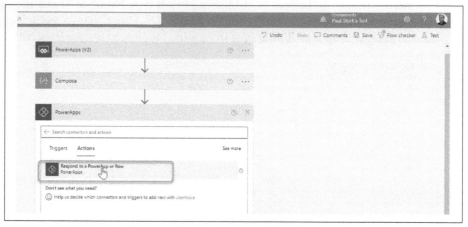

Figure 6-17. Inserting "Respond to Power App of flow" action

6. Click "+ Add an output" and choose the Text data type. Name the output "Result." Use the Dynamic content dialog to insert the outputs of the Compose into the "Enter a value to respond" field. Save the flow and return to the Solution (see Figure 6-18).

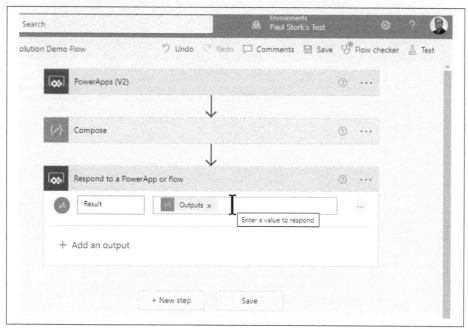

Figure 6-18. Configuring return value

7. Select the "+New" button and add a Tablet Canvas Power App to the Solution. Name the Solution "Demo App" (see Figure 6-19).

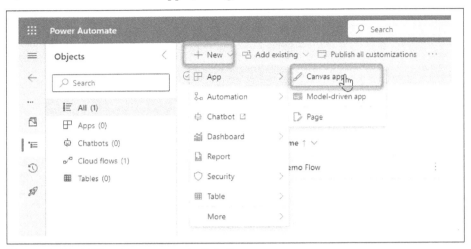

Figure 6-19. Adding Canvas app to Solution

8. Click Skip to close the Welcome to Power Apps Studio dialog. Insert and arrange the following controls on Screen1 as shown in Figure 6-20:

- Two Text input controls
- A Text label control
- A Button

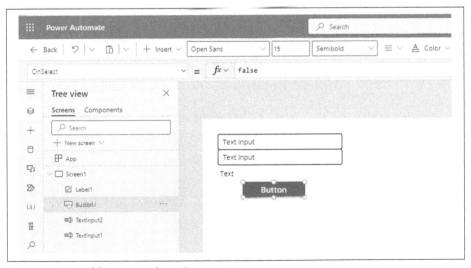

Figure 6-20. Adding controls to Canvas app

9. Select the Button on the design canvas, and click the Power Automate icon in the lefthand menu bar. Click the "+Add flow" link. Select the Solution Demo flow from the dialog (see Figure 6-21).

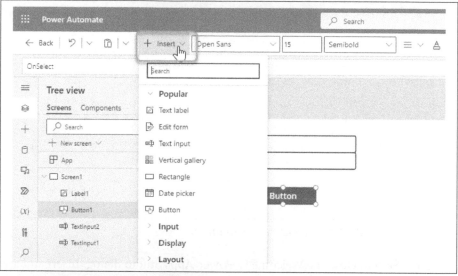

Figure 6-21. Adding a flow to the app

10. Set the OnSelect property of the Button to the following to trigger the flow with two input parameters (see Figure 6-22):

```
Set(return,SolutionDemoFlow.Run(Value(TextInput1.Text),
        Value(TextInput2.Text)))
```

The return variable will capture the value returned by the flow. Set the Text property of the label control to the following to display the result calculated by the flow:

```
return.result
```

Run the application. Fill in both Text input controls with numbers. Click on the Button. The result should be displayed in the Text label.

Figure 6-22. Adding flow run function

11. Save the application and use the back arrow in the upper left to return to the Solution. Click the Leave button in the dialog if prompted.

Power Virtual Agents

The Power Virtual Agents (PVA) application can be used to create conversational chatbots that users can interact with. PVA bots have tools for responding to a conversation, but they can't do calculations or directly retrieve data from a data source. For those kinds of actions, the bot calls a Power Automate flow. The process is similar to the one used in Power Apps. The flow is called, and any input parameters are supplied. Then, when the flow completes it sends output parameters back to the calling bot. The bot can then display those outputs to the user or use them to decide what to do next in the bot.

To use flows in a PVA bot, they must meet these requirements:

- The flow must start with the "When Power Virtual Agents calls a flow" trigger.
- The flow must be in a Solution stored in the same Dataverse environment as your bot.
- Flow values must be returned synchronously to the bot.

PVA stores bots and flows in the current environment's Default Solution automatically. The PVA designer does not provide the ability to manage custom Solutions directly like the Power Apps or Power Automate designers do.

Although it's not a requirement, flows normally end with the Return value(s) to Power Virtual Agents action to return output values back to the calling bot. If this action is not provided, the flow will still return control to the bot, but no output will be recorded.

Invoking a Flow from a Chatbot

A "Call an action" node can be added to the Chatbot design canvas for a Topic. That Node will prompt you to choose a flow or create a new one. The dialog will list all the flows that start with the "When Power Virtual Agents calls a flow" trigger in the current environment. As shown in Figure 6-23, the dialog will also let you launch Power Automate to create a new flow.

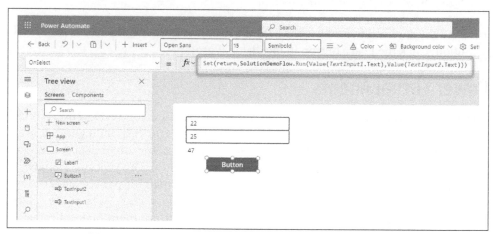

Figure 6-23. Adding a Call an action node

It will automatically generate a flow with the appropriate trigger and closing action. You can then build your flow by adding inputs, outputs, and actions between the two endpoints. Input and output parameters are added to the trigger and the final action in the same way that you added them to the flow for Power Apps.

Returning a Formatted Table of Results

The major difference between calling a flow in Power Apps and PVA is that bots cannot use the HTTP Response action to return an array of data. Only a single object with simple properties can be returned. To return a dataset to a bot, you need to format it as a table using the same Markdown formatting you use when creating an approval flow email in Power Automate. The details of the Markdown language, including examples, can be found in the Power Automate documentation (*https://oreil.ly/NH5hC*).

Exercise 6-4. Invoking a flow from a bot

In this example, you will create a simple chatbot that can check inventory for a part by name. It will then return what parts are in stock and how many there are.

1. Create a table in an Excel worksheet that contains the sample data shown in Figure 6-24. Store it on your OneDrive. This will be the data source for the flow to check.

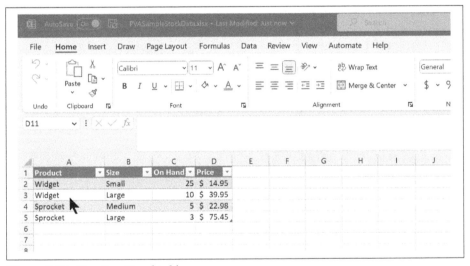

Figure 6-24. Creating Excel table

2. Return to your Solution in your developer environment and use the +New link to add a new Chatbot (see Figure 6-25). This will launch the Power Virtual Agents design site.

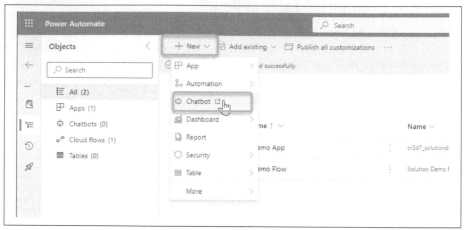

Figure 6-25. Adding a new Chatbot to the Solution

3. Type "Solution Demo Chatbot" as the name of your bot, and select English as the language the bot will use (see Figure 6-26). Wait for the chatbot to be created. This will take a few minutes.

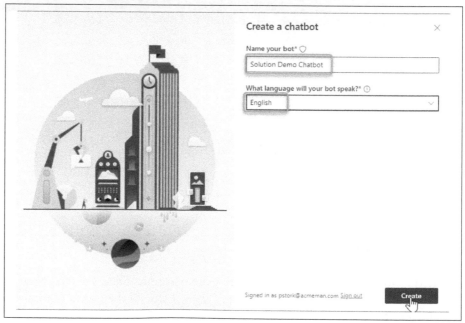

Figure 6-26. Creating a chatbot

4. Once the bot has been created, select the Topics tab in the lefthand toolbar (see Figure 6-27).

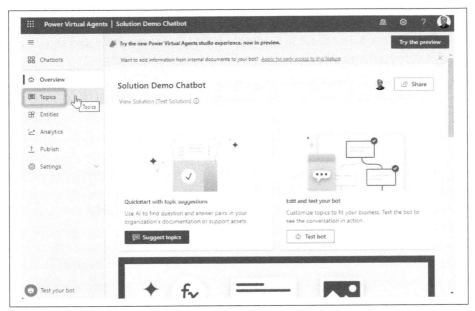

Figure 6-27. Navigating to the Topics list

5. Add a new blank Topic to the bot (see Figure 6-28). Topics are the keywords that trigger actions within the bot conversation.

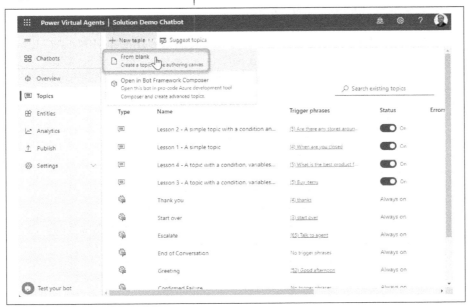

Figure 6-28. Adding a new blank Topic

6. Name the new Topic "Test Bot." Then add "test bot" (be sure it's all lowercase) in the Add phrases field, and press the plus (+) sign to add that trigger phrase (see Figure 6-29). Select the X in the upper right to close the panel and show the Topic's conversation path.

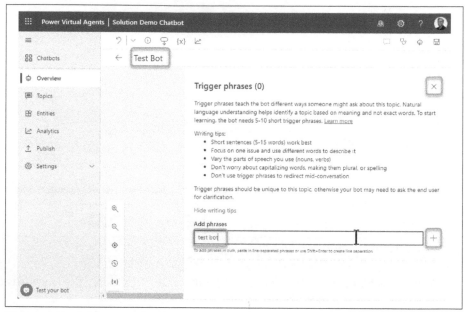

Figure 6-29. Adding trigger phrases

Select the plus (+) sign to add a node between the Trigger Phrases and the message node in the bot conversation path (see Figure 6-30). In the Add a Node dialog, select Ask a question. Type "What Product are you interested in?" as the question message, and select User's entire response under Identify.

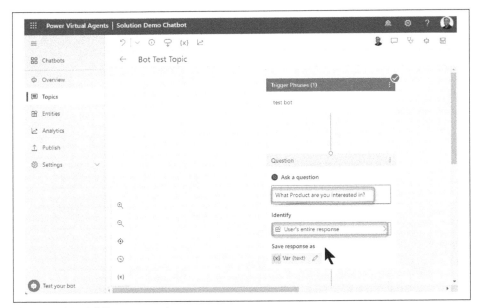

Figure 6-30. Adding a question

7. Select the plus (+) sign to add a node below the question node. In the "Add a node dialog," select "Call an action," and then choose to Create a flow (see Figure 6-31). This will launch the Power Automate website and create a simple flow with the PVA trigger and return value(s) actions. The existing flows in your Solution don't show because they aren't using the PVA trigger.

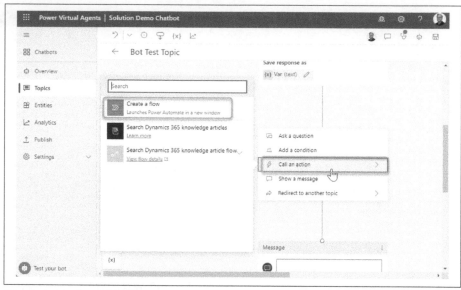

Figure 6-31. Creating a flow

8. Rename the flow to "In Stock Query." Then expand the trigger and use the "+Add an input" to add a Text input parameter. Change the name of the parameter to "Product" (see Figure 6-32).

Figure 6-32. Adding input parameter to trigger

9. Add an "Initialize variable" action between the trigger and the return value(s) actions. Type `varReturnTable` as the name of the variable. Select String as the Type of variable, and add the following as the initial value (make sure you add a carriage return after the second line so it looks like the screenshot in Figure 6-33):

```
| Product | In Stock |
     |-----------|-----------:|
```

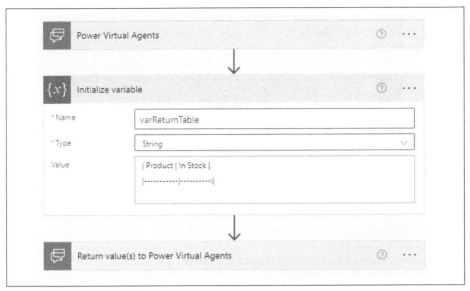

Figure 6-33. Initializing a variable

10. Add a "List rows present in a table" action after the "Initialize variable" action. If necessary, sign in to create a new Connection Reference for Excel Online. Fill in the "List rows" action as follows (see Figure 6-34):

Location
    OneDrive for Business.

Document Library
    OneDrive - **<<Your Tenant Name>>**.

File
    Choose the Excel file you created at the start of this example.

Table
    Table1.

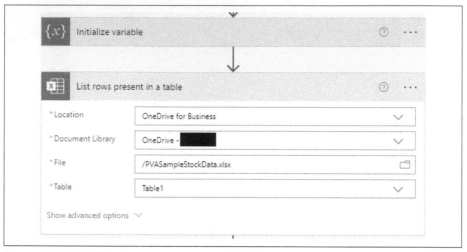

Figure 6-34. Adding List rows present in a table

11. Add a "Filter array" action after the List rows present in a table. Add the value dynamic content from the "List rows" action to the From field. Add the input parameter called Product to the left side of the filter and the Product field from the "List rows" to the right side (see Figure 6-35). Set the comparison to "contains." This will check to see if the Product in the table row is in the string supplied as input from the bot. The output will be an array of rows that match the product being requested by the bot.

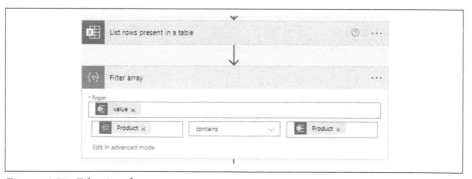

Figure 6-35. Filtering the rows

12. Add an "Apply to each" loop under the "Filter array" action. Insert the Body output dynamic content returned by the Filter array. Add an "Append to string variable" action inside the loop. The individual fields from the Filter array are not available directly as dynamic content, but we can access them by typing the JSON in the Expressions tab. Add the following JSON using the Expressions tab for each field:

- `items('Apply_to_each')?['Size']`

- `items('Apply_to_each')?['Product']`

- `items('Apply_to_each')?['On Hand']`

Add a pipe (|) symbol on each end of the string and between Product and On Hand. Make sure to add an additional carriage return after the last pipe so your "Append to string variable" action looks like the screenshot in Figure 6-36.

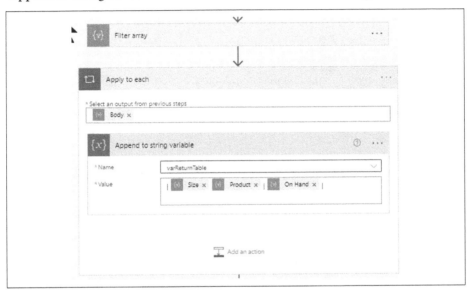

Figure 6-36. Appending array items to return string

13. Expand the "Return values()" action, and add a text Output parameter. Change the name to "Output" and insert the `varReturnTable` variable as the value to be returned. Save the flow and return to your PVA design canvas.

Figure 6-37. Returning formatted table as string

14. Click on the "Call an action" entry in the "Add a node" dialog. Select the In Stock Query flow you just saved. In the node that is added, select Var from the variable drop-down as the value for the Product (text) input parameter (see Figure 6-38).

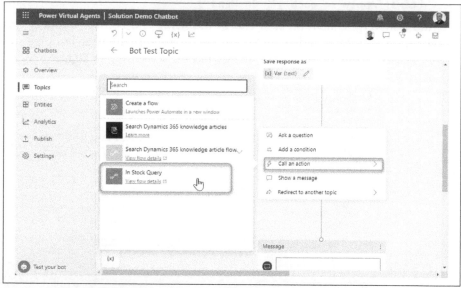

Figure 6-38. Selecting flow to call

15. Add the Output variable from the variable drop-down to the Message field. Save the edited Topic using the disc icon in the upper left. Select the Test bot icon next to the Save disc icon. This will open a chat window on the left where you can test your bot (see Figure 6-39).

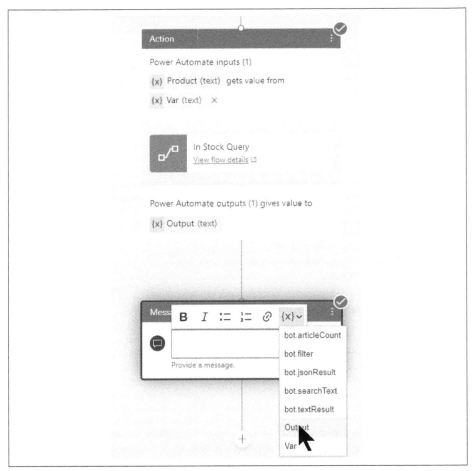

Figure 6-39. Adding flow Output variable to Message

16. Type "Test Bot" into the "Type your message" field. When the bot asks which product you are interested in, type either "Sprocket" or "Widget" into the message field. Wait for the bot to return the formatted response. Your screen should look like Figure 6-40.

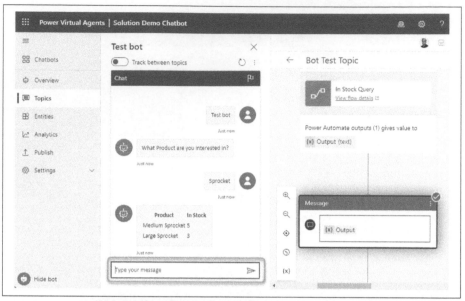

Figure 6-40. Testing the bot

Since bots can't process information directly, using Power Automate to retrieve and format data is a very common integration.

Power BI

To complete complex processing, Power Apps and PVA integrate with Power Automate by invoking flows using a manual trigger. For Power BI, however, there are many typical scenarios where Power Automate flows are used. These scenarios can be grouped together based on the triggers used in the flow. Here are the most common scenarios:

Recurrence Triggers

Can be used to schedule automatic distribution of Power BI reports or a periodic refresh of a dataset.

Automated triggers

Can be used to respond to data-driven alerts or other events generated by Power BI.

Manual triggers

Can be used to trigger flows that process Power BI data presented in a Power BI report. The Power BI connector contains eight Power BI–specific triggers, as shown in Figure 6-41.

Figure 6-41. Power BI triggers

The "Power BI button clicked" trigger is the one manual trigger. The other seven are automated triggers. Scheduling flows to refresh Power BI data is done with the regular recurrence triggers available in Power Automate.

Another difference regarding integration between Power BI and the other Power Platform applications is that you do not return values directly from the flow back to the calling Power BI report or dashboard. There are actions that you can use to add rows to an existing Power BI dataset or to refresh a report. But there is no Respond action like there is for Power Apps and Power Virtual Agents. The lack of a Respond action means that building flows to integrate with Power BI is essentially the same process as building other scheduled, automated, or instant flows.

Power Pages

Power Pages is the newest addition to the list of Power Platform applications that can be integrated with Power Automate flows. It can be used to create interactive, data-driven web pages that can be shared both inside an organization and with the general public. The application's low-code/no-code approach makes it easy to do this without requiring extensive knowledge of HTML. Like Power Apps and Power Virtual Agents, Power Pages focuses on the presentation of content but has very limited ability to retrieve and process data for display. Calling a Power Automate flow from a Power Page lets users retrieve information and display it on a web page.

Invoking a Flow from a Power Page

At the time of writing, support for triggering a flow from a button on a Power Page is available as a Preview feature. Features labeled as Preview should not be used in production implementation, since they may change or be withdrawn before they reach general availability. This is particularly true for the integration between a Power Page and Power Automate flow since it requires the use of JavaScript. So, it isn't a complete low-code/no-code implementation at present. This should change as the feature matures. If you would like to learn more about how to invoke a flow from a button on a Power Page, you can find a full walkthrough in the Power Automate documentation (*https://oreil.ly/e3hs1*).

Summary

In this chapter, you learned how to create Solutions to group flows together with other applications, flows, and bots in order to move them to another environment. You also learned how to make environment variables and Connection References to make those moves easier. Once you learned how to move related components between environments, you began practicing how to integrate Power Automate flows with other applications in the Power Platform to make them more powerful. Using these integrations, you can overcome the limitations of any of the platforms and develop robust automations that can transform your work.

But, as the flows become more complex, there are more chances to run into bugs and errors. In the next chapter, you will learn how to monitor and troubleshoot existing flows. You'll also see how you can build flows that adapt to errors without failing.

CHAPTER 7

Troubleshooting Tips

Whether they are standalone or integrated with other Power Platform applications, Power Automate flows are a very powerful tool for building low-code/no-code solutions to business problems. In Chapter 6, you learned how to integrate flows with other applications to make them more effective. However, these solutions are only helpful if they run without errors. As you work with Power Automate, you will occasionally encounter errors that can be caused by a multitude of issues. They may result from bad syntax in writing expressions, inconsistent data quality, or faulty logic when designing the flow. In this chapter, you'll learn the different ways you can find and remove errors from your flows. I'll also show you how to design your flows to automatically adapt to errors that may happen during a run.

Reviewing Run History

Every time a flow runs, it records a history log. These logs are kept for 28 days. Figure 7-1 shows a typical log history on the detail screen of a flow. Each log entry shows when the flow ran, how long it ran, and whether it was successful or not. You can also use the Edit columns link at the top of the list to add columns to the view for any input parameters that were given to the flow.

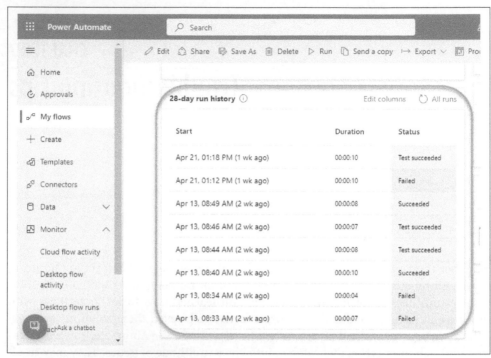

Figure 7-1. Flow run history logs

Filtering the All Runs View

The 28-day run history shows all the instances when the flow ran either successfully or unsuccessfully. But there are two special cases that are not included in the main view. The first is when the flow was using a polling-based trigger but wasn't triggered because there was no new data when the trigger was polled. The second case is when the flow wasn't triggered because the trigger itself threw an error. These two runs can be accessed by selecting the All Runs view in the upper-right corner of the 28-day history list. In the All Runs view, you can filter on any type of run, including runs where the trigger didn't fire, checks (no new data), and failed checks.

Selecting a flow from any of these lists will show you the status of each action in the flow for that run. Figure 7-2 shows an example of a history log with some failed actions.

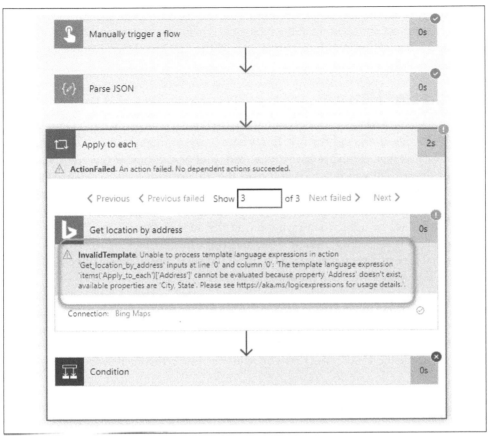

Figure 7-2. Sample flow run with error

Within the history log, you'll see the following symbols:

- Green circles with a checkmark indicate that the action completed successfully.
- Red circles with an exclamation point indicate that the action failed.
- Gray circles with an X indicate actions that were not executed.

 Failed container actions like scopes, conditions, or loops will be marked as failed if any action inside them fails. You will usually need to drill down to find the innermost failed action to get a meaningful error message. For loops, there are links to jump directly to the next or previous error.

Expanding an action that failed will show you the error message that was thrown by that particular action. Looking at the history will help you figure out where your flow failed and what caused it to fail. This is usually the first step when troubleshooting a flow.

Read the Error Message

Once you identify where your flow is failing, it's critical that you read the entire error message. People often read the first line where it says something like "Unable to process template language expressions in action" and assume that's the error message. But that doesn't tell you much. If you read the full error message in Figure 7-2, you will get to the spot where it says "'Address' doesn't exist, available properties are 'City, State.'" This gives you the details you need. In this case, the Address field in the data is null so it cannot be used when trying to get the address from Bing. You now know that the error is caused by missing data, and you can start looking for why that field isn't available. Error messages can be long and cryptic, but they usually point you in the right direction if you read the whole message.

Common Errors

There are many common errors that you will see when troubleshooting a flow. Understanding the kinds of errors you will encounter can help when trying to fix them.

Authentication Failures

One of the common errors that you can identify right from the error message is an Authentication failure. Authentication failures happen when the credentials used to connect to a data source are invalid. This may happen because a user password changed or permissions to a data source were altered. You can normally fix an authentication error by updating the connection being used in that particular action.

You can see a list of all the connections used by your flows in the Connections tab on *https://make.powerautomate.com*. Figure 7-3 shows a sample list of connections where some of the connections have failed. Clicking on the Fix connection link will take you to a Login dialog to fix the credentials being used by that connection.

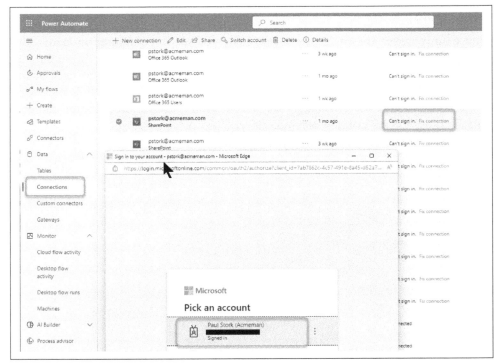

Figure 7-3. Fixing a connection

You can also use the ellipsis menu in the upper-right corner of an action to select a different connection or to log in to fix an invalid connection.

Action Configuration Errors

Another common error happens when one of the parameters in an action is misconfigured. This could happen because you loaded the wrong dynamic content in the field or because the content is null. The solution is to edit the flow to fix the configuration issue and then use the Resubmit button to run the flow again with the updated configuration.

The Coalesce() function can be used to replace null values at runtime with a default value. Coalesce() will interpret each parameter it is passed from left to right. It will then return the first parameter it runs into that is non-null. For example, Coalesce (items('Ap ply_to_each')?['fieldname'],'default Value') could be used when processing an array to substitute default value whenever the current item field is null.

Data Errors

Data quality issues are one of the major causes of action configuration errors. But data quality may be a problem even if the flow runs without errors. Expanding an action in a flow history will show you the inputs and outputs used by each action during a flow run. These inputs and outputs are often critical to finding and fixing problems in your flows. The history log will show you the values of inputs and outputs for most actions in a flow run (see Figure 7-4).

Figure 7-4. Action inputs and outputs

As you can see in Figure 7-4, sometimes the inputs or outputs are too large to display easily in the log. Selecting the Click to download link will download a JSON representation of the data and open it in your web browser. The download will be displayed with no formatting by default. It's a good idea to add a JSON formatter extension to your browser so the data will be displayed as formatted JSON. This will make it much easier to read. These extensions are available for any of the major browsers.

Microsoft's Edge browser has a built-in JSON viewer, but it isn't enabled by default. To enable the JSON viewer, do the following:

1. Navigate to edge://flags in your Edge browser.
2. Type "JSON" into the Search flags search box.
3. Select Enabled in the JSON Viewer drop-down menu.
4. Click the Restart button to reload your browser.

Logic Errors

The hardest type of errors to troubleshoot are problems with the logic of your flow. For example, let's say you want to send items in a list to users in an email. When you run your flow, it sends the email. But instead of getting one email with all the items, you get one email for each item. This is what happens when you put the "Send email" action inside the loop where you process the rows from the data source. To send one email, you need to put the "Send email" action after the loop finishes. But doing that means you no longer have access to the data inside the loop. So, it's not a simple fix. To solve this problem, you need to gather the information inside the loop and then save it to a variable or an HTML table so you can use it after exiting the loop. This is why it is critical to plan your flow before you start building it. Having a good idea of what the steps are and what order they should follow is critical to designing a successful flow. The flow may run, but if it doesn't do what you want it to, then it will need repair.

Monitoring and Tracking Cloud Flows

Reviewing the history log of a flow for errors requires being proactive. First, you need to know that the flow isn't working correctly. Finding non-working flows when you are still in the development process is easy. But how do you know that a production flow isn't working so you can begin troubleshooting what is wrong with it? That's easy if your flow does something like send you an email or make changes to a data source for you. But what if you are building the flow for a wider audience? You may not notice when a flow is failing because you don't see the outcome of the flow directly.

Aside from direct experience, there are two primary ways that you will know that your flows aren't working correctly. The first is that Microsoft will send you a weekly email notification listing any of your flows that fail. The second is by viewing a list of recent flow failures in the Monitor tab under Cloud flow activity on *https://make.powerautomate.com*.

Email Notifications

Flow failure emails are sent to the owner of the flow automatically. To make sure that your inbox isn't overwhelmed with failure messages, the emails are only sent once a week. All the flows that failed in the last week will be summarized in a single email. Figure 7-5 shows a typical failure notification. The email contains a link to the flow that failed and a count of how many times it failed in the last seven days.

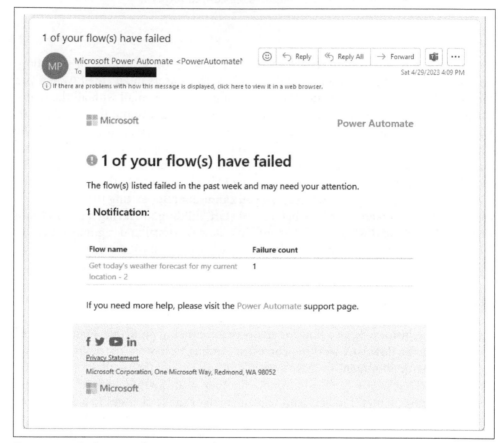

Figure 7-5. Failure notification email

The failure notification emails are sent automatically. You don't need to do anything to receive them. You can opt out of the emails or re-subscribe to start receiving them again using an online form (*https://aka.ms/flow-mail*).

Monitoring Cloud Flow Activity

You can also check on cloud flow activity on *https://make.powerautomate.com* or in the mobile Power Automate client application. On the website, select Cloud flow activity under Monitor in the lefthand toolbar to see a list of recent flow runs. Figure 7-6 shows a typical Cloud flow activity page. Using this screen, you can search for a specific flow, see flows that sent notifications, and see flows that failed. Clicking on a flow in the list will take you to the history log for that specific run.

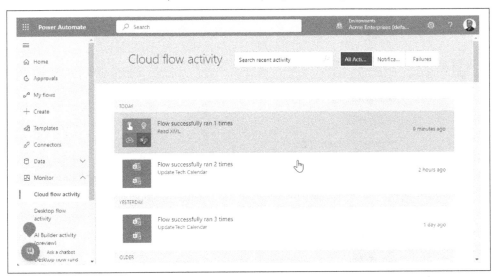

Figure 7-6. Monitoring cloud flow activity

You can also monitor cloud flow activity using the Power Automate mobile client application. Figure 7-7 shows the Activity tab in the mobile client. However, the mobile client only shows flows that are not Solution-aware. Solution-aware flows are flows that are created in a Power Automate Solution. A single Solution can hold multiple flows.

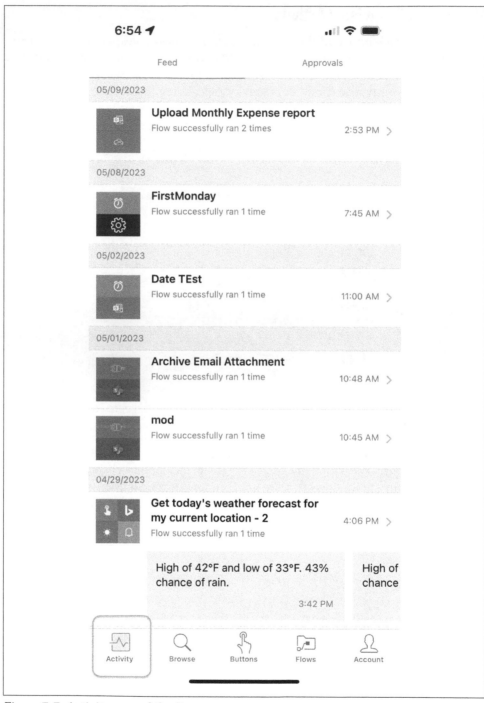

Figure 7-7. Activity on mobile client

View Analytics for Cloud Flows

There are also analytical reports available in the Power Platform Admin center. These Power BI reports will aggregate information from the 28-day history logs for an environment. They will display how many flows were run, what types of flows were run, new flows created, flows with errors, flows shared, and Connectors used. Figure 7-8 shows a typical analytics error report.

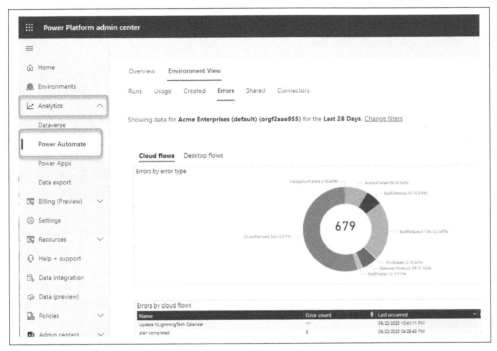

Figure 7-8. Analytics error report

The specific reports available to be viewed depend on the role of the administrator. This list summarizes what each type of administrator can see:

Environment administrator
  Can view reports for the environments that the administrator has access to

Power Platform administrator
  Can view reports for all environments

Dynamics 365 administrator
  Can view reports for all environments

Microsoft 365 Global administrator
  Can view reports for all environments

You can read more about the specific reports available in the Power Platform documentation (*https://oreil.ly/bg_Up*).

Improving Performance with Process Mining

Another tool for assessing flow performance is Process Mining, which is available on the flow details page. The Process Mining tool can search the flow runs you've made in the last 28 days and provide analysis that you can use to improve your flow. For example, Process Mining can tell you which actions in your flow are taking the most time and provide recommendations on how to improve your flow's performance. Figure 7-9 shows a typical Process Mining screen. The darker-colored rectangles in the flowchart denote actions (activities) that took longer to run. By default, Process Mining shows an aggregate of the variants (different versions of the flow), cases (different runs of the same version), and activities (unique actions in the flow). There are several ways to filter the data to figure out the bottlenecks and inefficient actions in your flow.

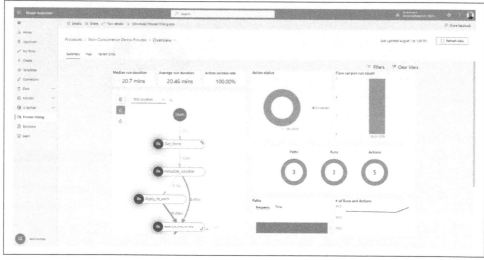

Figure 7-9. Process Mining screen

You can read more about how to use Process Mining in the Power Automate documentation (*https://oreil.ly/kkT3E*).

Fixing Flow Errors

Now that you have learned how to find flows that aren't working correctly, it's time to look at how to fix those errors. I'll show you some tips on how to isolate and identify errors so you can fix them. I'll also show you some techniques that you can use in your flows to automatically handle errors that occur while your flow is running.

Using the Flow Checker

The Power Automate Flow checker runs continuously while you are editing your flow and will help you identify and fix problems before you try to run your flow. The Flow checker identifies both errors (like using the wrong data type in a field) and warnings (like potential performance issues). Figure 7-10 shows the menu link on the toolbar that will open the Flow checker. The red dot icon populates over the Flow checker menu link and is an indicator that there are warnings or errors in the current flow.

Figure 7-10. Flow checker menu link

Selecting the Flow checker menu link will open a panel on the right side of the designer, like the one in Figure 7-11. The panel has entries for each error or warning that identify the specific action that is causing the issue. It also contains a brief description of the issue. If you fix the issue in the flow, the error or warning will disappear after a short period of time.

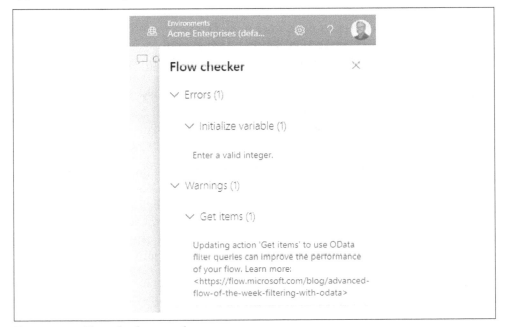

Figure 7-11. Flow checker panel

The Flow checker panel will also appear automatically if you try to save the flow while an error exists. You must fix all the errors before you can save the flow. You can save flows without fixing any warnings that are shown.

Using Compose Actions to Check Values

You've seen how you can review the history of a recent cloud flow run and how you can expand most successful actions to see what they used for input values, as well as the values that were output from them. But not all actions will give you that capability. Some actions, like a condition, will only show you whether the condition was successful or failed. So, it can be difficult to determine whether a condition is failing because you have the wrong condition or because the data is different than you expect. There will also be times when you want to look at the values used in actions that have failed. Failed actions will give you an error message, but they won't show you the actual inputs for that action. In these cases, you can add a Compose action just prior to the action that has the values you can't see. Then add to the Compose the same values you want to look at. When you run the flow the next time, you will be able to see the values even if the flow fails. Compose actions use untyped data, so you can add any type of value to the Compose and you will see the values.

Streamlining Testing

You will often have to run a flow multiple times to find and fix a specific error. This can become a time-consuming experience if the flow needs to retrieve large amounts of data or requires user interaction. During testing, you can use the Static Results option under the Settings of many actions to shorten the time it takes to complete each run by hardcoding the output from particular actions. For example, if you are testing an approval flow, you can hardcode the responses of the approvers so the flow won't send out emails but will act as though the approval responses were already received. Static Results can also be used to simulate an error when retrieving data from a data source.

To set the Static Results for an action, you should run the flow once and copy the Body output from the action you want to set. Then, access Static Results from the ellipsis menu of the action. Static Results will be disabled by default. Once enabled, you can click the icon to the right of the Static Result label (boxed in Figure 7-12), to switch the view to JSON mode. Once in JSON mode, you can insert the Body you copied from the sample run just after the Header {} line. Be sure to add a comma after the Header since you are adding another property. Figure 7-12 shows an Approval action that has been configured with a Static Result.

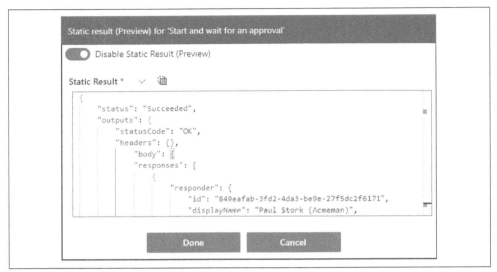

<figure>Static result (Preview) for 'Start and wait for an approval'

◉ Disable Static Result (Preview)

Static Result * ▾ 📥

```
{
    "status": "Succeeded",
    "outputs": {
        "statusCode": "OK",
        "headers": {},
            "body": {
            "responses": [
                {
                    "responder": {
                        "id": "849eafab-3fd2-4da3-be9e-27f5dc2f6171",
                        "displayName": "Paul Stork (Acmeman)",
```

Done   Cancel</figure>

Figure 7-12. Static Result (Preview)

Adjusting Run After Settings

Most programming languages have a structure called a `try-catch` block for organizing code. This structure can be used to handle predictable errors that occur during program execution, so the application doesn't fail. The `try` block contains the code that might fail with an error, and the `catch` block contains the code that handles or logs the error before continuing execution. It lets a programmer anticipate potential issues and provides a way for the application to continue running or exit in an orderly fashion.

Although Power Automate is a no-code/low-code system, it has a similar capability. Almost all flow actions have a Configure Run After entry in their ellipsis menu. This lets you configure what the current action will do if something happens in the action above it in the flow. You can configure an action to run when one of four possible events occur in the preceding action. You can choose to run the action after multiple different events:

Action is successful
 The preceding action ran successfully.

Action has failed
 The preceding action encountered an error (timeouts are not errors in this case).

Action is skipped
 The action was skipped because a condition was not met, a previous action failed, or it was in an alternate branch that the flow did not follow.

Action has timed out
> The preceding action timed out.

 Individual actions that access backend data sources will time out after two minutes. The entire flow will time out after it has been running for 30 days. There are also some actions like approvals where the specific timeout can be set in the settings of the action. The timeout can never be longer than 30 days.

Using the Terminate Action

When using the Run After settings to react to an error, sometimes you want to end the flow successfully even though an error has occurred. The Terminate action can be used to end the flow immediately with any one of three conditions: succeeded, failed, or canceled. If the flow is terminated as canceled, you can supply a custom error message and code. The Terminate action is also useful when you are testing so you can end a flow early to check a particular section of the flow for issues.

Using Scope Actions with Run After

The "run after" setting always applies to the previous action in a flow. But what if there are three or four previous actions that might throw an error? How do you respond to those? The answer is to enclose all of those actions in a single Scope action. A Scope is a container action that can hold one or more actions in a flow. One of the benefits of a Scope is that you can expand and contract the Scope to make a large flow more readable at a high level. But it can also be used when you are setting the "run after" of an action that follows a Scope. If any action inside the Scope fails or is timed out, then the whole Scope times out. So by using a Scope, you can have an action run based on what happens with one or more actions in a Scope.

 A few actions, like Initialize variables, cannot be enclosed in a Scope because they must be added directly to the main line of actions in a flow.

Exercise 7-1. Simulating a `try-catch` block

In this example, you will create a small flow that simulates appending information to a Text log. You will use Scope actions and Configure Run After settings to recover from a "file not found" error if the Text log doesn't already exist.

1. Create an instant cloud flow entitled "Write Log File" using the "Manually trigger a flow" trigger (see Figure 7-13).

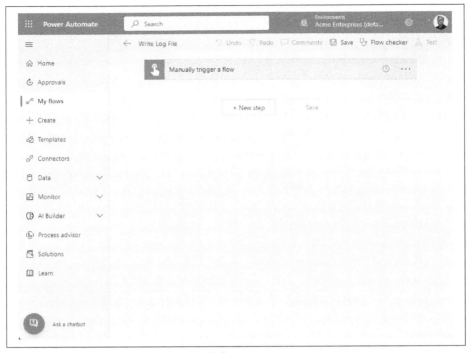

Figure 7-13. Creating an instant cloud flow

2. Add an "Initialize variable" action. Name the variable `varFileName` and select type String. Set the value field to *ErrorLog.txt*. This variable will hold the file name for your Log file (see Figure 7-14).

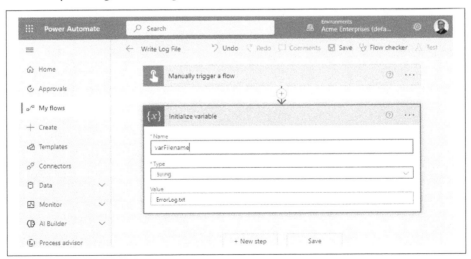

Figure 7-14. Initializing a variable

3. Add a Scope action and rename it "Try Block". This Scope will hold all the actions that might fail (see Figure 7-15).

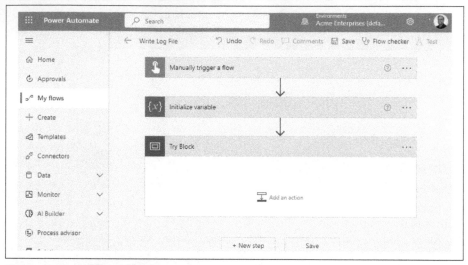

Figure 7-15. Adding a Scope

4. Add a OneDrive for Business "Get file metadata using path action to the Try Block Scope. Use the Dynamic content dialog to add the `varFilename` variable to the file path field (see Figure 7-16). Since you aren't specifying anything other than the filename, it will look in the root folder of your OneDrive.

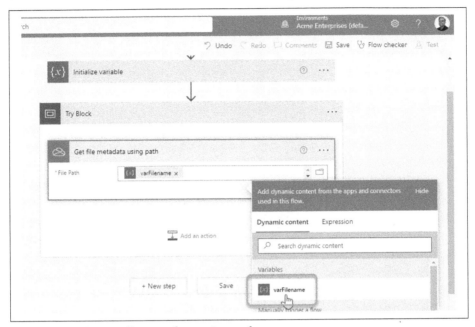

Figure 7-16. Getting file metadata using path

5. Add a Scope action and rename it "Catch Error." Use the ellipsis menu to select Configure Run After. Check the "has failed" checkbox, and uncheck the "is successful" checkbox. Click Done (see Figure 7-17). This Scope will now run if anything in the Try Block Scope fails.

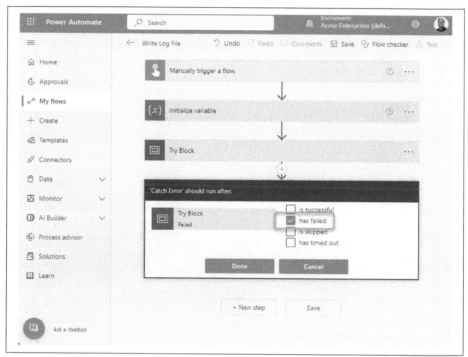

Figure 7-17. Adding Scope to run after an error

6. Add a OneDrive for Business "Create file" action to the Catch Error Scope. Use the Dynamic content dialog to add the following values to the action (see Figure 7-18):

- Folder Path: The path output from the "Get file metadata using path" action
- File Name: The varFilename variable
- File Content: Add the following using the Expressions tab:

```
Concat(formatdatetime(utcNow(),'MM-dd-yyyy HH:mm')
,' - ',
first(result('Try_Block'))?['outputs']?['body']?['message'])
```

This will create a text file with one line containing the current date-time and the first error message in the Try Block Scope actions.

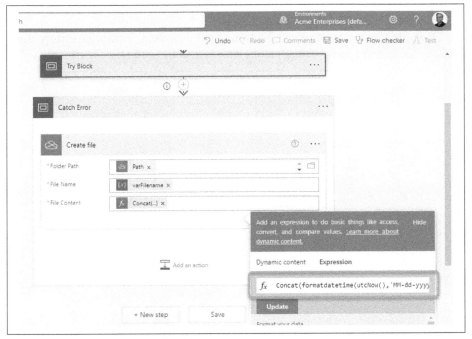

Figure 7-18. Creating a new log file

7. Click the plus (+) sign above the Catch Error Scope to add a parallel branch to the flow. Add a Scope action and rename it "Main Branch" (see Figure 7-19). This is the Scope that will now execute if the Try Block runs successfully.

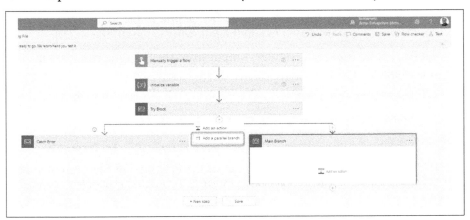

Figure 7-19. Adding Main Branch Scope

8. Add a OneDrive for Business "Get file content" action to the Main Branch Scope. Use the Dynamic content dialog to add the Id (unique identifier) output from the "Get file metadata using path" action to the File field. This will retrieve the existing file content so we can append a new line to the end (see Figure 7-20).

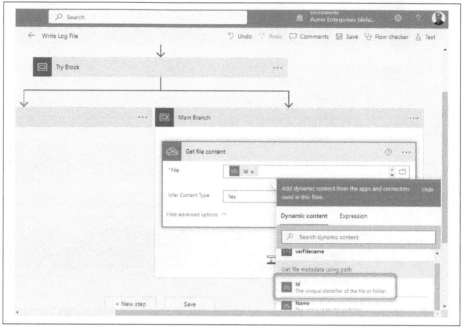

Figure 7-20. Getting existing log file content

9. Add a OneDrive for Business "Update file" action to the Main Branch Scope. Use the Dynamic content dialog to add the following values to the action:

   • File: The Id (unique identifier) output from the "Get file metadata using path" action

   • File Content: Add the following code using the Expressions tab:

```
Concat(outputs('Get_file_content')?['body'],
decodeUriComponent('%0A'),
formatdatetime(utcNow(),'MM-dd-yyyy HH:mm'),' - No Errors')
```

   • This will add a new line to the end of the existing log file content containing the current date-time and the text "No Errors" (see Figure 7-21).

Figure 7-21. Updating log file

10. Add a Scope action and rename it "Cleanup." Use the ellipsis menu to select Configure Run After. Check the "is skipped" checkbox and the "is successful" checkbox. Click Done. "Is skipped" needs to be checked for both Scopes in the parallel branches because one of the branches will always be skipped (see Figure 7-22).

Figure 7-22. Adding Cleanup Scope

11. Add a "Send me an email notification" action. Set the Subject field to Added Log Entry and the Body to "An entry was added to the Log file" (see Figure 7-23). This will send you an email saying that a log file entry was added.

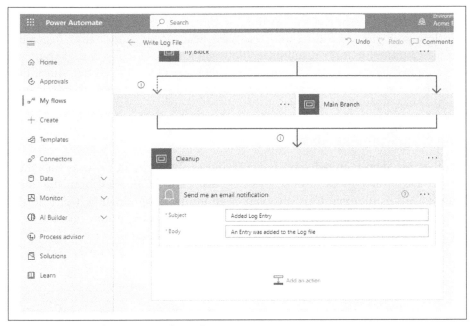

Figure 7-23. Sending an email notification

12. Save and run the flow twice. The first run should throw an error because the log file doesn't exist, so the flow will finish successfully by using the Catch branch. The second run should run without error and follow the Main Branch of the flow.

Resubmitting Flows

You've now learned how to find and fix flows that aren't running successfully. If your flow is using a manual trigger, it's easy to rerun the flow after you fix it. But what about flows that use automatic or recurrence triggers? How can you re-trigger them after the time has passed or the trigger event is concluded? Figure 7-24 shows the Resubmit link on the toolbar of a flow run opened from the history log.

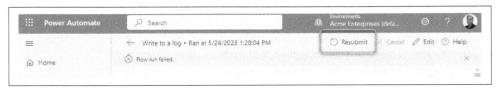

Figure 7-24. Resubmitting a flow

Once you've fixed the errors that are causing the flow to fail, you can return to the failed run in the history and select the Resubmit link on the toolbar. This will re-run the flow with the same data that was used when it was originally triggered. This doesn't guarantee that the resubmitted flow will run successfully. If the input parameters supplied by the trigger were incorrect, then the flow will still fail. But if the flow failed because actions were misconfigured or connections failed, then resubmitting the flow may help it run successfully.

Canceling Running Flows

Another problem that can arise when trying to fix errors in flows is that the error doesn't cause the flow to stop. In this case, you can't fix and resubmit the flow until after it finishes running. If the problem is an infinite loop, the flow won't finish until it times out after 30 days. Even if it's not in an infinite loop, it may take hours before the flow finishes. In these cases, you can select the running flow from the history log and cancel it using the Cancel link on the toolbar. Figure 7-25 shows the Cancel link on the toolbar as it appears in a running flow.

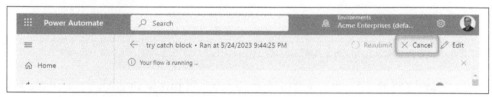

Figure 7-25. Canceling a running flow

Summary

In this chapter, you learned how to find, repair, and resubmit flows that don't work correctly the first time you run them. You also reviewed several ways to access different kinds of reports that detail how cloud flows are running.

So far in the book, I've focused on different types of cloud flows. In the next chapter, I'll introduce you to a completely different kind of flow—a desktop flow. Whereas cloud flows use connectors to access and manipulate information stored in data sources, desktop flows use your computer's UI to interact with websites and programs. Working directly with the UI eliminates the need for established APIs. This can make it easier to automate tasks that are done manually on your computer or interact with legacy programs that can't be accessed directly by cloud flows.

CHAPTER 8

Desktop Flows

Power Automate cloud flows are powerful, but they don't work in certain situations. For example, data may be stored in a source that doesn't have a connector or an API that can be used in a cloud flow to access the data. Or you may be trying to automate a manual process that someone does using a computer, terminal, or web page. The solution for these instances is Power Automate Desktop (PAD), which lets you create automated desktop flows that access information through the UI or a web browser on a computer desktop.

Using PAD, you can record actions performed on a computer desktop or a web browser. After creating the recording, you can edit the desktop flow. You can also create a desktop flow by dragging and dropping actions onto a workspace. These desktop flows can then re-run the actions on demand as needed. PAD provides a simple way to automate daily, repetitive tasks that you complete on your computer. This process of recording steps and replaying them is called Robotic Process Automation (RPA), which we discussed earlier in the book. But what is RPA, and how does it differ from the regular cloud flows that are built in Power Automate?

What Is Robotic Process Automation (RPA)?

RPA refers to the use of software robots known as "bots" to automate routine, repetitive tasks that are normally performed by human workers. RPA technology is designed to mimic human interactions with digital systems, allowing organizations to automate manual, time-consuming, and repetitive tasks. This frees up human workers to focus on more valuable and creative work. The goal of RPA is to increase efficiency, reduce costs, and improve accuracy by automating manual tasks. PAD is Microsoft's entry into the world of RPA.

Power Automate and PAD are both designed to be used to automate business processes. So, how is PAD different from regular Power Automate? The first difference is that Power Automate is a cloud-based platform, while PAD is a Windows desktop application that lets users automate tasks on their local computers. Both provide a visual, low-code environment for automating business processes. However, Power Automate is designed to work through APIs and connectors to access data sources, and PAD automates interactions through the local computer's UI. In summary, Power Automate is a cloud-based automation platform designed for automating workflows and business processes across different services, while PAD is a Windows desktop application designed for automating tasks and workflows on the local computer.

Prerequisites for Power Automate Desktop

The first step when installing the PAD designer is to make sure that your computer meets all the prerequisites. If you are using Windows 11 as your desktop operating system, you won't need to worry about this section since PAD comes preinstalled on Windows 11. But if you are running any other operating system, review the following list to make sure that you have all the prerequisites:

- A Microsoft or work or school account: PAD stores your desktop flows in either OneDrive consumer (Microsoft account) or the Dataverse database in one of your Power Automate environments (work or school account).
- A computer that runs one of the following 64-bit operating systems:
  — Windows 10/11 (Home, Pro, or Enterprise)
  — Windows Server 2016/2019/2022
- A computer with .NET Framework version 4.7.2 or later installed
- Microsoft Edge Chromium (version 80 or later), Google Chrome, or Firefox browser
- Environment with a Dataverse database (Office 365 accounts only)
- A keyboard attached to the computer
- An active internet connection

Depending on the account you use to sign in to PAD, there may be some limitations that apply to your use of the product. For example, if you use Windows 10/11 Home, you won't be able to record Selenium IDE desktop flows or use a cloud flow to execute a desktop flow.

Installing Power Automate Desktop

There are two different ways to install the PAD client: from a downloaded .MSI installer file or directly from the Microsoft store. If you have Windows 11, you won't need to install it because it comes preinstalled on this OS. The .MSI installer provides more control over the installation. Installing the PAD client from the Microsoft store will do a silent install and will not install optional components like the browser extensions or the machine runtime app. If you create a desktop flow that uses these features, you will be prompted to add them at that time.

Exercise 8-1. Installing PAD

In this example, you'll download the MSI installer to install PAD on your computer. If you have Windows 11, you can skip this exercise because the PAD client is already installed.

1. Log in to *https://make.powerautomate.com*, and select the "My flows" tab in the navigation bar on the left. On the "My flows" page, select the "Desktop flows" tab and click on the Install drop-down in the upper-right corner of the screen, as shown in Figure 8-1. This will give you the option of installing PAD or an on-premises data gateway. Select Power Automate for Desktop from the drop-down.

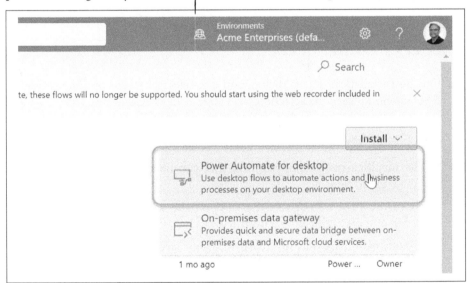

Figure 8-1. Installing PAD

2. Wait for *Setup.Microsoft.PowerAutomate.exe* to finish downloading. When it finishes, open the file. You will see a dialog window similar to the one in Figure 8-2. Click the Next button.

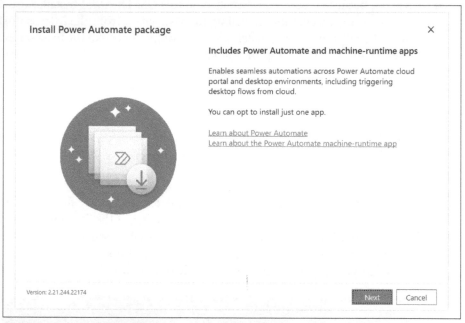

Figure 8-2. PAD install wizard

3. On the Installation details dialog, you can select different options related to the PAD client. Most of the selections will already be checked.

The installer allows you to install four different applications on your device:

- The desktop designer that you use to create, edit, and run your desktop flows

- The machine-runtime application that can be used to launch desktop flows from a cloud flow

- Microsoft Edge web drivers that support the web browser extensions used to record and play back interactions with websites in your web browser

- UI automation support for interacting with Java applications

Check the final checkbox to accept the terms of use. Your screen should now look like Figure 8-3. Click the Install button.

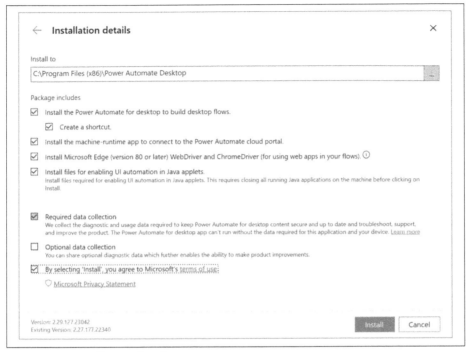

Figure 8-3. Installation detail options

4. Accept the User Account Control dialog, if it comes up, to allow the installer to make changes on your computer. Wait for the Installing package progress bar to complete, as seen in Figure 8-4.

Figure 8-4. Installation progress

5. On the final screen of the wizard, you will have the option to install browser extensions for whatever browsers you have installed on your desktop. Click the Close button, as shown in Figure 8-5, to exit the setup program.

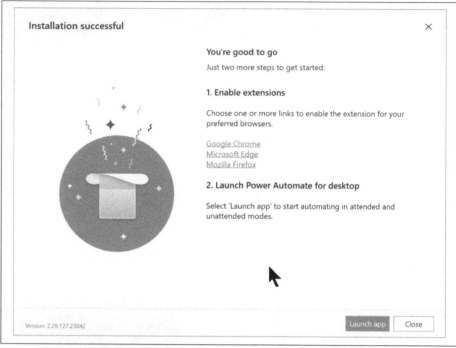

Figure 8-5. Installation successful screen

Machine Settings

Installing the machine runtime application is one of the optional elements available during installation of PAD. This application is required if you want to trigger your desktop flows from regular cloud flows.

Originally, PAD used the same on-premises data gateway as the rest of the Power Platform. But Microsoft deprecated the use of gateways by PAD in late 2022. Now, PAD registers devices directly with Power Automate in the cloud. When you install PAD on a computer, it is automatically registered in the default environment in Power Automate. If you don't want to call desktop flows from the default environment, you can use the machine runtime application to update the environment manually.

 You cannot connect a Windows 10/11 Home computer to the cloud to invoke desktop flows from a cloud flow.

You also have an option to create a machine group using the machine runtime application. Machine groups can be used to distribute your automation workload across multiple computers and optimize productivity. When you trigger a flow on a machine group, it is added to a queue. The first available computer in the group will then run the flow. You can read more details about how to manage machines and machine groups for PAD in the Power Automate documentation (*https://oreil.ly/ S1hNu*).

Licensing Requirements

PAD is free to use in attended mode on a Windows 10/11 desktop. But triggering a desktop flow from a Power Automate cloud flow requires a Power Automate per-user plan with attended RPA. A regular Power Automate or Power Apps per-user plan will not be enough. The Power Automate per-flow plan also doesn't include rights for running attended desktop flows. Figure 8-6 shows the retail licensing costs for Power Automate. Only the center license (per-user plan with attended RPA) will let you run attended desktop flows.

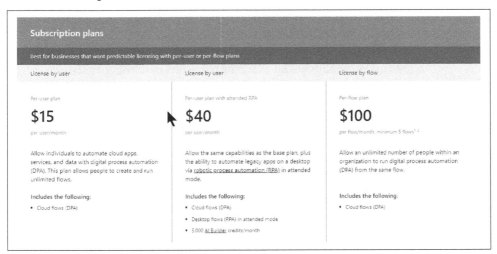

Figure 8-6. Power Automate plan pricing

There are two licensing options for running unattended flows. To run unattended flows on VMs or desktops that you provide to Power Automate, you must have an unattended RPA add on in addition to a Power Automate license. An alternative to this is to run unattended flows on machines provided by Microsoft. These "hosted" machines require a slightly more expensive add-on, but they help you avoid the cost of maintaining your own resources. Although the Power Automate per-flow license does not include attended RPA, it can be used as the base license for the unattended add-ons. But the add-ons cannot be combined with the standard Power Automate per-user license that does not include RPA.

You must purchase one add-on for each "bot" that you intend to run. In this case, a bot would be each machine or VM where you are running unattended flows or each flow if you are running multiple concurrent flows on a single machine. Desktop flows that are queued to run sequentially are considered one bot. Figure 8-7 shows the retail pricing for these add-ons.

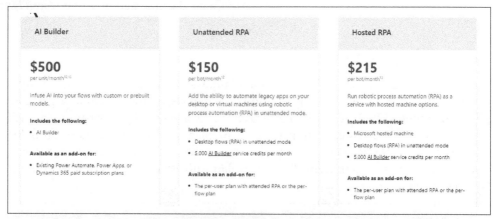

AI Builder	Unattended RPA	Hosted RPA
$500	**$150**	**$215**
per unit/month[2,1]	per bot/month[2]	per bot/month[1]
Infuse AI into your flows with custom or prebuilt models.	Add the ability to automate legacy apps on your desktop or virtual machines using robotic process automation (RPA) in unattended mode.	Run robotic process automation (RPA) as a service with hosted machine options.
Includes the following:	**Includes the following:**	**Includes the following:**
• AI Builder	• Desktop flows (RPA) in unattended mode	• Microsoft hosted machine
	• 5,000 AI Builder service credits per month	• Desktop flows (RPA) in unattended mode
Available as an add-on for:		• 5,000 AI Builder service credits per month
• Existing Power Automate, Power Apps, or Dynamics 365 paid subscription plans	**Available as an add-on for:**	
	• The per-user plan with attended RPA or the per-flow plan	**Available as an add-on for:**
		• The per-user plan with attended RPA or the per-flow plan

Figure 8-7. Unattended and hosted RPA pricing

AI builder credits are an added benefit when purchasing either of the unattended RPA add-ons. You can use these AI builder credits to build AI models for use in your cloud flows.

There are also two consumption-based licenses available for desktop flows. If you have an Azure subscription, you can set up a Pay-as-you-go plan to pay monthly for each desktop flow run that is not covered by a per-user or per-flow license. There is a different cost depending on whether the flow runs are attended or unattended. Figure 8-8 shows the retail pricing per-flow run for the attended and unattended plans. You can read more about Pay-as-you-go plans in the Power Platform documentation (*https://oreil.ly/3EJ27*).

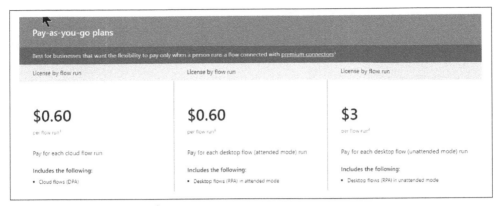

Figure 8-8. Pay-as-you-go licensing

Creating a Desktop Flow

Like cloud flows, desktop flows are a string of actions that are completed in a sequence. But the actions used to create a desktop flow are very different from the actions used to create cloud flows. Cloud flow actions are provided by the different connectors produced by Microsoft and other third-party companies. But all the actions available in a desktop flow are built directly into the desktop flow designer. Actions are added by dragging them from the action pane onto the main design surface. Once on the design surface, you will be able to fill in the fields provided in the action using static content or variables produced as output from previous actions in the flow.

Although desktop flows are made up of a sequential string of actions, that is where the similarity with cloud flows ends. There are several differences in the experience of creating desktop flows:

- The desktop flow designer is a client application, not a website.
- You can record your interactions with applications or web pages to create a desktop flow.
- Desktop flows don't use triggers.
- There are no functions available to create complex expressions.
- Error handing is built into each desktop action.

The actions you use and how they are added to the design surface is also a different experience. In cloud flows, you click a link to open a dialog box to select an action to add, but in desktop flows you drag actions from a sidebar onto the design surface. Exercise 8-2, later in this chapter, walks you through how it works in PAD. Before we get there, though, let's look at the design surface in the PAD client.

Exploring the Desktop Flow Design Surface

The desktop flow designer is divided into several sections. Figure 8-9 shows the designer with the different sections highlighted and alphabetically labeled. The following list describes what each section of the screen is used for:

A. Toolbar: Basic menu operations like Save, Run, or Record the flow

B. Subflows drop-down: Create and manage subflows

C. Actions pane: Categorized list of Actions

D. Workspace: Edit pane for desktop flows and subflows

E. Variables: Input, Output, and Flow variables

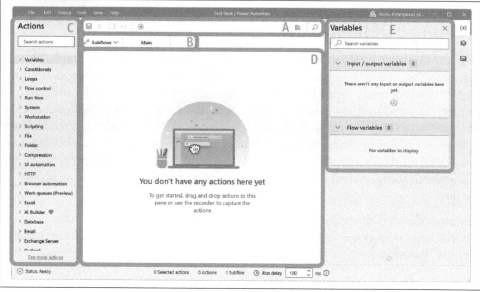

Figure 8-9. PAD designer

Most of your work will be done in the middle workspace pane. This central pane is a tabbed design surface that displays the main desktop flow and any subflows that were created for editing. When you execute a desktop flow, the pane will expand to take up most of the space in the application. When the flow switches focus to another window or starts a separate application, the entire designer will minimize. If there are any errors while the application is running, they will be highlighted in the workspace and displayed in a window at the bottom of the screen after the run is finished. Figure 8-10 shows a desktop flow that has stopped after an error occurred.

Figure 8-10. Flow designer with runtime error

Learning from Desktop Flow Examples

PAD provides several examples that will introduce you to what RPA can do. You can find all the available examples under the Examples tab in the designer. Examples can be very useful when trying to learn how to do something in a desktop flow. But like cloud flow templates, these examples are best used as learning tools, not as production-ready desktop flows.

Exercise 8-2. Creating an example desktop flow

In this example, you will create a new desktop flow using the example "Open a web page." This is one of the simplest examples, but it will show you how to interact with a different application on your desktop. The process that I describe here is the same for any of the examples in the designer.

1. Log in to *https://make.powerautomate.com*, and select the "My flows" tab in the navigation bar on the left. Select "Desktop flow" from the "+ New flow" drop-down. In the dialog that appears, click the "Launch app" button (see Figure 8-11). When prompted, click the Open button to launch the PAD client.

Figure 8-11. Launching the PAD client

2. Select the Examples tab and choose the Web Automation category (see Figure 8-12).

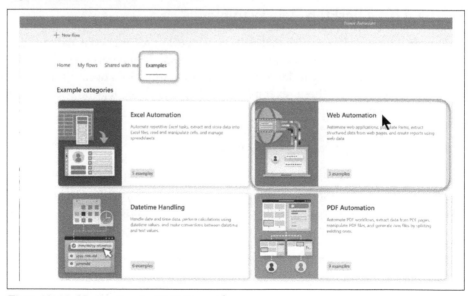

Figure 8-12. Navigating to PAD Examples

3. Hover over the second example, open a web page, and click on the pencil icon to edit the example flow (see Figure 8-13). Wait for the desktop flow designer window to open.

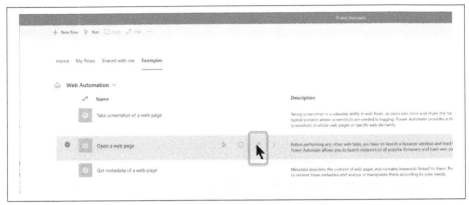

Figure 8-13. Loading the "Open a web page" Example

4. Click on the "Got it" button to close the dialog box (see Figure 8-14).

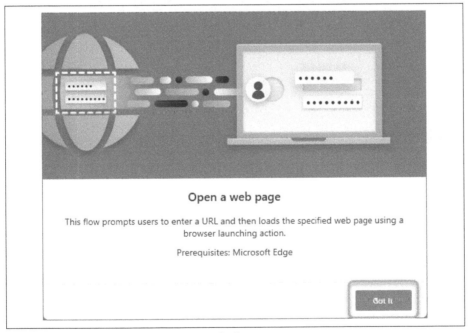

Figure 8-14. Successfully loaded example flow

5. Select Run on the toolbar to run the Example flow (see Figure 8-15).

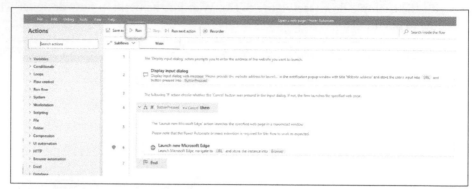

Figure 8-15. Running the Example flow

6. The flow will pause on the first action and display a dialog box asking for user input. Type "dontpapanic.com/blog" into the dialog box and click OK (see Figure 8-16).

Figure 8-16. Running Example flow

7. A web page will be displayed (see Figure 8-17).

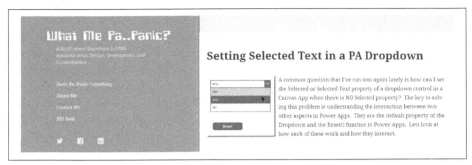

Figure 8-17. Web page displayed by flow

8. Select the Power Automate icon from the task bar at the bottom of the screen to return to the completed flow. Select Save As on the File menu to save a copy of the desktop flow under a new name. After Saving the flow, you can Exit the designer (see Figure 8-18).

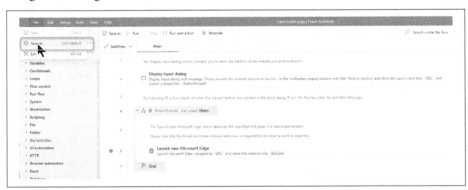

Figure 8-18. Saving a copy of the Example flow

Recording User Interactions

Examples are good learning tools, but they rarely do exactly what you want a desktop flow to do. Desktop flows are usually designed to duplicate a manual process that you do on your computer. To turn those manual steps into a desktop flow, you can use the built-in recorder. Using the recorder, you can create the basics of your flow and then edit the flow produced to fine-tune the details. Some actions, like conditionals or loops, can't be recorded so they will need to be added later. The recorded flow may also contain extra actions that aren't necessary and that should be removed. Editing a recorded flow is almost always a requirement, but recording a set of steps will still save time as you are creating new flows.

 PAD originally used two different recorders: a Windows recorder for desktop apps and a Selenium IDE recorder for interacting with web browsers. Both recorders have now been deprecated and replaced by the current recorder that can record both desktop and web browser interactions.

When recording your interaction with a desktop application or a web page, PAD identifies UI elements that you interact with. For most applications and web pages, PAD looks inside web pages and applications to pick up the identities of the UI elements used by the application or web page. For example, a text input field in a web form may have been assigned a unique ID by the web designer. If there is no unique ID, then PAD will use the control tree location of the element. In some cases, the recorder may not be able to identify specific UI elements. The application may not expose their accessibility API, or it may have other technical limitations that block the recording process. When this happens, there is a setting that lets you use image-based recording. Image-based recording uses image recognition and optical character recognition (OCR) to identify specific UI elements on the screen and extract text from them. Image-based recording must be enabled using the context menu drop-down before starting the recording, as shown in Figure 8-19.

Figure 8-19. Enabling image-based recording

Exercise 8-3. Recording navigating a website

In this example (*https://oreil.ly/MSkRr*), you will use PAD to record your actions on the screen while interacting with a website. You will start by opening a web browser and navigating to my blog. On the blog, you will navigate to a page where you can send an email to me. After filling in the required fields and sending the email, you will close the browser and stop recording. I don't use these emails for anything other than responding to you if you ask a question.

1. Open the Start menu on your computer. Type "Power Automate" into the Search bar and select the Power Automate App icon to start PAD (see Figure 8-20). As a desktop application, PAD can be launched from the Power Automate website, as we did in Exercise 8-2, or from the Start menu.

Figure 8-20. Launching PAD

2. Create a new desktop flow named "Recorder Demo" (see Figure 8-21).

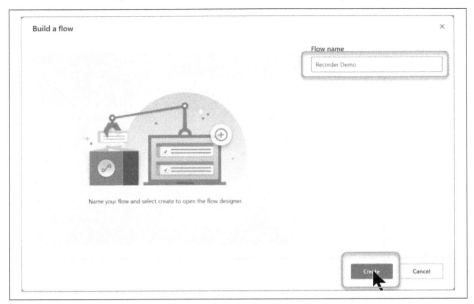

Figure 8-21. Creating a new desktop flow

3. Select the Recorder button from the toolbar above the design surface (see Figure 8-22).

Figure 8-22. Opening desktop recorder

4. In the Recorder dialog window, select "Launch new web browser" from the context menu (see Figure 8-23). Choose Microsoft Edge (or another browser where you've installed the Power Automate extension). A browser window will open.

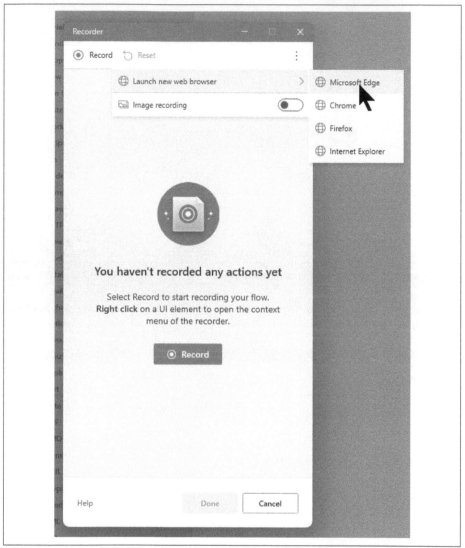

Figure 8-23. Launching web browser for recording

5. In the Recorder dialog window, click the Record link on the toolbar to start recording (see Figure 8-24).

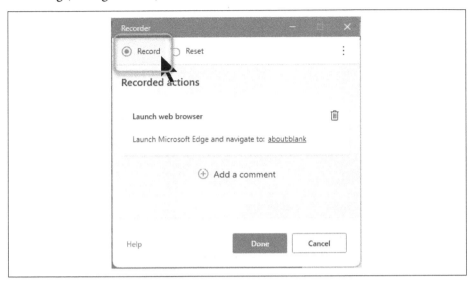

Figure 8-24. Starting the recording

6. In the browser window, hover your mouse over the address bar until you see the red outline. The red outline means that the recorder has identified this as a UI element. Right-click the Address bar and select "Populate text field" from the context menu. A dialog box will appear. Type *"https://www.dontpapanic.com/ blog"* into the dialog box and click "Add text" (see Figure 8-25).

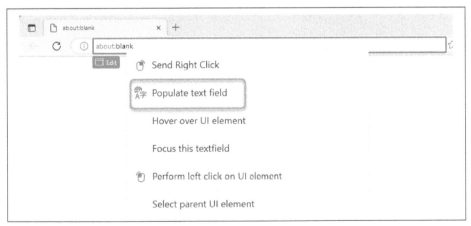

Figure 8-25. UI element context menu

7. After the web page loads, hover over the Contact Me link in the left sidebar until it is outlined in red (see Figure 8-26). Click on the Contact Me link, which is an HTML anchor tag on the web page. A web form will be loaded.

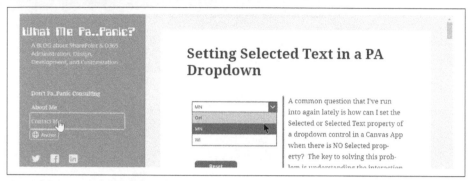

Figure 8-26. Anchor tag UI element

8. Click on the Your Name field in the Contact Me form. After it is highlighted in red, type in your name. Use the same process to fill in the Your Email, Confirm Your Email, Correct Response, and Your Message fields with appropriate information (see Figure 8-27).

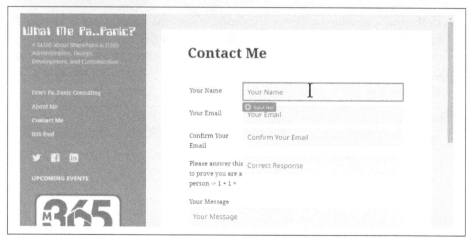

Figure 8-27. Filling in Contact Me form

9. Hover over the consent checkbox until it is highlighted in red and then click the checkbox (see Figure 8-28).

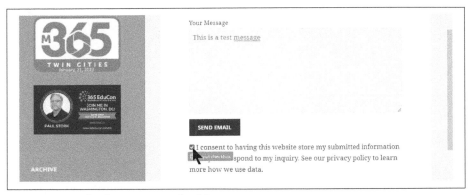

Figure 8-28. Checking consent checkbox

10. Hover over the Send Email button until it is highlighted in red. Click the Send Email button (see Figure 8-29).

Figure 8-29. Clicking Send Email button

11. Wait for the Success message to appear (see Figure 8-30).

Figure 8-30. Message sent page

12. Close the browser window. It's a best practice to start and close an application as part of a desktop flow. This helps the flow correctly identify which application you are interacting with (see Figure 8-31).

Figure 8-31. Closing your browser

13. Go back to the recorder dialog; you may have to open it from your taskbar if it's been minimized. Click on the Done button to stop recording and return to the desktop flow designer (see Figure 8-32).

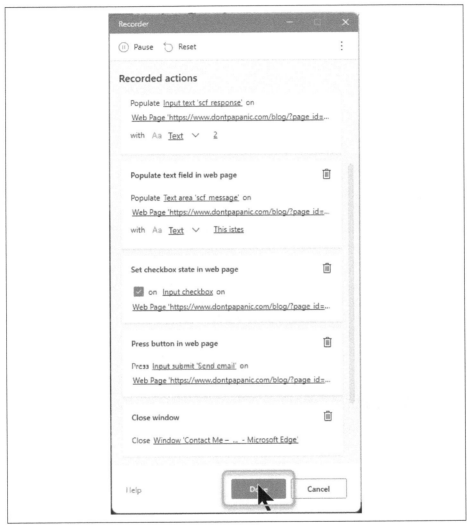

Figure 8-32. Stopping recording

14. In the designer, click on the Run link in the toolbar to try running the script. Recorded scripts will often require editing to remove extra steps or fix errors (see Figure 8-33).

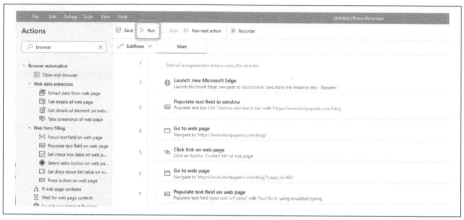

Figure 8-33. Finished recording and running the script

If you want to use PAD to automate something that you now do manually on a computer, recording the steps can be a great way to start. But recordings often have extra steps that are unnecessary or are missing steps that might keep them from failing if something isn't exactly where it should be. For example, a browser window may have been recorded when it wasn't full screen, but playback has the browser maximized. This usually means that recorded desktop flows will need additional editing after you record them.

Adding and Editing Actions

An alternative to using the recorder to create a new desktop flow is to create it directly in the designer. To create a flow from nothing, you need to find the action you want in the Actions pane on the left of the design surface. Then you can either double-click the action to add it to the end of the current desktop flow or drag it into the designer and drop it where you want it to be inserted. After inserting the action on the design surface, a modal dialog will open, displaying fields for any parameters that need to be configured. Input parameter fields may be text fields, drop-down menus, or checkboxes. Some of the parameter fields may be filled in with default content. You can also directly edit the values or use variables already in the flow to set the values.

Figure 8-34 shows an action to launch a new instance of the Microsoft Edge browser. The Launch mode and Window state fields are set to defaults that you can change. The Initial URL is blank and must be filled in with the URL of the website you want the browser to display. The small {x} at the end of the Initial URL field can be used to insert a variable value from the flow.

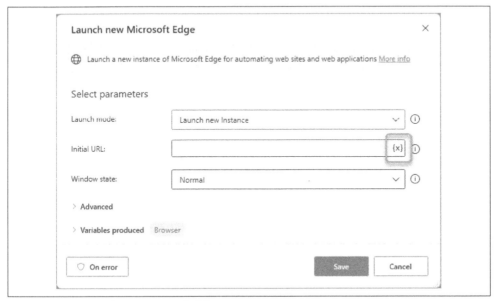

Figure 8-34. Launching Microsoft Edge action

Working with Variables

Variables are created as output from most actions in PAD. You can also create variables manually using the "Set variable" action. Variable names are enclosed by percentage signs (%), a symbol that is considered a special character in PAD. Any string enclosed inside percentage signs will be evaluated as a variable name. If you want to use an actual percentage sign as a value, then it should be preceded by another percentage sign like this: %%. Figure 8-35 shows a typical "Set variable" action.

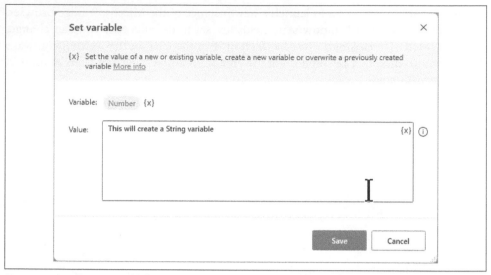

Figure 8-35. "Set variable" action

Percentage sign notation can also be used inside the "Set variable" action to do calculations and store the resulting value as a different data type. For example, adding "%3*15%" to the Value field of a "Set variable" action will result in a numeric value type variable with a value of 45. Using "%15>12%" will result in a Boolean value type variable with a value of True. Using percentage sign notation, you can create complex expressions containing hardcoded values, variable names, arithmetic and logical operations, comparisons and parentheses.

You can also create variables that are a list of values using the "Create new list" action. In Power Automate, this would be an array. Once a list variable has been created, you can populate the list using the "Add item to list" action. List variables can be processed using looping actions, like "For each," or you can use percentage notation to access a list value directly by using an index enclosed in square brackets. For example, if you had a list variable named "Sample List," you could access the second record of the list using "%SampleList[1]%."

The percentage sign notation provides a lot of flexibility when working with variables in PAD. But unlike cloud flows, there are no expressions available for use in PAD that accept variables as parameters. The closest thing to functions in Power Automate are the properties available with different variable values based on data type. Figure 8-36 shows the dialog for adding a variable to an action. The SampleList variable has a Count property that contains the number of items in the list, and the SampleString variable has several properties available. The specific properties available will depend on the data type of the variable. There are also actions available that will do the same things as these properties. But those produce new variables rather than providing just the values, like functions, in Power Automate.

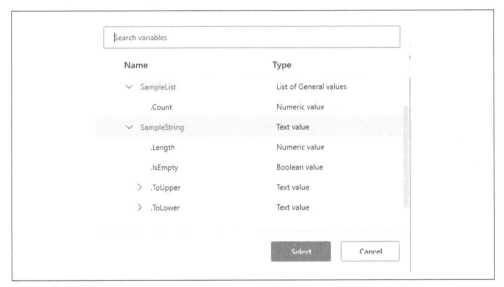

Figure 8-36. Variable dialog

One last feature of variables in PAD should be mentioned. As shown in Figure 8-37, a specific variable can be marked as sensitive. Marking a variable as sensitive will hide the value of the variable at runtime in the designer or a log of the flow run. In Figure 8-37, you can see that the value of SensitiveVar has been hidden. For example, if the desktop flow uses a password stored as a variable to log in to a site, this would prevent that value from being visible to anyone else.

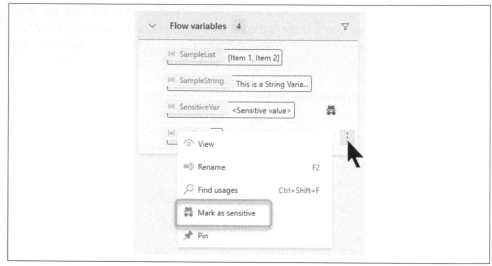

Figure 8-37. Marking a variable as sensitive

Handling Errors

There are two types of errors associated with desktop flows: design-time errors and runtime errors.

Design-time errors occur when you are configuring the actions you add to the design surface. For example, you may forget to provide a value for a required parameter. Design-time errors will be displayed as you are creating the flow and must be fixed before you can run the flow.

Runtime errors, also known as exceptions, are generated when you run your desktop flow and it fails. For example, let's say you misspell a file path in one of the actions, so the file is not found. When a runtime exception is thrown, the execution of the flow will be interrupted, and the flow will not progress. In regular Power Automate, you handle these kinds of exceptions by setting the Run After property of the next action in the flow. In Power Automate desktop, each action has On Error settings that can be used to specify what happens if an exception is encountered.

You can configure what an action does when it encounters an error by clicking the On Error button at the bottom of the action to open a modal dialog. The dialog will have two or three sections that you can use to configure what the flow will do in case an error is encountered. Figure 8-38 shows a typical On Error dialog.

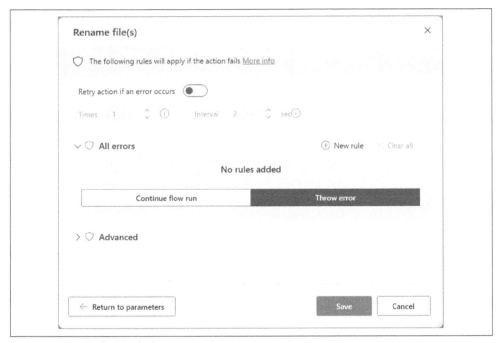

Figure 8-38. On Error dialog

The first section in the dialog can be used to retry the action if it fails. You can set both the number of times to retry the action and the delay between retries. The second section can be used to add rules on what happens if any error is generated by the action. The third section, under Advanced, can be used to configure rules for specific types of errors that the action might throw. The rules added for all errors or specific errors can be used to do things like store a value in a variable or run a subflow. They can also be used to specify how the flow will continue if you ignore the error.

There is also an "On block error" action that you can add to the flow. The "On block error" action can be used to group multiple actions together and apply the same On Error settings to all of the actions. The "On block error" settings do not include an Advanced section since the settings apply to all of the errors in a group.

Exercise 8-4. Unzipping an archive to a specific location

If you are able to create a cloud flow to automate a process, this is usually the better approach. Cloud flows don't require that your computer be on or that you be logged in to do their work. But there are cases where actions don't exist in cloud flows to easily implement a manual process. One example of this is adding a directory structure and files to a ZIP archive. Cloud flows have a built-in action for extracting an archive, but you need to buy a third-party connector to create an archive. However,

PAD does have an action that can zip files into an archive. In this example, you will use PAD to zip a directory structure of files and add it to a ZIP archive.

1. Using Windows Explorer, create a directory in the root of Drive C: called *Temp*. Add a subdirectory to it called *Level 1*. Copy some files to *Temp* and *Level 1* (see Figure 8-39).

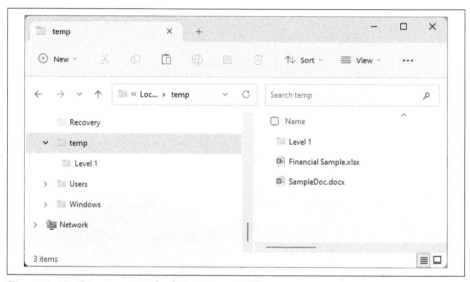

Figure 8-39. Creating sample directories and files

2. Using PAD, create a new desktop flow and name it "Zip Files" (see Figure 8-40).

Build a flow   ×

                                                    Flow name

                                                    Zip Files

Name your flow and select create to open the flow designer.

                                            Create   Cancel

Figure 8-40. Creating a new desktop flow

3. In the Actions pane, expand the Message boxes category and double-click on Display input dialog. Set the fields to the following values (see Figure 8-41):

Input dialog title
    File Path to Zip

Input dialog message
    Please enter the folder path of the files to Zip

Default value
    C:\temp

This action will prompt the user for a directory path to ZIP when the flow is started.

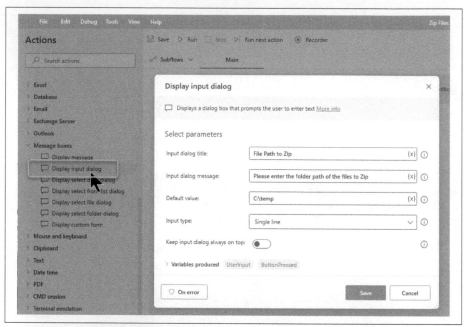

Figure 8-41. Adding input dialog action

4. In the Search Actions text box, type "Zip." Drag and drop the ZIP files action into the designer below the "Display input dialog" action. Set the fields to the following values (see Figure 8-42):

Archive Path
> C:\Archive\backup.zip (or another filename in some other existing folder on your computer)

File(s) to ZIP
> %UserInput% (This is the output variable from the previous action.)

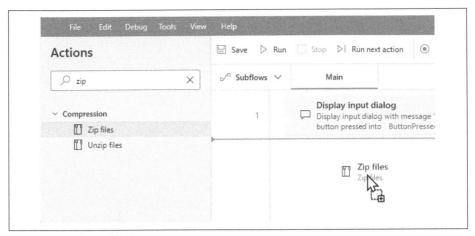

Figure 8-42. "Zip files" action

5. In the "Zip files" action, click the On Error button at the bottom. Select the Advanced link to open the Advanced error handling. Click on "Failed to zip files" to define when the flow can't zip the files (see Figure 8-43). The default is Throw error. Instead, select Continue flow run, and leave the Exception handling mode set to Go to next action. Click Save to close the Dialog.

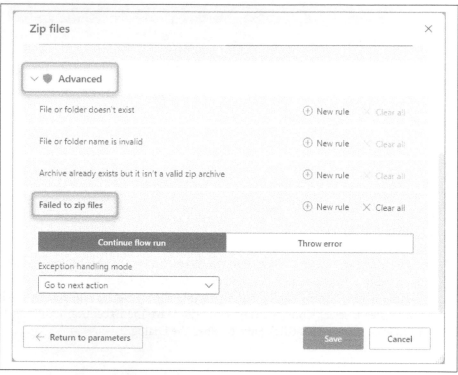

Figure 8-43. Configuring on error

6. In the designer, click on the Run link in the toolbar to try running the script. Check the ZIP file that was created to see if all files and subdirectories were included. Delete the destination folder and run the flow again. Since you configured error handling, the flow still runs without error.

Calling a Desktop Flow from a Cloud Flow

Up to this point in this chapter, all the desktop flows you have worked with have been attended flows that are executed manually on your computer from PAD. But what if you want to run a desktop flow on a particular schedule or on a different computer where you aren't logged in? To do that, you'll need to call the desktop flow from a cloud flow. This is where the concept of attended versus unattended flows comes in.

Attended Versus Unattended RPA

Desktop flows can be run either in an attended or unattended mode. Flows run in attended mode by default. This mode reuses the Windows user session of the currently logged-in user who is running the flow. This makes attended mode the preferred choice when you are running a desktop flow that requires human supervision or pauses for the user to make choices.

The one potential issue with running in attended mode is that it uses your current session and desktop. This makes it hard for you to do anything else while the desktop flow is running. Sometimes you want to run one or more desktop flows on VMs or on dedicated computers on your network. To do that, you can use a cloud flow to run the flows in unattended mode. Unattended mode is best for applications that do not need human supervision.

When running unattended, Power Automate automatically creates and signs into a remote desktop (RDP) session on the target computer. Once the unattended flow finishes, Power Automate automatically signs out from the device and reports the success or failure of the flow.

Unattended flows have some specific limitations:

- Windows 10/11 computers can't run unattended flows if there is a current user session.
- Windows Server computers can run unattended flows if there is a current user session, but different credentials must be used.
- Flows cannot be launched with elevated privileges.
- User interaction with the flow is prohibited because the desktop screen is locked while running in an RDP session.

Passing Parameters to and from a Desktop Flow

When you call a desktop flow from a cloud flow, it's common to want to provide some data for the flow to process and get some results back. To do that, you need to create Input and Output variables in the desktop flow. You create Input or Output parameters by clicking the plus (+) icon on the Input/output variables panel and selecting either Input or Output from the drop-down, as shown in Figure 8-44.

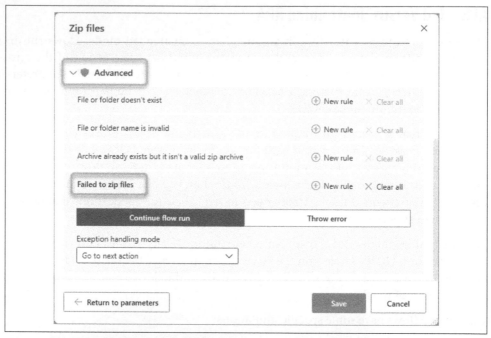

Figure 8-44. Creating Input and Output variables

A dialog will then be opened where you can name your variable, select what type of data it holds, and specify a default value. Input and Output values can have the following data types:

Text
> A simple string value

Number
> An integer or floating point number

Boolean
> True or False

Custom Object
> A JSON object with one or more properties

List
> A JSON array of simple values or objects with no key names

Data table
> A JSON array of objects, otherwise known as a data table

Input variables will show up as fields in the Power Automate "Run a flow built with Power Automate for desktop" action. Output variables will appear as dynamic content associated with the action after the desktop flow runs.

Exercise 8-5. Calling an attended desktop flow

One of the most common scenarios when calling a desktop flow from a cloud flow is to do it at a scheduled date and time. In this example, you will set up a recurrence flow to call the desktop flow you created in Exercise 8-4. For testing purposes, you'll set it to run every five minutes. But if you change the settings of the recurrence trigger, this flow could run the desktop flow once a week or once a day.

1. Open the desktop flow you created in Exercise 8-4. We need to adapt it to accept a path from the cloud flow that invokes it. To do that, create a new Input variable and fill in the fields with the following values:

Variable name
    UserInput

Data type
    Text

Default value
    C:\temp

External name
    Folder Path

Click Save (see Figure 8-45). A dialog will be displayed saying that the variable name is already in use. Click Continue to merge this new variable with the existing variable from the Display Input dialog action.

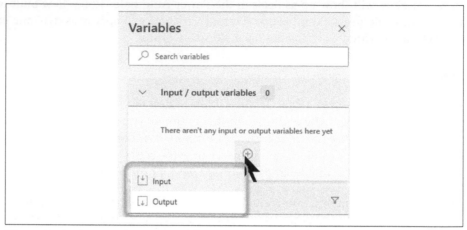

Figure 8-45. Creating Input variable

2. Now that you've created the Input variable for `FilePath`, you no longer need the original "Input dialog" action. Delete the "Display input dialog" action using the ellipses context menu that is displayed when you hover over the action (see Figure 8-46).

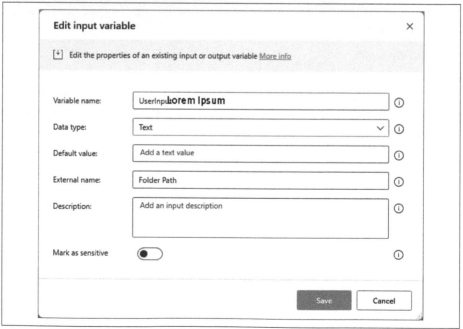

Figure 8-46. Deleting Input dialog action

3. Use the File menu to Save the desktop flow and Exit the designer (see Figure 8-47).

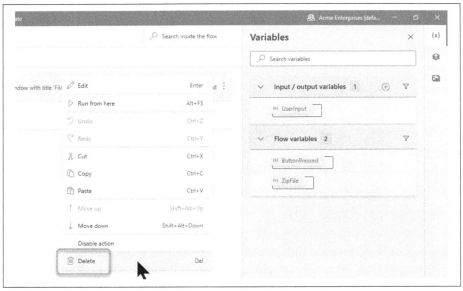

Figure 8-47. Saving and exiting from designer

4. Click the Windows Start button and type "CMD" in the Search bar. This will open a command prompt window. In the window, type "whoami." Press Enter. Copy the computername\username or domain\username that is returned. You will use this to create a machine connection to your desktop from a cloud flow (see Figure 8-48).

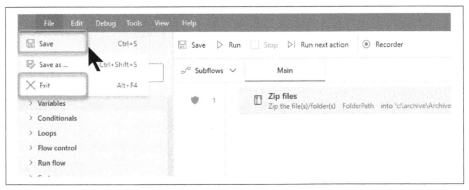

Figure 8-48. Determining logged-in user

5. Create a scheduled cloud flow. Name it "Run Desktop Flow." The Starting field will default to the current time and date. Set the Repeat every field to 5 minutes. This will start the flow every 5 minutes. Click the Create button (see Figure 8-49).

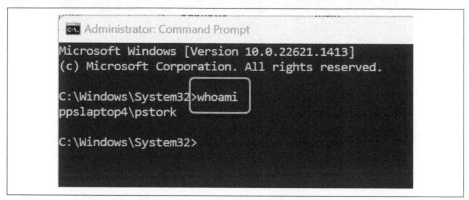

Figure 8-49. Creating scheduled cloud flow

6. Click on New Step to add an action to the flow. Type "desktop" into the Search bar and select "Run a flow built with Power Automate for desktop." You will see that this action is a premium action and requires higher-level licensing (see Figure 8-50).

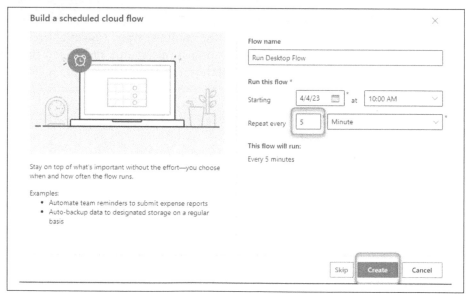

Figure 8-50. Running a desktop flow action

7. Create a new connection directly to your desktop machine (see Figure 8-51). Fill in the fields as follows:

Connect
    Directly to machine.

Machine
    Choose your desktop from the drop-down.

Domain and username
    Type the values returned by the "whoami" command in step 4.

Password
    Your login password.

Figure 8-51. Desktop flow machine connection

8. Once the machine connection is created, you can fill in the other fields in the "Run a flow built with Power Automate Desktop" action. Select Zip Files from the list of desktop flows available on your computer. Select Attended as the Run Mode. Unattended mode has additional licensing and computer requirements that would be hard to guarantee for this exercise.

Once you have selected the Desktop flow to run, the action will refresh to show you any Input parameters you added to the application. Type "c:\temp" into the Folder Path field (see Figure 8-52).

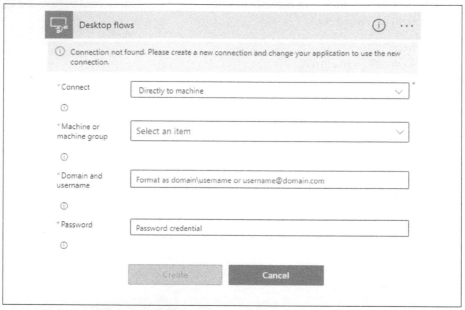

Figure 8-52. Running desktop flow action

9. Save your cloud flow. Wait five minutes. In the left sidebar, select "Desktop flow runs" under the Monitor tab. Your desktop flow run should be marked Succeeded. You can click on the run to drill down and see more details (see Figure 8-53).

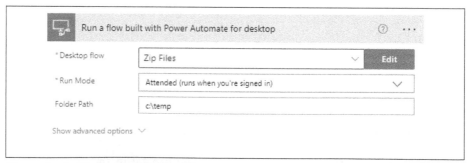

Figure 8-53. Monitoring desktop flow runs

Summary

In this chapter, you learned how to create desktop flows that interact directly with the UI of your computer. These flows can be used to automate manual processes without the need for APIs or prebuilt connectors. That makes them perfect for automating legacy applications or systems that only have a web interface. As you've seen, desktop flows can also be used when a could action does not exist for what you want to do. This book is primarily about Power Automate cloud flows, but desktop flows are a related concept that is often confused with Power Automate cloud flows. It's important to know how to use both.

In the next chapter, I'll cover another type of flow that is different from both a cloud flow and a desktop flow. Business process flows provide a checklist of tasks in a business process—which may include manual tasks, desktop flows, and even cloud flows—with the goal of guiding people through a complex process.

CHAPTER 9

Business Process Flows

Cloud flows are used to automate business processes where there is a connector or API. Desktop flows can automate manual tasks done on a computer. But what if you have a business process that involves multiple people or groups of people completing different sets of tasks? This is when you use a business process flow (BPF). BPFs provide a visual checklist of the tasks that need to be completed to achieve a result. They can be used to track the progress of data collection and completion of individual or group tasks. This type of tracking helps coordinate the work of multiple people and groups and will increase the consistency and completeness of data entered as part of the process.

What Is a Business Process Flow?

BPFs coordinate groups of people who are completing a set of related tasks. For example, when onboarding a new employee, there are a number of tasks that need to be accomplished by different people in a particular order. The following list summarizes a typical set of onboarding tasks:

- Security needs to create a user account and assign appropriate levels of access.
- HR needs to enroll the new employee in the company health insurance and benefits program.
- A manager needs to request a work phone and computer for the new employee.
- A welcome message needs to be sent to the new employee with this information.

In this BPF, someone in the corporate security department would create a user account for the new employee and assign their starting access. Someone in HR would then add the employee to the company health insurance and benefits program. The new employee's manager would submit a request for a work phone and a computer.

Finally, a welcome email would be automatically sent to the new employee with all this information. Each stage along the way is the responsibility of a different group or person, and some of the stages depend on the previous stage being completed before they can begin. Coordinating these kinds of activities is what a BPF does.

A BPF is made up of Stages, where each Stage contains one or more Steps. There are four kinds of Steps that can be added to a Stage. The following list summarizes each type of Step available:

Data Step
Sets the value of a field in the Dataverse table associated with the BPF

Action Step
Adds a button to the Stage that executes a Dynamics action or Workflow

Flow Step
Adds a button to the Stage that will run an instant Power Automate cloud flow (this Step type is still in preview and may change before it gets to general availability)

Workflow
Automatically runs a Dynamics workflow when exiting the current Stage

 Dynamics actions and Workflows shouldn't be confused with Power Automate flows. Dynamics actions implement business processes like making a phone call, sending an email, or triggering a workflow. Dynamics Workflows provided a functionality similar to Power Automate that is specific to Dynamics. They are legacy implementations that can still be used in a BPF. This book focuses on the newer implementation of Power Automate flows.

Each BPF is attached to a Dataverse table. The Stages of the flow are then displayed at the top of a form in a model-driven application that is created using that Dataverse table. Figure 9-1 shows what a BPF looks like in the context of a model-driven application created for a Dataverse table. You can see the name of the BPF and the various Stages of the flow displayed across the top of the form. The current Stage is expanded to show the Steps for that stage. At the bottom of the Stage, there is a Next Stage button that will move the flow to the next Stage.

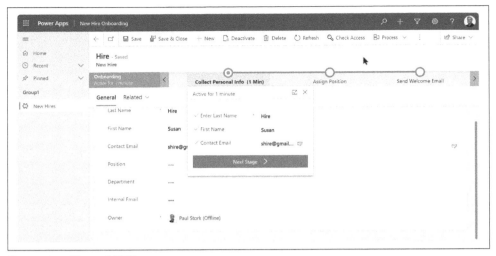

Figure 9-1. Typical BPF

Creating a Business Process Flow

BPFs must be built as part of a Solution. The BPF, the Dataverse table it's attached to, and any cloud flows called by the BPF should all be part of the same Solution.

When Power Automate was first released, you could create a BPF from the "+ New flow" link in the My flows tab. As of August 2022, you can no longer create or manage BPFs directly from Power Automate. Now, they must be built inside a Solution.

Once you have a Solution with a Dataverse table, you can create a BPF using the + New drop-down in the Solution Objects menu. The path in the drop-down is + New > Automation > Process > Business process flow. Figure 9-2 shows the panel that opens for creating a new BPF. You must supply a Display name, which will be used with a prefix to generate a Name for the flow. You will also have to pick a Dataverse Table to attach the BPF to. The BPF will appear on Forms in the table when a record is created.

Figure 9-2. Create a new BPF

Prerequisites

There are two prerequisites that must be in place to create a BPF. First, you must have one of the following licenses:

- Power Apps per-user
- Power Automate per-user
- Dynamics 365 license

A Microsoft 365 license does not have sufficient permissions to create BPFs. Second, you must have a Dataverse table to attach the BPF to. BPFs are triggered when a new record is created in the Dataverse table associated with the BPF. BPFs can capture data to multiple fields in several tables, but there is always one primary table that controls the start of the BPF.

Limitations

There are a number of limitations that you should be aware of when working with BPFs:

- A Dataverse table can only support a maximum of 10 activated BPFs.
- A BPF can reference a maximum of 5 Dataverse tables.
- A BPF can contain a maximum of 30 Stages.

- Each Stage can have a maximum of 30 Steps.
- Branch conditions must be based on Steps in the previous Stage.
- Multiple conditions can be added to a Branching Rule, but they must all be connected using either "And" or "Or." There is no way to group conditions.
- Branches can only be stacked up to 10 levels deep.

Adding Stages and Steps

After you create a new BPF in a Solution, it will open in a drag and drop designer interface in the Power Apps website, as shown in Figure 9-3. The panel on the right of the screen has two tabs: Components and Properties. The Components tab contains two categories of objects: Flow and Composition. Objects under the Flow category can be added to the main flow. Objects in the Composition category can be added to an individual Stage in the flow. The Properties tab is used to change the properties of a Stage or other object selected on the design surface.

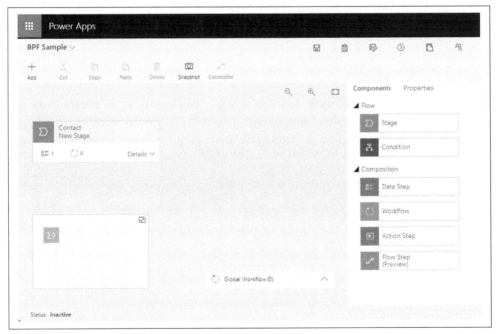

Figure 9-3. BPF in Power Apps designer interface

When you drag a Stage or Condition from the Components tab onto the main design surface, squares with plus signs appear, as shown in Figure 9-4, to show where you can drop them.

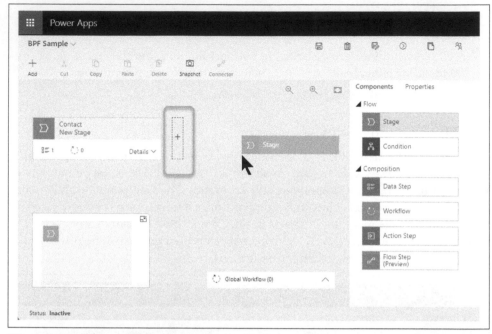

Figure 9-4. Adding a Stage

If you expand the Details drop-down of a Stage, you can drag an object from the Composition section of the Components tab onto a similar area in the Stage. Figure 9-5 shows a Flow Step being added to an existing Stage. Data Steps, Action Steps, and Flow Steps can be added before or after any Step in the Stage. Workflows can only be added at the end of the Stage.

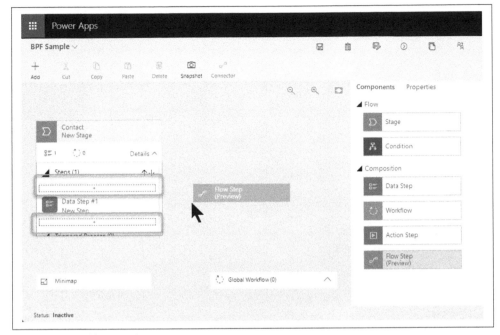

Figure 9-5. Adding a Flow Step

If you click on any Stage or Step in the design surface, you can modify the properties of that particular object. Property changes are not automatically saved, so you must click on the Apply button to commit the change. This step is frequently forgotten, which leads to a lot of added work.

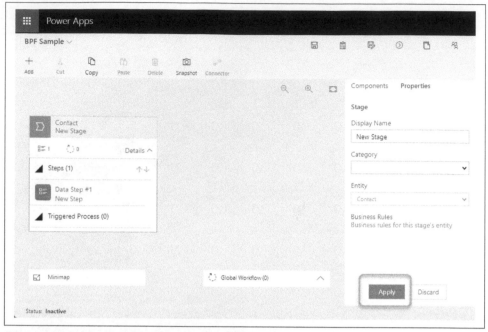

Figure 9-6. Setting Stage and Step properties

Once the Stage, Condition, and Step tiles have been added to the designer, you can rearrange them using drag and drop.

Managing Security Roles

Not everyone in your organization will need access to a new BPF. By default, only users with the System Administrator or System Customizer role will have access to the BPF. You can create a Security Role in the Solution to give additional users access to the whole BPF.

Validating and Activating a BPF

The final steps before using a new BPF are to Validate and Activate the flow. Validating the BPF checks it for syntax errors or missing information. Once the flow has been Saved and Validated, you can Activate the flow. Activating the flow makes it available in the views of model-driven applications built on the Dataverse table that initiated the flow. Figure 9-7 shows where the Validate and Activate menu entries are in the BPF editor.

Figure 9-7. Validating and activating a BPF

Example Introduction: Creating a BPF

In the following example, you will create a simple BPF for an employee-onboarding process. The process will have four different stages:

- Collecting personal information from the new hire
- Assigning a position and internal email address to the new employee
- Setting the Department field in the employee's record, if they aren't a manger
- Sending a welcome email to the new employee's personal email address

One of the Stages will be skipped if the employee is a manager, and a Power Automate cloud flow will be used to send the welcome email.

Exercise 9-1. Creating a Dataverse table

The BPF will be used to gather and process information for a new employee that has been just hired. The first thing you will need is a Dataverse table to store the information that is gathered by the BPF.

1. Create a new Solution named "BPF Onboarding." Select the CDS Default Publisher as the Publisher and click Create (see Figure 9-8).

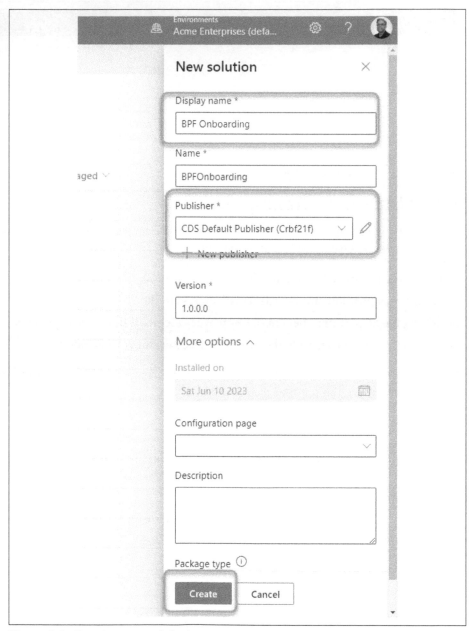

Figure 9-8. Creating a new Solution

2. Use the New+ link in the Solution menu to create a new Dataverse table named "New Hire" (see Figure 9-9). This table will hold the information collected by the flow. Click Save.

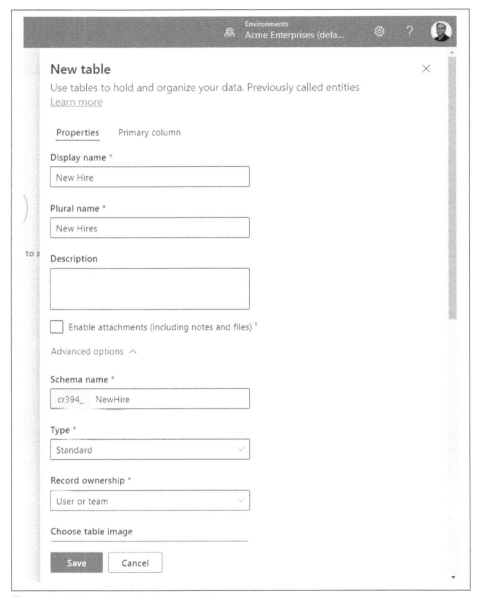

Figure 9-9. Creating a Dataverse table

3. Select the Columns link in the Schema section of the new table. Use the ellipsis menu to Edit the Name column and change the Display name to Last Name (see Figure 9-10). Click Save.

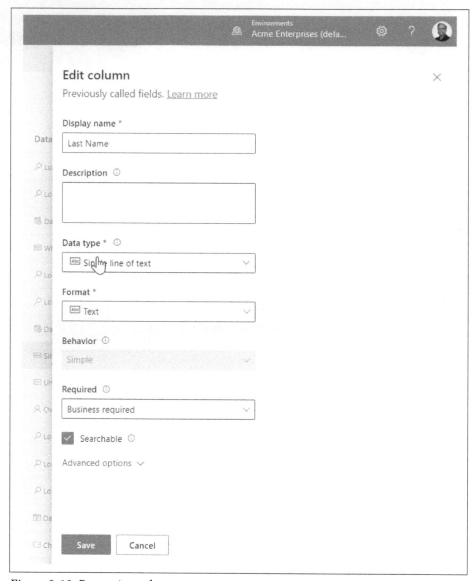

Figure 9-10. Renaming column

4. Use the "+ New column" link on the menu to add the following columns with the specified data types and formats (see Figure 9-11):

   • First Name

     — Data type: Single line of text

     — Format: Text

- Contact Email
  — Data type: Single line of text
  — Format: Email
- Internal Email
  — Data type: Single line of text
  — Format: Email

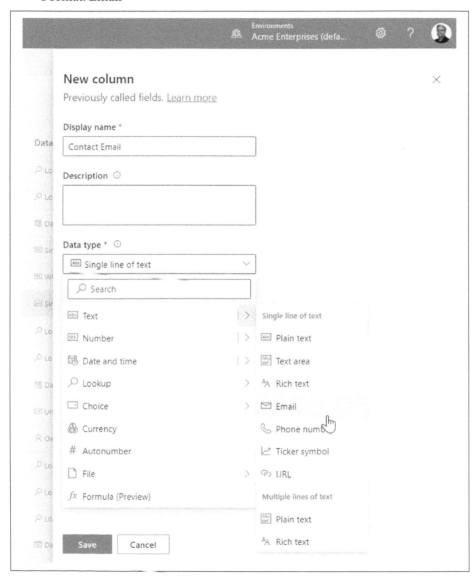

Figure 9-11. Creating text columns

5. Use the "+ New column" link on the menu to add a choice column named Position. Select the Yes radio button to "Sync with global choice." Select the "+ New choice" button to create a new global list of choices (see Figure 9-12). Syncing with a global choice value will let us use the same set of choices in another table without having to re-enter them. This makes long-term maintenance easier.

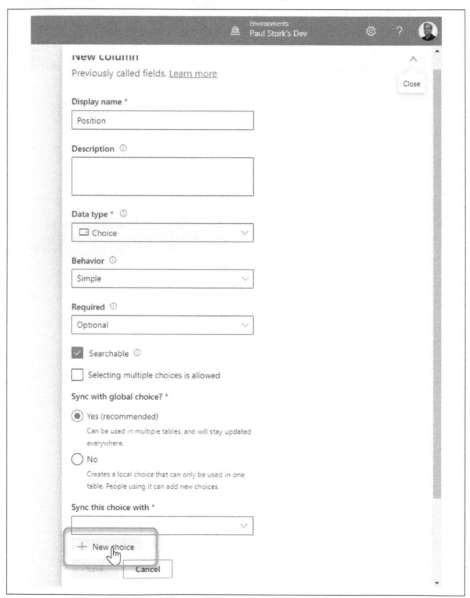

Figure 9-12. Creating a synced choice column

6. Type "Position Choices" into the Display name field of the Choice list. Add the following choices to the list by filling in the Label field.

- Analyst
- Consultant
- Manager

Click the "+ New choice" link to get another Label and Value. Accept the default Values suggested. The default values use a prefix from the publisher. You can change the Values, but they must be unique in the environment. Click Save (see Figure 9-13).

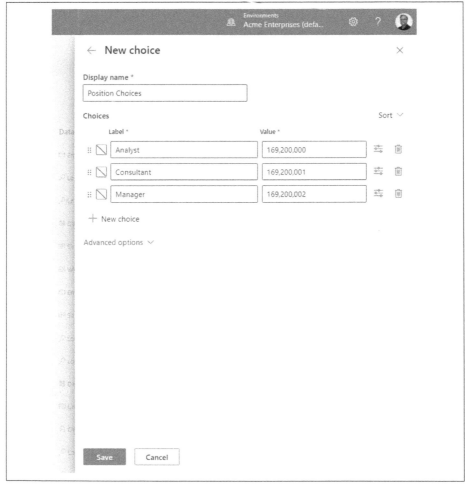

Figure 9-13. Creating global position choices

7. After creating the Position choices, select Position Choices from the "Sync this choice with" drop-down in the Position column you created earlier. Click Save (see Figure 9-14).

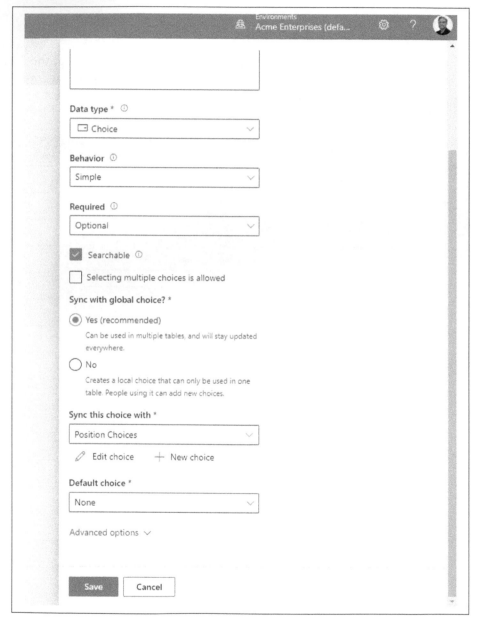

Figure 9-14. Setting global choices to sync with

8. Use the "+ New column" link on the menu to add a choice column named "Department." Select the No radio button for "Sync with global choice." Add Local Choices for Sales, Support, and Administration as local choice values. Creating the values locally is easier, but it means they can't be reused in another table. Click Save (see Figure 9-15).

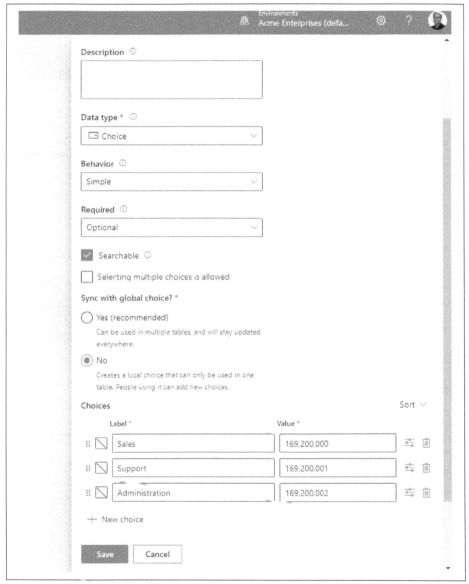

Figure 9-15. Creating local choices

9. Use the breadcrumb to return to the New Hire table page. Select Forms. Edit the Main Form. If prompted to preview the form, open the form in a new tab. Drag and drop each of the columns you created to the form (see Figure 9-16). Save and publish the form.

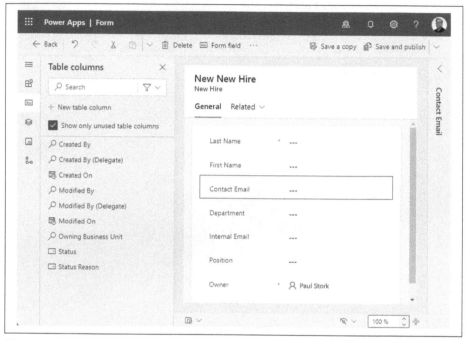

Figure 9-16. Adding fields to table Main Form

Exercise 9-2. Building a cloud flow to trigger from the BPF

One of the Steps in our BPF will be to send a welcome email to the new employee after all the onboarding tasks are completed. To do this, we'll use a regular cloud flow. In this example, you'll create a cloud flow that can be called when you create the BPF in the next example.

1. Using the + New link in the Solution menu, create a new instant cloud flow. Name the cloud flow "Send Welcome Email." Select the "When a flow step is run…" trigger. Click Create (see Figure 9-17).

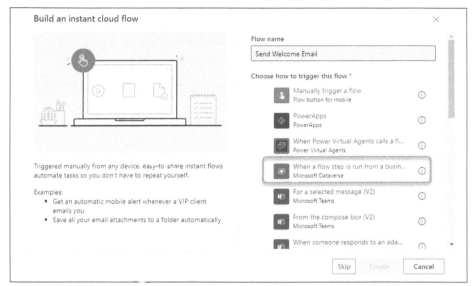

Figure 9-17. Creating an instant cloud flow

2. Add a Dataverse "Get a row by ID" action to the flow. Select New Hires as the Table name, and insert "BPF Flow Stage Table Row ID" in the Row ID field (see Figure 9-18). The trigger doesn't contain any of the data that the BPF Stage is processing, but it does contain the Table Name and Row ID of the record being processed. Retrieving this record will give you access to the data being processed.

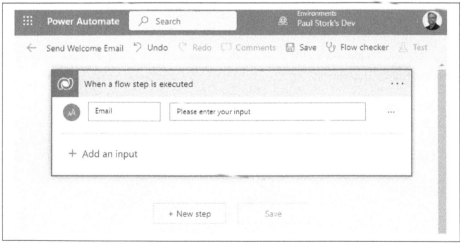

Figure 9-18. Adding text input to trigger

3. Add a "Send an Email (V2)" action to the flow. Click the "Add dynamic content" link under the To field, and add the Contact Email you retrieved in the previous action to the field. Add "Welcome" to the Subject field and type some text in the Body (see Figure 9-19). Save and close the flow.

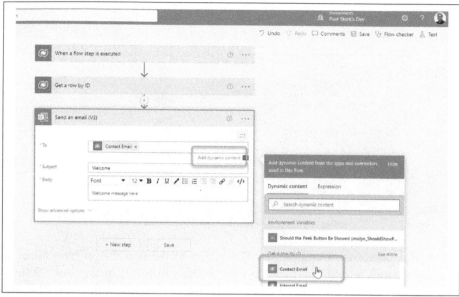

Figure 9-19. Sending an email

Exercise 9-3. Building a BPF

Now that you have created the cloud flow and table that you'll need, you can start creating the BPF itself.

1. Return to the Solution Objects page and use the + New link on the menu to create a new BPF called Onboarding. Select the New Hire table that you created in the previous example as the Table that uses the BPF. Click Create (see Figure 9-20). The new BPF will open in a designer in the Power Apps website.

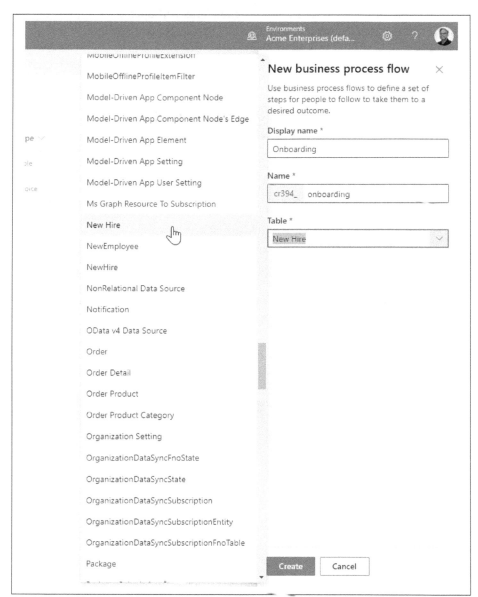

Figure 9-20. Creating a BPF

2. Select the first new Stage in the designer. This will open the Properties panel on the right side of the screen. Change the Display Name to "Collect Personal Information." Category can remain blank, since that is only used to tie into Dynamics 365 activities, and Entity is already set to the New Hire table (see Figure 9-21). Click Apply.

Figure 9-21. Renaming first Stage

3. Click on the Details drop-down in the Collect Personal Information Stage to expand the Stage. Select Data Step #1 and change the Step Name in the Properties panel to "Enter Last Name." Select the Last Name field in the Data Field drop-down. Select the Required checkbox. Checking the Required box will force users to enter a last name before moving on to the next Stage in the BPF (see Figure 9-22). Click Apply.

Figure 9-22. Renaming Data Step

4. Switch back to the Components tab and drag and drop a Data Step to the area below Data Step #1 (see Figure 9-23). Change the Step Name to "First Name" and select the First Name data field. Click Apply. Repeat this action to create a Data Step for the Contact Email data field. Click Apply.

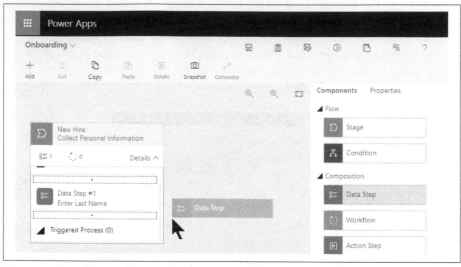

Figure 9-23. Adding a Data Step

5. Switch back to the Components tab and drag and drop a new Stage next to the existing Stage (see Figure 9-24). Rename the Stage as "Assign Position" and create Data Steps for Position and Internal Email. Remember to Click Apply each time you make a change.

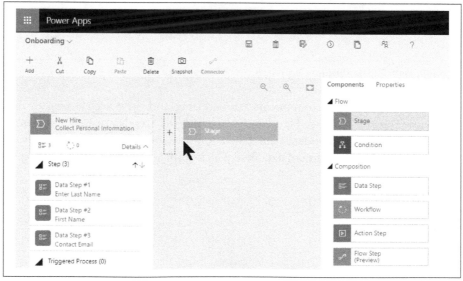

Figure 9-24. Adding a second Stage

6. Drag and drop a Condition next to the Assign Position Stage. Set the Display Name of the Condition to Is Manager, and configure the Rules as when Field Position Equals Value Manager. Click Apply (see Figure 9-25).

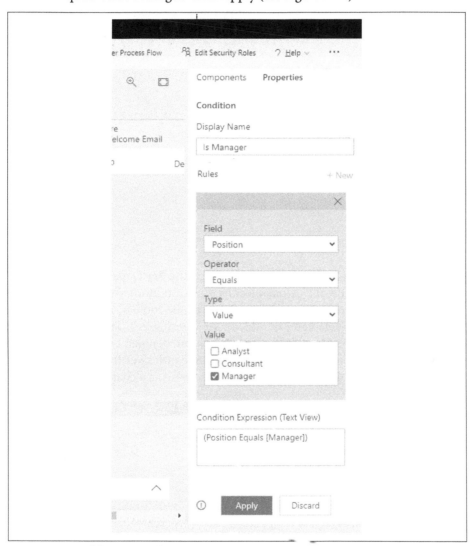

Figure 9-25. Adding a Condition

7. Drag and drop a new Stage into the Yes branch, denoted by the green checkmark, of the Condition. Name it "Set Department." Configure the Data Step with the Step Name Department and pick the Department Field (see Figure 9-26). Remember to Click Apply each time you make a change.

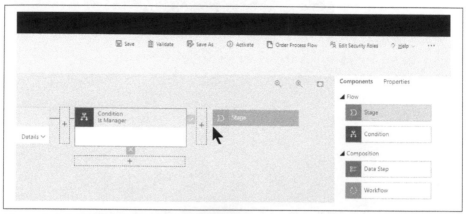

Figure 9-26. Adding Stage to Yes Condition

8. Drag and drop a new Stage to the right of the Set Department Stage. Name it "Send Welcome Email." After selecting the Condition you added earlier, select Connect from the Connector drop-down in the toolbar, then click on the Send Welcome Email Stage you just added (see Figure 9-27). This will create an alternate path from the No output of the Condition, denoted by the red X, to the next Stage. This will ensure that the flow continues whether the condition is True or False. Remember to click Apply each time you make a change.

Figure 9-27. Adding a final Stage

9. Drag and drop a Flow Step above Data Step #1 in the Send Welcome Email Stage. Set the Display Name to "Trigger Welcome Email flow" and click Apply (see Figure 9-28).

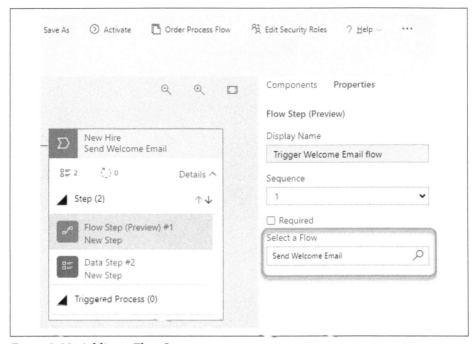

Figure 9-28. Adding a Flow Step

10. Select the Data Step #2. Click Delete on the toolbar (see Figure 9-29).

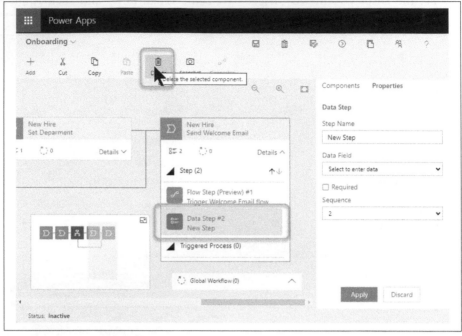

Figure 9-29. Deleting Data Step

11. Save and Activate the BPF (see Figure 9-30). This will make it available for use in a model-driven application built around the New Hires table.

Figure 9-30. Activating and Saving the BPF

Exercise 9-4. Testing the BPF with a model-driven application

BPFs provide a visual checklist in the context of a model-driven application, based on the table you chose when you created the BPF. In this example, you will create a simple model-driven application so you can test your new BPF.

1. Use the +New link in the toolbar to create a new model-driven app. Name the app "Test BPF." Click Create (see Figure 9-31). Your new model-driven application will open in a designer.

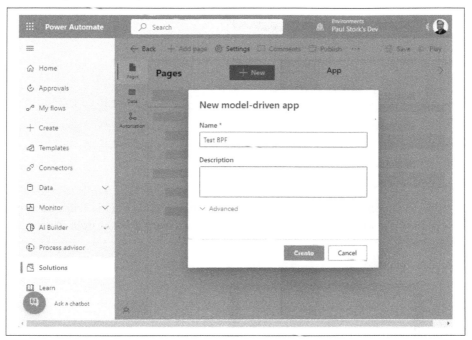

Figure 9-31. New model-driven application

2. Click the +New button. Add a new Dataverse table page (see Figure 9-32). Click Next.

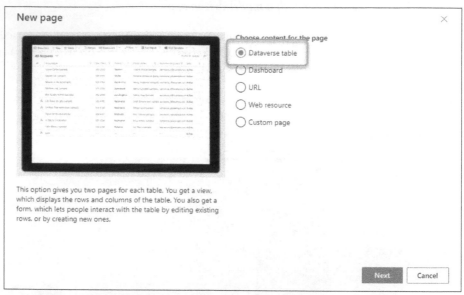

Figure 9-32. Adding a Dataverse table

3. Type "new" in the Search box and check the New Hire table to add it to the model-driven application. Click Add (see Figure 9-33). This will add the Main Form from the table as the default page of the model-driven application.

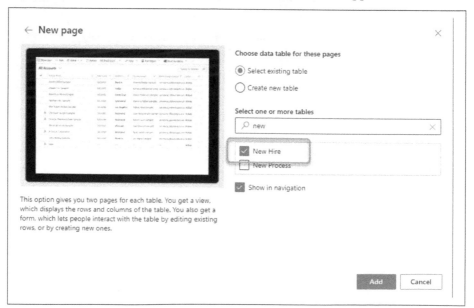

Figure 9-33. Selecting New Hire table

4. Use the toolbar to Save, Publish, and Play the application (see Figure 9-34). Wait until each action finishes before proceeding.

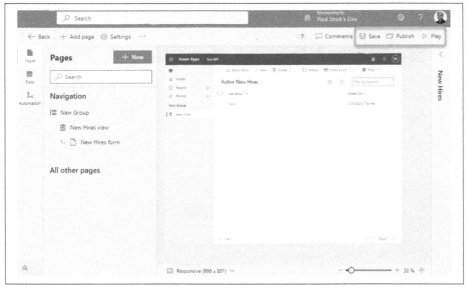

Figure 9-34. Saving, publishing, and playing the application

5. Use the +New link on the menu to add a new Record to the New Hires table. The Test BPF should appear at the top of the form (see Figure 9-35). Click on Last Name in the form and fill in your Last name.

Figure 9-35. Adding a new record

6. Click on Collect Personal Information to expand the first Stage. Fill in your first name and a personal email address. Click Save (see Figure 9-36). You will not see the button to proceed to the next Stage until you save the changes you make. Click the Next Stage button to move to the next Stage.

Figure 9-36. Filling in data in Test BPF

7. Select a Position from the drop-down and add a fake email as the internal email of the new test employee. Click Next Stage (see Figure 9-37). Remember, if you pick Manager for the Position, you will be routed to a third Stage to select a Department before going to the final Stage.

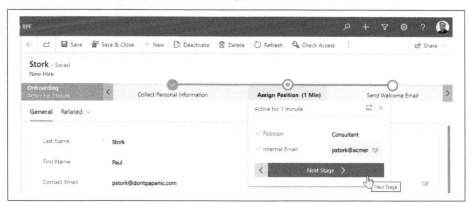

Figure 9-37. Completing Assign Position Stage in Test BPF

8. Click the Run Flow button to run the cloud flow you created in Exercise 9-2 (see Figure 9-38).

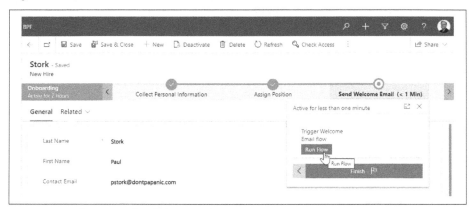

Figure 9-38. Running cloud flow in Test BPF

9. The first time you run the cloud flow, you will be prompted to sign in and approve the permissions used by the Outlook connector to send the email (see Figure 9-39). This prompt will only happen the first time you run the flow.

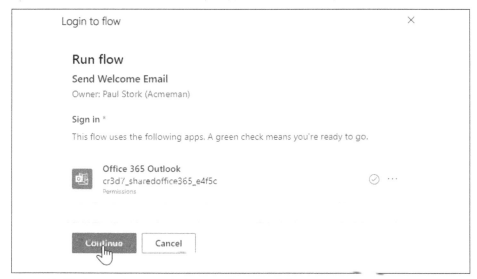

Figure 9-39. Approving permissions on first cloud flow run

10. After the OAuth permissions for the connection have been approved, you will see a dialog where you can run the flow. If you had added any input parameters to the trigger in the flow, you would be prompted to provide them here. Click "Run flow" (see Figure 9-40).

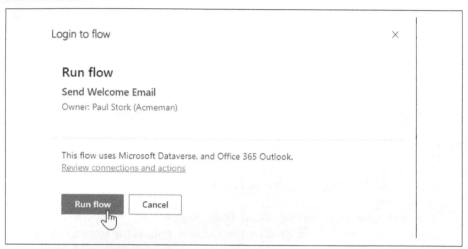

Figure 9-40. Running the flow

11. Once the flow run completes, you will see a confirmation that the flow ran successfully. You can review the log of the flow's run by clicking on the Flow Runs Page link. Click Done to close the dialog and return to the last Stage (see Figure 9-41).

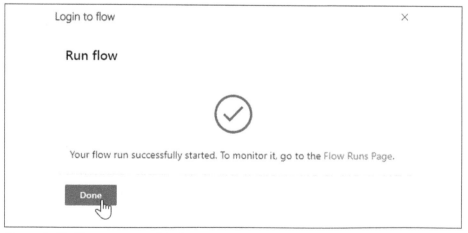

Figure 9-41. Flow run completed

12. Your BPF is now complete. Click the Finished button to mark it as done. Then, click the Save & Close button on the top menu to go back to the records list in the New Hires table (see Figure 9-42).

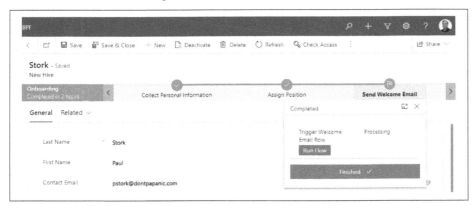

Figure 9-42. Finalizing flow run

Summary

In this chapter, you learned how to create BPFs that let you collaborate with other people on complex processes that involve more than one task. BPFs can be used to collect information, run Dynamics 365 actions and workflows, and trigger a cloud flow. These BPFs are tied to a Dataverse table and triggered when a record is created in that table. They are then displayed in the context of a model-driven application. These flows are primarily used by Dynamics business users, but they can be used by anyone who has a license that covers premium connectors since this requires a Dataverse connection.

While the main topic of this book is Power Automate cloud flows, coverage would not be complete if we didn't also examine desktop flows and business process flows since they fall under the Power Automate product line. Even if you don't use business process flows directly, a flow that has individual embedded flows to do specific tasks is a useful design concept. If you have to build complex processes in the future, this type of design may be useful.

That brings us to the end of this book. In the Conclusion that follows, I'll provide you with some additional resources that you can use to continue learning more about Power Automate.

Conclusion

Congratulations! Unless you're the kind of person who likes to read the last chapter of a mystery before reading the full book, you've just finished learning about what Power Automate is and how it can help improve efficiency and accuracy in your work. As you've seen, Power Automate can create flows that turn mundane, boring, and repetitive tasks into automated tasks that run on their own. This will free you up to concentrate on tasks that are more interesting and that generate more value for you and your organization.

This book has taken you on a journey that I'm convinced will change how you manage information from now on. But the journey doesn't end here. Now it's time to start looking at the information you manually process each day and start using Power Automate flows to make those tasks easier. I'm sure you'll encounter a few bumps along the way, as we all do, but I'm convinced that you've learned enough in this book to begin that next stage of your journey.

There is another reason why this isn't the end of the road for your learning experience: Power Automate is always evolving with new features, triggers, and actions. Microsoft is constantly changing and expanding the capabilities of the platform. These changes are both exciting and challenging. They're exciting because they let you expand the way you use Power Automate. But they're also challenging because, as time passes, things that used to work will stop working due to the changes. This means you'll sometimes have to fix a flow that worked fine last month. The best way to be aware of these changes, so you can take advantage of new features and be prepared to fix things that break, is to frequently review the Power Automate roadmap (*https://oreil.ly/iYJ38*). The roadmap will provide you with details about new features and changes that are being tested. It will also tell you when they will be available in Public Preview and when they are scheduled for General Availability release. If you know what new features are coming, you will be better prepared to take advantage of them or fix something that breaks because of them.

No single book, website, or video collection will provide you with everything you need to know about Power Automate. The key is really to start using the product to automate things. As you find more and more uses for Power Automate flows, you'll also encounter problems where you'll need to learn something new to accomplish your goal. These problems will provide you with your best opportunity to really improve your knowledge and understanding of Power Automate. You were introduced to one resource for this kind of learning early in the book: templates. The templates provided with the product are rarely a perfect solution, but they do provide good examples of different ways to approach automating specific tasks. Take the time to examine them and learn how they work. That will move you forward as you learn more about how to automate things with Power Automate flows. But don't stop there. In the next section, I'll provide some suggestions on where you can find other resources to continue your learning journey.

Where Can I Learn More?

Since there is always more to learn, I want to share some resources that you can use to continue your journey toward mastery of Power Automate. There is a wealth of good resources out there waiting for you to find them, and this section details a few that I have found useful as I've improved my knowledge of Power Automate.

Power Automate Documentation

The first resource I suggest is the Power Automate documentation (*https://oreil.ly/giEGY*). Some questions that can be answered by reading the documentation include what syntax or data type to use. Additionally, Microsoft provides extensive, up-to-date documentation on all the connectors they create, which includes descriptions of the triggers and actions in the connector. The descriptions of each trigger/action also include the syntax for calling them and the data types of both the input and output fields. As I mentioned in Chapter 7, one of the most common errors in Power Automate is something like "expected array but got string." This normally happens because you aren't clear on the data type of the dynamic content that you are inputting or because you don't know what it should be. So, to avoid these types of errors, it's always a good idea to check the documentation to see which data types are expected for input and output.

The documentation also contains links to articles about topics like using Solutions to distribute flows, using flows in Microsoft Teams, and general best practices. Ultimately, the documentation is your encyclopedia of information about all things Power Automate. It may be dry reading, but it is well worth the time.

Microsoft Learning Website

Another great resource for taking your knowledge of Power Automate to the next level is the Microsoft Learning website (*https://oreil.ly/xLj4_*). This website provides Learning Paths that will walk you through a specific concept in Power Automate. Each Learning Path is broken down into modules that deal with a specific topic, like getting started with Power Automate or planning and managing your Power Platform environment. Each module contains short lessons, or units. The prerequisites and objectives for each module are also clearly stated. The information contained in these lessons is similar to the information in the official documentation, but it is presented in a more directed manner. Instead of reading a long article, each lesson is a series of pages and illustrations that explain the topic. If you know what you are looking for, the documentation may be a more efficient resource, but if you just want to learn about a specific aspect of working with Power Automate, the Learning Paths, modules, and lessons are a great way to get started.

Additional Resources

Although I tried to make this book a thorough review of how to use Power Automate, I'll be the first to admit that it doesn't cover everything. When I was originally contacted by O'Reilly to write this book, it was supposed to be about 75 pages shorter. As time went on, the book continued to increase in size. My publisher was gracious enough to let me expand the page count quite a bit before we finished, but I still found myself having to discard some topics as I wrote to stay within a reasonable page count. That's a fairly long explanation for why you may want to also consult other books on Power Automate to supplement your knowledge. Different authors bring a different perspective to the topic, and each book will have something new to offer you.

One of the books I would like to highlight is *Building Solutions with the Microsoft Power Platform* (*https://oreil.ly/buildSolutionsMPP*) by Jason Rivera (O'Reilly). Jason was one of the technical reviewers on this book and is very knowledgeable about Power Automate and the Power Platform in general. If you are interested in learning more about the possibilities for integration that I mentioned in Chapter 6, then take a look at Jason's book. It provides an overview of all the applications in the Power Platform and will give you great insight into what's possible in Power Apps, Power Pages, and Power BI in addition to Power Automate.

Video tutorials are also a great resource. There are a number of very talented people who have created a variety of videos about specific topics in Power Automate. I would recommend checking out content from the following people:

- Reza Dorrani (*https://rezadorrani.com*) is a Microsoft Principal Program Manager and former MVP. I met Reza on the Power Platform forums. He is a very knowledgeable individual, and he creates excellent videos that are easy to follow.

- Damion A. Bird (DamoBird365) (*https://oreil.ly/448Im*) is a fellow Super User on the Power Platform forums. Like Reza, he makes great videos on Power Automate. I've watched him solve some really difficult problems for people on the forums, and he is a great resource to learn from.

- Anders Jensen (*https://oreil.ly/4jT4K*) is a fellow MVP who specializes in robotic process automation (RPA). His videos are excellent if you want to learn more about Power Automate Desktop.

Additional Help

No matter how good you get at using Power Automate, there will be times when you design a flow that just won't run. So, it's important to know where you can turn when you need more help. You will of course get to know other people who are learning Power Automate. Even if you are a more advanced user, sometimes you just need a different set of eyes to look at your design to find the problem. Even a novice may spot something that an experienced citizen developer doesn't see, due to their preconceptions on how a design should work.

If you still need help, I suggest you post a question on the Microsoft Power Automate community forum (*https://oreil.ly/_SKpn*). Microsoft sponsors a public forum where you can post questions or problems and get help solving them for free. I spend a lot of time on the forum answering questions, and a lot of the knowledge I've imparted in this book comes from learnings that I gained through helping out there. Try posting a question, and if you want, you can tag me (@Pstork1) to draw my attention to it. But you may find that you get an answer before I get a chance to read and respond.

Finally

That brings us to the end of this book. I hope you've enjoyed your journey learning how to build Power Automate flows. In a time when so much depends on timely and accurate processing of information, the value of automation tools like Power Automate cannot be overstated. As organizations and individuals, we live in an increasingly fast-paced and interconnected world. The ability to automate repetitive and time-consuming tasks is critical to maintain a competitive edge. Power Automate offers an opportunity for even non-programmers to build sophisticated and powerful workflows that free us from mundane tasks and allow us to focus on what truly matters: innovation, creativity, and problem-solving.

I won't say "farewell" because I'm sure our paths will cross again. But I will say "goodbye for now," and, above all, have fun working with Power Automate.

Index

Symbols

A

B

C

templates (see also Visio)
  how to use, 43
  learning from, 54
  using flow templates, 45-54
Terminate action
  overview of, 148
  using for error handling, 230
testing, streamlining, 228
timeouts, 135
toLower() function, 115
Tracked Properties feature, 137
trial license, 17, 28-36 (see also licensing requirements)
Trigger Conditions feature, 139-146
triggers and actions (see also individual actions; individual triggers)
  adding actions, 94-97
  adding comments, 131
  adding dynamic content, 97-106
  adding notes to, 132
  anatomy of flows, 19-22
  basics of, 85, 94
  changing action settings, 133-137
  choosing triggers, 89-94
  copying actions, 130
  deleting and replacing triggers, 90
  filtering triggers, 91
  finding correct connector, 85-89
  renaming actions and triggers, 131
  trigger settings, 137-146
  using Action ellipsis (...) menu, 128-133
  using JSON, 107-113
  working with expressions, 114-128
troubleshooting (see also error handling)
  common errors, 218-221
  dynamic content, 104, 106
  monitoring and tracking cloud flows, 221-226

reviewing run history, 215-218
try-catch blocks, 229

U

"Update file properties" action, 151
"Update file" action, 236
"Update item" action, 142
Upper() function, 153
user interactions, recording, 256-266

V

values
  checking with Compose actions, 228
  returning results to Parent flows, 158-163
  returning to Power Apps, 192-199
variables
  environment variables in Solutions, 183-187
  working with in PAD, 267
Visio
  BPMN flowcharts, 72-77
  designing flows with, 71
  exporting templates, 77-82
  exporting workflows to Power Automate, 82
  prerequisites for, 72

W

"Wait for an approval" action, 170
"When an HTTP request is received" trigger, 158
Windows licensing, 19

Z

"Zip files" action, 275

About the Author

Paul Papanek Stork is the owner and principal architect at Don't Pa..Panic Consulting. He has worked in the IT industry for over 35 years and has been awarded the Microsoft Most Valuable Professional (MVP) award for the last 16 consecutive years. In addition to being a frequent book contributor and conference speaker, Paul is currently one of the only triple Super Users on the Microsoft Power Platform forums, where he answers questions and troubleshoots issues on Power Apps, Power Automate, and Power Virtual Agent.

Colophon

The animal on the cover of *Learning Microsoft Power Automate* is a zebu (*Bos indicus* or *Bos taurus indicus*), also known as humped cattle. Some believe them to be the oldest domesticated breed of cattle in the world, having been domesticated in the Indus Valley as much as 6,000 to 7,000 years ago.

Zebu have a large fatty hump above their shoulders, drooping ears, upward-curving horns, and a large flap of loose skin around their neck called a dewlap. They are well adapted to warm climates and have a high tolerance for heat and drought, and these adaptations have led to them being introduced to other parts of the world, particularly Africa and Brazil. They have also been crossbred with many other varieties of cattle to produce new breeds. While zebu can be found in many countries, the largest herds are in Brazil and India.

The zebu population is large and worldwide, so they are therefore not listed on endangered species lists. However, many of the animals on O'Reilly covers are endangered; all of them are important to the world.

The cover illustration is by Karen Montgomery, based on an antique line engraving from *Shaw's Zoology*. The cover fonts are Gilroy Semibold and Guardian Sans. The text font is Adobe Minion Pro; the heading font is Adobe Myriad Condensed; and the code font is Dalton Maag's Ubuntu Mono.

O'REILLY®

Learn from experts.
Become one yourself.

Books | Live online courses
Instant answers | Virtual events
Videos | Interactive learning

Get started at oreilly.com.

©2023 O'Reilly Media, Inc. O'Reilly is a registered trademark of O'Reilly Media, Inc. | 175_J v0187s

Milton Keynes UK
Ingram Content Group UK Ltd.
UKHW032141280923
429584UK00002B/2

9 781098 136369